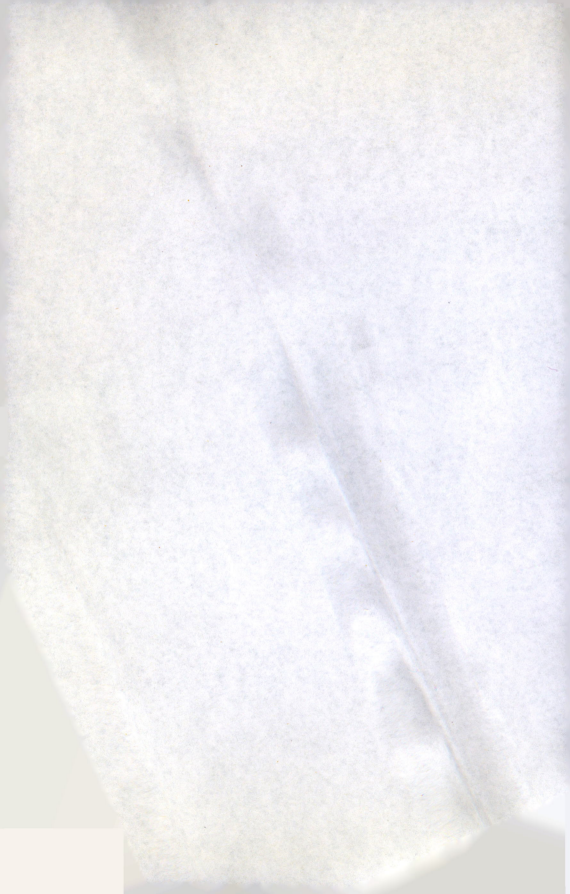

The GM Debate

The GM Debate tells the story of an unprecedented experiment in large-scale public participation: the government-sponsored debate about the possible commercialisation of genetically modified (GM) crops in the UK, which took place in 2002–03. The book provides a unique and systematic account of the debate process, setting it within its political and intellectual contexts, and examining the practical implications of this development for future public engagement initiatives.

The authors produce a conceptually informed and empirically based evaluation of the debate, drawing upon detailed observation of both public and behind-the-scenes aspects of the process, data on the views of participants in debate events, a survey of public views, and details of media coverage. They analyse the design, implementation and effectiveness of the debate process, and provide a critique of its official findings.

The book will be of interest to a wide readership of researchers, policy-makers and students, concerned with cross-disciplinary aspects of risk, decision-making, public engagement, and the governance of technology.

Tom Horlick-Jones is an independent researcher and consultant, currently based at Cardiff School of Social Sciences, Cardiff University. He was team leader of the debate evaluation project.

John Walls is a Senior Research Associate in the School of Environmental Sciences at the University of East Anglia.

Gene Rowe is Head of Consumer Science at the Institute of Food Research in Norwich.

Nick Pidgeon is Professor of Applied Psychology in the School of Psychology at Cardiff University.

Wouter Poortinga is an RCUK Academic Fellow in health and risk communication in the Welsh School of Architecture at Cardiff University.

Graham Murdock is Reader in the Sociology of Culture at Loughborough University.

Tim O'Riordan is Emeritus Professor of Environmental Sciences at the University of East Anglia.

Genetics and Society

Series editors:

Paul Atkinson, *Associate Director of CESAGen, Cardiff University*;
Ruth Chadwick, *Director of CESAGen, Lancaster University*;
Peter Glasner, *Professorial Research Fellow for CESAGen at Cardiff University*;
Brian Wynne, *member of the management team at CESAGen, Lancaster University*.

The books in this series, all based on original research, explore the social, economic and ethical consequences of the new genetic sciences. The series is based in the ESRC's Centre for Economic and Social Aspects of Genomics, the largest UK investment in social-science research on the implications of these innovations. With a mix of research monographs, edited collections, textbooks and a major new handbook, the series will be a major contribution to the social analysis of new agricultural and biomedical technologies.

Forthcoming in the series

Governing the Transatlantic Conflict over Agricultural Biotechnology (2006)
Contending coalitions, trade liberalisation and standard setting
Joseph Murphy and Les Levidow
978–0–415–37328–9

The GM Debate (2007)
Risk, politics and public engagement
Tom Horlick-Jones, John Walls, Gene Rowe, Nick Pidgeon, Wouter Poortinga, Graham Murdock and Tim O'Riordan
978–0–415–39322–5

New Genetics, New Social Formations (2006)
Peter Glasner, Paul Atkinson and Helen Greenslade
978–0–415–39323–2

New Genetics, New Identities (2006)
Paul Atkinson, Peter Glasner and Helen Greenslade
978–0–415–39407–9

Local Cells, Global Science (2007)
Embryonic stem cell research in India
Aditya Bharadwaj and Peter Glasner
978–0–415–39609–7

Growth Cultures (2007)
Life sciences and economic development
Philip Cooke
978–0–415–39223–5

The GM Debate

Risk, politics and public engagement

Tom Horlick-Jones, John Walls,
Gene Rowe, Nick Pidgeon,
Wouter Poortinga, Graham Murdock
and Tim O'Riordan

 Routledge
Taylor & Francis Group

LONDON AND NEW YORK

First published 2007 by Routledge
2 Park Square, Milton Park, Abingdon, Oxon OX14 4RN

Simultaneously published in the USA and Canada
by Routledge
270 Madison Avenue, New York, NY 10016

Routledge is an imprint of the Taylor & Francis Group, an informa business

© 2007 Tom Horlick-Jones, John Walls, Gene Rowe, Nick Pidgeon,
Wouter Poortinga, Graham Murdock and Tim O'Riordan

Typeset in Garamond 3 by
Florence Production Ltd, Stoodleigh, Devon
Printed and bound in Great Britain by
MPG Books Ltd, Bodmin

British Library Cataloguing in Publication Data
A catalogue record for this book is available
from the British Library

Library of Congress Cataloging in Publication Data
The GM debate: risk, politics and public engagement/
Tom Horlick-Jones . . . [et al.]
        p.cm.
    Includes bibliographical references and index.
    1. Genetically modified food.   2. Genetically modified foods –
Government policy – Great Britain.   3. Genetically modified foods –
Great Britain – Public opinion.   I. Horlick-Jones, Tom.   II. Title:
Genetically-modified debate.
TP248.65.F66G62 2007
306.4'6–dc22   2006025541

ISBN10: 0–415–39322–1 (hbk)
ISBN10: 0–203–94593–X (ebk)

ISBN13: 978–0–415–39322–5 (hbk)
ISBN13: 978–0–203–94593–3 (ebk)

Contents

Figures

Tables

Boxes

Preface

When we began the work of evaluating the *GM Nation?* public debate in 2002, none of us could have imagined how much of our lives the debate would come to occupy. As we finalise this book, almost four years have passed. Our initial evaluation report was published early in 2004. A stream of papers, addressing different aspects of the evaluation exercise, have already appeared in the technical journals, or are still finding their way through the academic publishing process. We feel it is now the time to publish a monograph-length account of the debate, which provides a considered examination of the key issues, and which will be of interest, we hope, to both scholars and practitioners of various kinds.

The central focus of our work has been on producing a high-quality and rigorous evaluation of the *debate process*, and one which has allowed us to make a range of practical and specific suggestions about how such an exercise might be organised more effectively in the future. As well as addressing the effectiveness and quality of the debate, the book documents a process of methodological development. The hybrid approach that we adopted to carry out the evaluation was a plural one, combining qualitative and quantitative methods. It was also cross-disciplinary, drawing on a range of methodological and conceptual perspectives from across the social sciences. In terms of evaluation theory, we have attempted to adapt a rigorous, criterion-based approach in ways that have allowed us to learn from the process, and which has been open to the identification of emergent findings.

We should make clear at this stage what the book is *not* about. It does not seek to provide a detailed examination of the wider domestic and international politics of, and regulatory struggles over, transgenic crops and food. Neither does it consider the relative merits or otherwise of the technology in question. While we all have personal views about the substantive topics of the debate, our analytic stance for the evaluation exercise has been one of unflinching even-handedness and *methodological indifference* towards the outcome of the debate process. Similarly, while we appreciate that, in principle, processes of engagement with the lay public offer a means of improving the quality of public decision-making and enhancing the democratic process, we also recognise the dangers in seeing such initiatives as a panacea. In practice, such desirable outcomes will necessitate processes that are characterised by careful design and effective organisation. Our book makes clear that a corresponding body of coherent design knowledge does not yet exist. We have attempted to make a contribution towards developing such a body of knowledge.

Turning now to acknowledgements, we recognise that during the period in which the work reported in this book was conducted, we incurred a colossal debt in terms of practical support. We are therefore pleased to have this opportunity to thank a number of individuals and organisations.

First, we thank the members of the *GM Nation?* Public Debate Steering Board for providing us with the opportunity to act as accredited evaluators, and for their cooperation as the process unfolded. We feel that we must also acknowledge the impressive levels of dedication and commitment they displayed in conducting this task. As pioneers in developing new practical forms of deliberative democracy they faced an enormous challenge, yet they managed to acquit themselves with distinction, given the complex problems and enormous workload they faced. We are also most grateful to the debate secretariat, and staff at COI Communications and Corr Willbourn Research and Development, for their patience and helpful assistance. While we have been critical of many specific aspects of the implementation of the debate, we appreciate that this work entailed navigating largely uncharted waters. Our criticisms should not, therefore, be interpreted as casting any doubts about their general competence and professionalism.

The evaluation project would not have been possible without the cooperation of a large number of participants in the debate, across a range of modes of involvement. Many found the time to speak with us, sometimes at length, and to complete our questionnaires. We are indebted to them all. Our work was supported by the Leverhulme Trust (RSK990021), and by two awards from the Economic and Social Research Council (ESRC), including one from the *Science in Society* programme (L144250037). Additional support during the preparation of this manuscript was provided by the ESRC *SCARR* programme (RES-336–25–0001).

Peter Glasner first suggested that we write this book, and we are pleased to thank him, and his fellow editors Paul Atkinson, Ruth Chadwick and Brian Wynne, for inviting us to contribute to the monograph series associated with the journal *New Genetics & Society*. We also thank the two anonymous readers appointed by Routledge, both of whom provided supportive and helpful comments.

We are pleased to acknowledge the role of numerous colleagues who helpfully provided assistance with the data collection, and with whom we have discussed many of the issues raised in the book. We thank in particular: Nick Bailey, Katie Begg, Karen Bickerstaff, Mick Bloor, Ann Bruce, Jacquie Burgess, Matthew Harvey, Emma Hughes, Alan Irwin, Kevin Jones, Mavis Jones, Jenny Kitzinger, Irene Lorenzoni, Carl Macrae, Greg Myers, Judith Petts, Jonathan Rosenhead, Peter Simmons, Andy Stirling, Joyce Tait and Colin Young. We are grateful to Tee Rogers-Hayden for kindly providing us with some of her unpublished research findings. We also thank Michelle Corrado and Claire O'Dell at Ipsos MORI for their friendly cooperation.

All nine chapters of the book have been written and re-worked extensively for this publication. Inevitably, in places, the text draws upon fragments of our papers which have appeared elsewhere. We have been careful to identify all such sources in the list of references. We gratefully acknowledge permission to reproduce various materials in this book: Blackwell Publishing for diagrams which first appeared in the journal *Risk Analysis*, and Sage Publications for a revised and enlarged version of a paper from the journal *Public Understanding of Science* (as Chapter 7). We also thank Edna Einsiedel, the editor of *Public Understanding of Science*, for her co-operation and support. Finally, we thank COI Communications and David Lewis, the artist, for permission to reproduce the cartoons which appear as Figures P.1 and 7.3.

Tom Horlick-Jones
Pontcanna, Cardiff, July 2006

Figure P.1 A cartoon produced as stimulus material during the *GM Nation?* debate

1 The origins of the debate

The *GM Nation?* public debate, which took place during 2002–03 was, for the UK, an unprecedented experiment in large-scale public participation. It amounted to an extended process of information collection and provision, consultation and discussion, about a controversial technology: namely genetically modified (GM) crops, and related matters such as GM-derived food. The debate, which was sponsored at 'arm's length' by the British government, was underwritten by a commitment by the government to take its findings into account when making a decision about the possible commercialisation of GM crops in the UK. Despite suffering from a number of imperfections, the debate was successful in generating widespread interest and considered discussion about complex matters of science and policy among relatively large numbers of the lay public. Such developments would have been unthinkable in policy circles just a decade before.

This book charts the history of the debate, and examines some of its key implications. It does so in an admittedly limited way: the central focus of our work has been concerned with carrying out a systematic (and independent) evaluation of the debate's implementation. In this respect, the book provides one of a small number of rigorous evaluations of such processes that may be found in the literature. As officially accredited evaluators of the debate, we were given unique behind-the-scenes access to virtually all aspects of the debate process. We are, therefore, in a position to provide a comprehensive assessment of the strengths and weaknesses of this unique experiment.

Despite our somewhat technical focus, we have formed some clear views about a range of contextual features that need to be considered in seeking to understand why the debate took place. We also appreciate the importance of what the experience of the debate says about the nature of governance in contemporary Britain: both narrowly in terms of regulatory controls on technological innovation, but also more widely in glimpsing something of the emerging politics of risk in the early years of the twenty-first century.

The debate may be seen as a concrete manifestation of a trend towards *citizen engagement*: a notion that has become a central motif in public policy discourse within many democratic countries. A greater role for the voice of the lay public in decision-making has come to be regarded as an important component of 'good governance', and, in practical terms, is seen as having the potential to address a number of perceived, potentially problematic, 'deficits of democracy' faced by contemporary public administrations: shortages of knowledge, trust and legitimacy (CEC, 2001; DETR, 1998; OECD, 2001). Significantly, this 'deliberative turn' (Dryzek, 2000) poses important questions about decision-making over innovation and technology management; in particular in cases where the technology in question is associated with some degree of controversy, involving conflicts in underlying values and motivations. In such cases, how are expert knowledge and the needs of the market to be reconciled with strongly held beliefs and value commitments among the citizenry?

These international trends in thinking about democratic processes have been reflected within the sentiments expressed in the 'modernising government' programme of Britain's New Labour administration (Blair, 1998; Her Majesty's Government, 1999). They also resonate with a number of recent substantive developments within the British policy-making community, including the state's adoption of risk management as a basis for administrative practice (Cabinet Office, 2002; Horlick-Jones, 2005a, 2005b; NAO, 2000, 2004; Rothstein *et al.*, 2006), and a decisive move away from a 'deficit' model of public (mis)understanding of science (which stresses public ignorance of technical facts; see Irwin and Wynne, 1996) towards an advocacy for engagement with the lay public and their values (Cabinet Office 2002; House of Lords, 2000; POST, 2001).

Such changes may be understood partly in terms of responses to large-scale social and economic shifts, and attempts by the British state to reconcile tensions within the nexus of scientific and technological developments, social values and expectations, and market pressures (Walls *et al.*, 2005a). However, they also appear to reflect the impact of a number of high-profile government and corporate failures in recent years, perhaps most notably the BSE/CJD disaster (Jasanoff, 1997; Phillips, 2000). A further important factor seems to have been a pre-occupation within British government circles about the need to 'regain' a perceived loss of trust in public institutions (Löfstedt and Horlick-Jones, 1999; Poortinga and Pidgeon, 2003b; Walls *et al.*, 2004).

The technology in question – genetic modification – had been controversial, in international terms, for many years (Bauer and Gaskell, 2002; Gaskell and Bauer, 2001; Toke, 2004), and the period running up to the announcement of the debate was characterised by many unresolved tensions. In Britain, the continuing market uncertainty over GM-related products had been signalled by their withdrawal from supermarket shelves during the late 1990s. A de facto moratorium on GM crop cultivation was coming to an end, corresponding to the imminent results from field-scale evaluations of the impact of GM crops on farmland biodiversity. All cultivation of GM crops in Britain continued to be threatened by a sustained programme of opposition, including trial crop destruction by environmental activists. In international terms, the US was threatening to take action against the European Union (EU) through the World Trade Organisation (WTO) on the basis of its allegedly anti-free market position on GM products (Toke, 2004).

Whatever the motivation behind the GM debate, the need for a thorough evaluation of its implementation, and a measure of its performance against a range of appropriate criteria, seems undeniable. In this way lessons from this important experiment may be learned, with a view to performing such public debates more effectively in the future. In this chapter we set the stage for the detailed discussion of the debate that is to follow. We do so by tracing some important features of the institutional, political and cultural landscape that provided the backdrop against which the debate came into existence. We also describe how we came to have a close involvement with the debate process. We conclude the chapter by first noting the relevance of the debate to some wider issues in the scholarly and policy-related literatures, and then finally by providing some signposts to assist the reader in navigating the text.

The GM controversy

Recent years have seen a widening gulf between Europe and a number of regions of the world in terms of both governmental policies towards GM-related agricultural practice and associated regulatory controls, and consumer views towards GM-derived products, with the most stark contrasts being between Europe and the US (Bauer and Gaskell, 2002; Wiener and Rogers, 2002). Indeed, by 1998 almost three-quarters of the global land area planted with GM crops was located in the US (Anderson, 1999). US-based corporations, backed by the US government, were pushing for unhindered entry to European markets – for both GM seeds, modified to resist tailor-made herbicides (typified by Monsanto's *Round Up Ready* soya) and GM products, particularly modified soya beans (a basic ingredient in many supermarket foodstuffs).

Given the apparent enthusiasm for GM agriculture in North America, it is easy to forget the level of controversy that existed there in the mid-1970s, leading to a prominent group of US scientists calling for a moratorium on 'recombinant DNA' experiments. There was a widespread fear of the possible adverse effects of releasing genetically modified organisms into the environment. This level of controversy, and a recognition of the need for 'genetic engineering' to be governed by special levels of regulation, led to the establishment in the UK in 1976 of the Genetic Manipulation Advisory Group, or GMAG (Bennett *et al.*, 1986; Fincham and Ravetz, 1991). GMAG was, for its time, a highly unusual government advisory committee, including as it did representatives of the 'public interest'. In this way it was designed to promote a discussion of technical matters in their wider social, political and ethical contexts. GMAG was a short-lived experiment, and is now rarely mentioned in the literature on GM, however, in many ways its existence prefigured the recent developments in institutional innovation that led to the establishment of the GM debate.

Despite these cautious beginnings, in recent years biotechnology has become a diverse, and potentially lucrative, area for technological development and industrial innovation. Indeed, in a widely reported speech to the Royal Society in London in 2002, British Prime Minister Tony Blair pointed to its key potential role in securing the UK's future prosperity. In that speech he warned against resistance to new scientific developments that amounted to 'a retreat into a culture of unreason' (Blair, 2002: 10).

The political and regulatory trajectory that led to the fears underlying Blair's statement have been documented very effectively elsewhere (Bauer and Gaskell, 2002; Gaskell and Bauer, 2001; Levidow and Carr, 2000; Toke, 2004; Wiener and Rogers, 2002), and to address this background in detail would take us far beyond what is possible within the confines of this book. Therefore, in the following paragraphs we simply attempt to capture something of the mood of the times leading up to the GM debate.

As Gaskell and Bauer (2001: 4) note, the year 1996 proved pivotal in a developing period of controversy. The concerns of scientists who had investigated the potential environmental hazards of extensive GM crop plantings (e.g. Rissler and Mellon, 1996) were beginning to attract increasing attention. There were two main sources of anxiety: that the habitats supporting rare species and biodiversity might be degraded or destroyed (here, the Monarch butterfly was later to become a case in point), and that traits from GM crops might be transferred to other plant varieties contaminating neighbouring crops and generating unwanted 'superweeds' that had developed resistance to targeted herbicides. Tensions were brought to a head in 1996 when it emerged that the first shipment of GM soya beans from the US arrived in Europe with EU labelling rules not yet in place, prompting the launch of an anti-GM campaign by a number of pressure groups.

During the next two years, the level of controversy in Europe about the GM issue continued to rise. A vigorous campaign by two leading environmental pressure groups, Greenpeace and Friends of the Earth, argued for the protection of organic crops from 'GM contamination', and against the introduction of GM crops and foodstuffs. Meanwhile, a concerted campaign of direct action by environmental activists sought to destroy all trial GM crops. These tensions culminated in the public row in 1998 over the sacking of a scientist, Arpad Pusztai, from the Rowett Institute in Aberdeen. Pusztai had claimed to find evidence of adverse effects in rats caused by them consuming GM food. These claims had been hotly contested by the scientific establishment, including a critique by the prestigious Royal Society of London (Rowell, 2003: 79–102). In June 1998, Prince Charles, an enthusiastic advocate of organic farming,[1] called for a public debate on whether to allow GM crops to be grown in Britain. The following month, English Nature, the government's official advisory body on wildlife conservation, called for a three-year moratorium on commercial planting.

Also in 1998, pressure groups successfully mobilised a campaign to persuade supermarkets to withdraw GM foodstuffs from their shelves. Marks & Spencer agreed to remove all GM ingredients from the foods on its shelves, and Waitrose and the Co-op promised to make their own-brand ranges GM free. Other supermarkets began to start sourcing from non-GM food supplies, and indeed, one of them, the Iceland chain, decided to market on the basis that none of its own-brand products would contain GM material. In this way, businesses responded not only to uncertainty about consumer preferences, but also, in the context of a perceived rising environmental consciousness in the UK, appear to have sought to capitalise on emerging marketing opportunities. Prior to 1998 the EU had, in fact, approved nine GM products, but from October 1998 had agreed to stop approving any more products for planting or import. Retailers were refusing to stock GM food, and the market in GM products began to fail. As Grabner *et al.* (2001: 28) put it, 'as a wave of scepticism flowed over Europe, the process of product approval ground swiftly to a halt'. Faced with a mounting crisis, the EU used the revision of Directive 90/220 as a device to introduce a de facto moratorium on the production and sale of GM crops in Europe.

The moratorium existed in the UK between 1998 and 2003. Initially the biotechnology industry regarded this state of affairs as just a 'breathing space' before a 'managed process of commercialisation' could begin. The moratorium was sustained by a voluntary agreement between government and industry; the latter represented by five companies – representing the biotechnology industry, crop protection companies, seed producers, farm produce distributors and farmers' interests – known as the Supply Chain Initiative on Modified Agricultural Crops (SCIMAC; discussed in detail in Toke, 2004). During this period, SCIMAC worked with regulatory bodies to agree a set of best practice guidelines for the growing and harvesting of GM crops. The moratorium in Britain eventually expired at the end of a programme of farm-scale trials, designed to investigate the impact on biodiversity of herbicide resistant GM crops (AEBC, 2001). The findings from these trials were published in the autumn of 2003 (Hawes *et al.*, 2003).

In global political terms, the EU moratorium fuelled pre-existing tensions between Europe and the US over regulatory approaches for transgenic crops (Levidow and Carr, 2000; Wiener and Rogers, 2002). According to the EU, its 'precautionary'-based regulation was prudent, and responsive to significant uncertainties in the possible risks posed by these crops. However, in May 2003, the US and a number of cooperating countries announced that they would file a case through the WTO against the EU. The moratorium, they argued, was illegal and not based upon 'sound science'. Moreover, they suggested that it was harmful to both agriculture and the interests of the developing world (e.g. Toke, 2004).

Of course, Britain's membership of the EU imposes certain obligations regarding the licensing of crops and, indeed, EU rulings had made clear that 'GM free zones' were illegal within European law. When, in March 2003, the EU GM products approval process was re-started under EC/2001/18, serious questions were raised about the credibility of holding a public debate about the cultivation of GM crops in the UK. Indeed, the timing of this development was unfortunate, occurring as it did just a few months before the public aspects of the *GM Nation?* debate were scheduled to 'go live'. As we note in Chapter 3, news of the activation of the approval process prompted the Chair of the debate's Steering Board to write to the Secretary of State, seeking reassurances about the government's goodwill.

The form of the EU regulatory framework for GM crops, and of the wider WTO obligations provided an important backdrop to the *GM Nation?* debate. The negotiations over the EU GMO Directive EC/2001/18 had resulted in a tough regime that laid greater emphasis on the environmental assessment of any proposed GM crop. However, it also included a somewhat ambiguous clause providing member states with the discretion to take appropriate measures to avoid unintended 'contamination' of other crops by GM species. In practice, the UK government found itself squeezed between an essentially techno-scientific regulatory framing of 'sound science', and uncertainty about the political repercussions of accepting GM species for domestic cultivation (see discussion in Toke, 2004).

The debate went ahead, but doubts remained in some quarters about the value of 'national' public debates about issues where individual nation states have limited scope for autonomous action. Such concerns were reinforced by an important development that occurred whilst we were finalising the text of this book. The threatened WTO action by the US, Canada and Argentina, which had been taken, had led to a preliminary ruling in which the WTO had found against the EU.[2] At the time of writing, the full implications of this decision, with a final ruling pending, have yet to become clear.

The public mood

Throughout the period immediately prior to the GM debate, there was considerable uncertainty about the likely behaviour of consumers with respect to GM products. Opinion polls suggested that consumers were far from convinced of the much-vaunted virtues of GM-related products, with the Eurobarometer survey indicating rising levels of opposition to the technology in many European countries, including Britain (Gaskell *et al.*, 2003; Gaskell and Bauer, 2001). Such polls indicated that GM food was an area where the lay public had relatively little faith in the competence of government regulation. This is perhaps unsurprising given the recent history of food-related controversies in the UK, culminating in the BSE/CJD disaster.

The polls indicated that up to a third of people neither supported nor opposed GM food: attitudes that earlier focus group-based studies had variously interpreted as 'ambivalence' (Grove-White *et al.*, 1997: 1) or 'an instability between optimism and playing safe' (Petts *et al.*, 2001: 92). The existence of a substantial portion of the lay public holding such ambivalent views was a clear finding from the survey work that formed part of our debate evaluation exercise, as will be discussed in later chapters.

In the light of these apparent consumer attitudes, supermarkets were loath to stock GM food, fearing the potential risk to their reputations if seen to be abandoning their no-GM policy.[3] A public relations campaign in Europe by the multinational corporation Monsanto in 1998 had been recognised as a failure (Bauer and Gaskell, 2002: 351). This state of affairs led the largest industry firms to form an association, the Agricultural Biotechnology Council, with the primary objective of counteracting anti-GM claims made by environmentalists. By the time that the *GM Nation?* debate took place, an earlier mood of confrontation had shifted to one in which industry had begun to respond to calls for public dialogue, and to present its position in terms of being 'committed to listening and responding to issues surrounding GM technology'.

Given the sometimes obscure technical details of GM, and the high level of public ambivalence associated with its agricultural applications, media accounts of these issues require particular attention. Here, we have in mind the extensive literature that has examined the role of the media in shaping public opinion, in agenda-setting, and in 'amplifying' or 'attenuating' the perceived significance of certain risk-related issues (Gamson and Modigliani, 1989; Kitzinger, 2000; Murdock, 2004; Murdock *et al.*, 2003). This literature points to the significance of how media accounts are 'framed': providing ways of talking about issues, and highlighting specific aspects of the situation by constructing stories around particular themes. In addition, 'templates' organise the overall structure of reporting by suggesting analogies and comparisons with salient past and contemporary events.

While risk as a theme has been central to media coverage of GM, we note that from the outset, however, the GM story was never solely about risk. It was also about corporate power and political accountability: themes that were developed in two other major news frames, one focused on the location of control over the development of GM, and the other on distrust of government and the Prime Minister. The 'control' frame mobilised worries that the future of GM in Britain would ultimately be determined 'offshore', first in the EU and second in the US, operating through the WTO. The 'distrust' frame drew on popular suspicions that government policy had been captured by corporate interests and that an ideological commitment to 'free' markets took precedence over public concerns (Marquand, 2004).

The emerging 'risk' and 'control' frames were consolidated in February 1999 when GM emerged as a major news story, with a group of scientists demanding that Pusztai's findings be re-examined. Eight days later an opinion poll published in the *Independent on Sunday* revealed that over two-thirds of those questioned (68 per cent) were worried about eating GM foods. The paper publicised these findings as part of a concerted campaign for comprehensive food labelling, and a three-year freeze on the development of GM crops, which it had launched at the start of the month. Five national dailies also launched campaigns on potential food risks. The slogans were clear and explicit; 'Food scandal' (*The Guardian*), 'Genetic Food Watch' (*Daily Mail*), 'Label Frankenstein Foods' (*Daily Mirror*) and 'Stop GM foods' (*The Independent*).

In orienting stories about GM, the major media template was provided by the UK's recent experiences with bovine spongiform encephalopathy (BSE), more popularly knows as 'mad cow disease'. A systematic content analysis of items on GM appearing in the national press in early 1999 revealed that a quarter contained explicit reference to BSE (Durant and Lindsey, 2000). Plausibly, the activation of this template had two major consequences. First, it strengthened anxieties about the risks to human health posed by untested techniques by anchoring them in vivid reminders of patients dying from the wasting disease vCJD. Second, it resurrected memories of early warnings ignored, dissident scientists pilloried, and senior politicians and officials closing ranks to defend commercial interests against the public interest in safe food (Marquand, 2004). When a general sample of the adult population were asked in January 1999 which sources they trusted to advise them on the risks posed by BSE only 4 per cent nominated government ministers and 17 per cent government scientists (House of Lords, 2000). Once the emerging news template had highlighted the similarities between the two situations it seems plausible that this legacy of suspicion was transferred to GM.

In February 1999 the Prime Minister gave his personal backing to industry assurances that GM foods were safe to eat. He went on to argue, five days later, that banning GM products would damage the development of the UK's biotechnology industries, and so seriously undermine Britain's efforts to lead the international race to develop a knowledge-based economy. Claims were subsequently made that the UK government's Science Minister, Lord Sainsbury, had commercial links with companies owning and developing GM technologies.[4] At the same time, media coverage of popular protests, such as demonstrations outside supermarkets and activists destroying crops, served to cement a fourth major media frame: one centred on a notion of the scale and depth of popular opposition.

One powerful representation in media coverage came in the form of the phrase 'Frankenstein', or 'Franken-', foods. The figure of Frankenstein, the over-reaching scientist in Mary Shelley's cautionary tale, who sets out to assemble a perfect life form, but manufactures a creature that ends up destroying him, is a familiar image from horror films, comic books and fancy dress costumes. The use of the image captures anxieties associated with the unknown effects of GM in a graphic, and immediately understandable way. This lent itself to popular press reporting, perhaps most notably in the *Daily Mirror*'s front page featuring a digitally manipulated portrait of Tony Blair as the monster under the headline 'The Prime Monster', followed by the text 'Fury as Blair says: I Eat Frankenstein food and it's safe'.

Other sources of such resonant media imagery included the theme of nuclear contamination, and the figure of the Grim Reaper, the biblical harbinger of death. News photographs of GM activists engaged in destroying crops often captured them dressed in the kind of anti-contamination suits associated with workers at nuclear installations. Such associations also entered the coverage in more subtle forms. *The Independent*, for example, chose to illustrate a story headed 'Ministers told to study GM cancer risks' (on 2 May 1999) with a cartoon showing a husband completely encased in a protective suit saying to his wife 'I'm just popping down to the greengrocers'. The figure of the Grim Reaper was also widely used by GM protesters, and extensively circulated through news photographs of street demonstrations and field invasions. Here was an image with the potential to mobilise deep-seated anxieties about the arbitrary nature of death and destruction, for which there is no equally powerful expression in secular iconography.

By mid-1999 the news coverage of GM had crystallised around a handful of core frames – risk, control, distrust and opposition – anchored in recurring phrases such as 'Frankenstein Foods', and widely used images of contamination suits and Grim Reapers. After this initial peak of media attention, coverage dropped back to relatively low levels. As we will see in Chapter 8, the dominant definitions of the situation that formed in this key phase remained a readily available set of cultural resources: ones that were drawn upon extensively in constructing media coverage during the *GM Nation?* debate.

The birth of the debate

The handling of GM issues presented the British government with a difficult challenge. The government was broadly supportive of biotechnology as a potential contributor to the creation of an innovative science-based economy, which, after all, has been a central objective of the entire New Labour programme. However, an unequivocal embracing of GM might have been viewed as politically risky. What might be described as a 'somewhat precautionary' approach to full commercialisation of GM crops has resulted (Levidow and Carr, 2001; Oreszczyn, 2005), entailing a substantial review of the regulatory framework for biotechnology (OST, 1999).

During the 1990s a number of changes took place that served to shape the form of this review. We have already mentioned the various domestic and international controversies, and the adverse media coverage. Within government, important developments were occurring in thinking and practice about the handling of risk. In 2002 the British government's Cabinet Office – the central policy-making body of the state machinery – published a report (Cabinet Office, 2002) which recognised that risk management, which it describes as 'getting the right balance between innovation and change on the one hand, and the avoidance of shocks and crises on the other', is 'now central to the business of good government' (ibid.: 2). In many ways this document may be regarded as consolidating into policy a number of trends that led to the GM debate, including moves towards openness, extended consultation, stakeholder engagement, and the use of 'arm's length' bodies as sources of risk information.

These developments in governmental style may be understood in terms of wider currents. Two factors appear to have been especially influential. First, global developments in the nature of capitalism have had an enormously important impact on the state structures of Western nations, leading to the adoption of private sector-inspired policies such as de-regulation, cost-cutting and performance-driven resource allocation (Hood, 1991; Osborne and Gaebler, 1992). Second, during the last two decades a number of risk-related policy failures and crises have taken place. It is important to appreciate the extent to which these events concentrated the minds of those in government, as well as ringing alarm bells throughout the corporate world. In particular, the official inquiry into BSE (Phillips, 2000) identified necessary changes in risk handling practices that amounted to nothing less than a fundamental shift in culture and behaviour in UK risk policy and institutions. These changes included a recognition of the need for openness to 're-establish' trust and credibility; an overhaul of the use of scientific advice by government; and changes in how risk and uncertainty should be managed and communicated.

New Labour came into power with a commitment to 'modernise' government. In practical terms, the new governance of risk has taken two, overlapping forms: the adoption of the private sector machinery of *corporate governance*, with its underlying concern with control and accountability; and a citizen engagement agenda. The latter reflects thinking in international policy networks about citizen engagement, which we have already mentioned. It also appears to draw upon a strand of management thinking that advocates a need to be responsive to stakeholder needs. Interestingly, a congruence emerges here between the notions of *citizen* and *shareholder* (Horlick-Jones, 2005a, 2005b). With these changes a new interest in issues of transparency, stakeholder views and ethical considerations came into regulatory discourse.

The impact of these developments on the regulatory framework for biotechnology was significant. First came the restructuring of the Advisory Committee on Releases to the Environment (ACRE). Prior to the reforms, eight of the thirteen members of ACRE had links with the biotechnology industry. The reforms resulted in ten of the thirteen members being replaced by scientists without direct links with the industry (Toke and Marsh, 2003).[5] However, most far-reaching in this broadening of the base of the regulatory apparatus was the establishment of two new standing advisory bodies. This development led directly to the establishment of the *GM Nation?* debate.

The two novel institutional forms recommended by the 1999 Cabinet Office review were the Agriculture and Environment Biotechnology Commission (AEBC) and the Human Genetics Commission (HGC). While not possessing direct regulatory responsibilities, these multi-stakeholder bodies were charged with the responsibility of providing government with strategic advice regarding the wider social and political implications of the technologies in question. The establishment of the AEBC appears to have been an attempt to institutionalise in microcosm the existing dynamics of the GM controversy. Among the voices present around the table were those from seed companies, organic and conventional farming, and environmental and consumer lobbying organisations (Walls *et al.*, 2005a). The establishment of the AEBC therefore constituted, in itself, a move towards a greater degree of stakeholder engagement in the regulatory process.

The origins of the *GM Nation?* debate lie in recommendations contained in the first AEBC report, *Crops on Trial*, which was published on 10 September 2001. The report was an examination of the farm-scale evaluations, or 'field trials', designed to investigate the impact of GM cultivation on biodiversity. One of the conclusions to the report suggested that the results of the field trials, while a necessary condition, would not be a sufficient one on which to base a decision to proceed with commercialisation of GM crops. To the consternation, we understand, of certain key figures in central government, the report recommended the need for a public debate. Specifically, it concluded that public policy on GM should 'expose, respect and embrace the differences of view which exist, rather than bury them' (AEBC, 2001: 12). It went on to call for 'an open and inclusive process of decision-making around whether GM crops being grown in the [field trials] should be commercialized, within a framework which extends to broader questions' (ibid.: 19) and for the future role of GM crops within UK agriculture to be considered in 'a wider public debate involving a series of regional discussion meetings' (ibid.: 25).

It should be noted that the AEBC recommendations, despite being produced by a group of individuals associated with a highly disparate range of views on GM-related issues, were recognisably influenced by a distinct critical perspective on matters concerning technology, risk and society. This perspective (see e.g. Wynne, 1987, 1992) argues that ostensibly neutral 'scientific' risk assessments possess implicit social and political framings. Such framings, it is suggested, serve to exclude a range of wider considerations and value-commitments, and so alienate lay public caught up in conflicts about the control of technology, leading to an erosion of trust in regulatory and other official bodies. This perspective is strongly associated with a commitment to the democratisation of science and technology, a matter to which we return at the end of this chapter. As we will see, the role of lay framings came to play a central role in the design of the debate. It is interesting to speculate on the extent to which all the membership of the AEBC, and indeed Ministers and government officials involved in discussions about the possibility of holding a debate, fully appreciated the radical nature of the critique embedded within the debate recommendations.

In January 2002, the government (UK government, Scottish Executive and the Department of the Environment in Northern Ireland, with the National Assembly of Wales replying separately) asked the AEBC to provide advice on how best to organise such a public debate, including 'how to determine the public acceptability of GM crops'.[6] In her subsequent letter to the AEBC (dated 25 July 2002) the Secretary of State responsible for the debate, Margaret Beckett, confirmed the government's wish, first indicated on 31 May, that a 'public dialogue on GM' should take place. The government, she stated, was committed to a 'genuine, balanced discussion, and also to listening to what people say'. At this stage she also set out the three-component form that the overall programme of dialogue would take. These components included a review of the scientific evidence headed by the Chief Scientific Advisor, David King, and an economics study to be produced by the Strategy Unit; part of the Cabinet Office. The intention was 'to create a dialogue between all strands of opinion on GM issues'. A budget of £250,000 was allocated for the public debate, and a timetable established in which the final report on the debate was to be submitted to government by June 2003.

With this letter, the government published a detailed note responding to the AEBC advice submitted on 26 April. The terms of reference for the overall programme of dialogue were specified as follows:

- to identify, using methods that focus on grass roots opinion, the questions which the public has about GM issues, avoiding as far as possible the polarisation that has characterised so much of the discussion to date;
- to develop, from this framing of the issues and through a wholly open process, the provision of comprehensive evidence-based information to the public on scientific, economic and other aspects of GM;
- to provide people with the opportunity to debate the issues openly and to reach their own informed judgements on this subject;
- to provide information to government on how questions raised by the public have shaped the course of the debate, including on the scientific, economic and other aspects of GM.

In September 2002, the creation of an independent Public Debate Steering Board (PDSB) was announced, to be chaired by Professor Malcolm Grant, the existing Chair of the AEBC. It was made clear that members of the Steering Board would serve in their personal capacity, rather than as representatives of particular organisations or constituencies with which they were associated. The PDSB was to operate on similar lines to those established by the AEBC, namely to hold its meetings in public, and to publish minutes on the debate website.[7] It was also announced that the AEBC secretariat would provide administrative support for the debate, and that COI Communications (formerly the Central Office of Information) – an 'arms-length' government agency that specialised in public relations – would become the main contractor, or executive agency, for the debate.

As we discuss in detail in Chapter 3, the design of the debate adopted by the PDSB for implementation was remarkably close to the initial design proposed to government by the AEBC. This took the following form: a preliminary series of workshops, designed to allow a range of lay perspectives to frame the terms of the process; an open engagement phase, comprising public meetings, availability of information materials, a website, and the opportunity to comment on the issues or complete a questionnaire; and a series of focus groups that were conceived as providing some degree of 'control' over possible bias arising from the public engagement perhaps only attracting participation by those with fixed pre-existing views.

How we got involved

At the time the GM debate was proposed we had been monitoring the work of the AEBC for a period of some eighteen months. The emergence and functioning of new institutional forms such as the AEBC was of considerable relevance to our work on the changing patterns of risk perception and risk governance in the UK (the *Understanding Risk* programme, 2001–06). The agreement by government for a full-scale public debate to take place was therefore a development of great significance for this wider programme of work.

Accordingly, we decided to commit sufficient resources to allow us to follow the course of the debate. We were pleased to note that the initial AEBC guidance to government on the conduct of the debate recognised the need for a systematic evaluation of the process, although we were disappointed to learn that the debate budget was insufficient to allow the Steering Board to fund its own systematic evaluation. Clearly an appointment by competitive tendering would have been more satisfactory from the point of view of evaluating a publicly accountable process. Fortuitously, we found ourselves in a position of being able to fund a fairly extensive programme of evaluation work from our existing research budget, and so in August 2002 we wrote to the AEBC, expressing interest in having a substantive involvement in the process of evaluating the debate process.

In our letter we observed that we were confident about having the necessary skills to carry out an evaluation that would be both robust and methodologically sound. We also expressed a commitment that this work would be independent of any of the bodies involved in the debate. In September 2002, we were invited to present a detailed proposal to the debate's Steering Board (Horlick-Jones *et al.*, 2002), and on the basis of our proposed methodology we were appointed as the official evaluators of the debate. This quasi-contractual arrangement was achieved by means of a formal exchange of letters, which were subsequently posted on the debate's website.

A summary of the early findings from our evaluation work on the debate was submitted as an invited contribution to the House of Commons Environment, Food and Rural Affairs Committee inquiry in October 2003 into the conduct of the debate. That memorandum was subsequently published as part of the official report of the inquiry (Horlick-Jones *et al.*, 2003b). In February 2004, we published a full evaluation report (Horlick-Jones *et al.*, 2004), which was launched at a conference staged at the Royal Academy in London. This 182-page report was posted on the *Understanding Risk* programme website, and distributed to key stakeholder organisations inviting comments. As noted in the Preface above, in addition to the preparation of this book, the evaluation exercise has generated a growing number of technical papers (Horlick-Jones, 2004, 2007; Horlick-Jones *et al.*, 2006a, 2006b, in press, a, in press, b; Pidgeon *et al.*, 2005; Pidgeon and Poortinga, 2006; Poortinga and Pidgeon, 2004b; Rowe *et al.*, 2005, 2006, in press; Walls *et al.*, 2005a, 2005b).

Some wider questions

Although this book is focused fairly tightly on the nuts and bolts of the GM debate, by necessity it also engages with a great many wider issues in intellectual and policy debates. Clearly it is not simply an exercise in social science theory. Rather, it reports on an application of social science methods and thinking to matters of considerable practical relevance. Nevertheless, the story we have to tell intersects with, and has a bearing on, a number of sometimes highly contested areas of scholarship that relate to the nature of the contemporary world, and how best public policy decisions should be made. In this section we reflect briefly on some of these wider themes.

We mentioned the establishment of the advisory committee called GMAG back in the 1970s, in response to the initial worries and controversies about what was then called 'genetic engineering'. As far as we are aware, at that time there was no serious suggestion that the issues in question should be debated in ways that *directly* involved the lay public. In this respect there are features of the contemporary world that are very different from the one that existed just thirty years ago.

Perhaps the most influential attempt to theorise contemporary sensibilities to risk-related issues is provided by the 'Risk Society' thesis associated with Ulrich Beck (1992, 1995) and Anthony Giddens (1990, 1991). Certainly, a significant shift in anxieties about health and environmental risks appears to have taken place in recent years (Glassner, 1999; Pidgeon *et al.*, 2003). These efforts have not been without criticism (e.g. Dingwall, 1999; Horlick-Jones, 2005a; Rose, 1999), and indeed, this shift has hardly been monolithic, with resistance to new technologies by no means a universal feature of contemporary societies. Indeed, one need look no further than mobile telephones to find a case of market saturation rather than wholesale disquiet. Nevertheless, there are worries that over-cautious regulatory regimes may prove pathological (Burgess, 2004; but see Timotijevic and Barnett, 2006).

Arguably the most important features of contemporary Western societies with a bearing on the need for governments to adopt public engagement, are rising public expectations of what is necessary for 'the good life' (Berger, 1987), and an enhanced propensity for consumer mobilisation. Two crises in recent years illustrate this latter tendency: the affair in 1994 concerning the disposal of the Brent Spar, an oil storage platform in the North Sea jointly owned by Shell and Exxon (Löfstedt and Renn, 1997); and the ongoing disaster concerning BSE/CJD and British beef, which emerged in 1996 (Jasanoff, 1997; Maxwell, 1997). Both crises resulted in shifts in market behaviour that caused concerns in government offices and corporate boardrooms alike. The potential for a similar impact on consumer behaviour has been clear in connection with claims in the UK regarding the possible dangers associated with the combined Measles-Mumps-Rubella (MMR) vaccination. All these risk controversies have been characterised by key protagonists – government, industry and pressure groups – basing their arguments in terms of claims of authoritative knowledge. In this sense, public arenas, which form the focus of considerable media attention, take on the character of quasi-judicial contests with 'expertise' being invoked to support competing positions (Horlick-Jones, 2004). In this sense, the contemporary situation in Europe increasingly resembles an earlier era in North America (Huber, 1991).

How, then, can one understand the provenance of the GM debate? Thirty years ago, one of us argued for enhanced citizen participation largely in liberal-reformist terms (O'Riordan, 1976). Contemporary theorists such as Dryzek (2000) would argue that such exercises allow the state to avoid a crisis of legitimacy. Neo-Marxist analyses might see the debate as in some sense a 'tactical' deployment of participation as a policy tool, as part of a 'tapestry' of coordination measures which seek to optimise capital accumulation (Jessop, 2002; Walls *et al.*, 2005a). For some governance theorists, the debate might be a signpost on the inexorable trajectory from top-down monolithic govern-ment towards regimes with much greater levels of plurality and participation (see e.g. Rhodes, 1997). Followers of Michel Foucault might regard it as an exercise in 'governmentality', an attempt by the state to incorporate its citizens, and so create discipline, as part of a strategy of 'neo-liberalism' (Rose, 1999).

Certain members of the PDSB told us that they regarded the debate as an opportunity to open up the 'sound science'-based regulatory procedures within agricultural biotechnology to wider social and ethnical perspectives. In this respect their views seem to have been influenced by the 'social and political framing' critique of risk assessment in technology management mentioned above.

For contemporary policy analysts, the question remains: why enter into extended engagement with stakeholder groups and the wider lay public? In fact, an increasingly 'corporate' state might see many potential benefits, including:

- enhancing credibility and public trust;
- enhancing the quality of public decision-making;
- establishing legitimacy for decisions;
- gathering knowledge from, and providing knowledge to, stakeholder groups;
- taking into account possible misgivings about policy among stakeholder groups, and avoiding associated potentially expensive difficulties;
- highlighting and promoting wider discussion and debate about issues that the government regards as important, yet may, in formal terms, have limited powers to address.

Of course, the very notion of a 'better' decision is an intensely political one, and one or more of these objectives may prove dominant in the motivations of the government in question, or whichever stakeholder group is calling for the engagement exercise to take place. In practice, real-world participation exercises are shaped by a powerful *realpolitik*, with what is ostensibly a 'fair debate' being embedded within a matrix of underlying concerns and agendas.

Indeed, when evaluating the *GM Nation?* debate, we found that while all stakeholder groups, including those 'for' and 'against' GM, supported the idea of a public debate, they possessed rather different ideas of what the debate should be about. These views serve as a useful reminder that public debates of this nature inevitably entail political manoeuvring, resulting in a need for would-be evaluators to be particularly careful in assessing the quality of the data they collect.

At a technical level, it is important to recognise that the more intractable issues that may arise in public controversies often cannot be resolved by appeal to 'the facts' if competing arguments are differently 'framed'; in other words competing perspectives are based upon different ways of 'looking' at the problem issue (Schön and Rein, 1994). As we discuss in Chapter 7, according to this perspective, engagement processes such as the *GM Nation?* debate may be seen as attempts to incorporate and reconcile competing perspectives, subject to the practical constraints and opportunities afforded by the character of the issue in question. In this way, there is a need for engagement processes to strike a balance between *processes* that allow different voices to be heard, and *techniques* that allow technical and other knowledges to be captured, and so to inform the process of deliberation. Seen in this way, the quality of public decision-making can be enhanced by maximising the volume and range of knowledge being taken into account, and the diversity of perspectives on the matter at hand (Funtowicz and Ravetz, 1992; see also Horlick-Jones, 1998; Petts, 1997; Wynne, 1991).

We recognise that some of the most energetic advocates for extended participation in public decision-making see 'engagement' as a vehicle for achieving wider goals than simply enhancing the quality of decision-making about specific matters. These include those who view participation as a way of attending to what is often described as a malaise in the health of the democratic system, characterised by: a loss of trust in government, a perceived culture of political 'sleaze', widespread lack of interest in politics, reduction in numbers voting at elections, and so on (see e.g. Involve, 2005).

Others see participation as a means of achieving radical change. For instance, 'upstream engagement' (opening the process of technological innovation to wider scrutiny at a very early stage in its development; see Wilsdon and Willis, 2004) is seen by some as a way of 'democratising' science and technology. This agenda draws on a body of sociological studies of the nature of scientific knowledge (which we again consider in Chapter 7). These studies have revealed the contingency underlying the apparent neutrality and objectivity of scientific knowledge. Some scholars (e.g. Irwin and Wynne, 1996) seek to use this degree of contingency as an opportunity to address questions about science such as: 'who owns it?'; 'who benefits from it?'; and 'to what purpose should it be directed?'. As we understand it, according to this perspective, upstream engagement provides an opportunity to shape basic science, and the trajectory of technological development, in more democratically accountable directions, while it is still being formed.

Such proposals raise a host of difficult conceptual and practical underlying issues, ranging from the extent to which constructionist analyses are able to capture the material nature of technologies (see e.g. Button, 1993; Horlick-Jones, 2007; Horlick-Jones and Sime, 2004; Hutchby, 2001) to possible adverse impacts on the process of innovation. Early forms of engagement also raise a number of technical questions which we address in this book, including the representativeness of participation in such interventions, and the difficulty of avoiding a biased pre-framing for issues that are sufficiently obscure as to be difficult for the lay public to grasp.

We will return to this discussion of wider issues at the end of the book, in Chapter 9.

The structure of the book

Here, we provide an outline of the remaining parts of the book.

The next chapter provides a detailed examination of the methodological foundations of the approach we adopted to evaluate the debate. This includes a discussion of the evaluation criteria we used – normative and sponsors'– and the reason why we chose to also consider a set of criteria inferred from participants' observations about events in which they took part.

Chapter 3 sets out a brief chronology of the debate, and discusses how the various component parts unfolded in practice. It also examines the various datasets we included in our evaluation exercise, and how these data were collected. A map is also provided that shows how the various criteria with which we worked are considered in the subsequent chapters.

Chapter 4 presents the first part of the evaluation, focusing on 'process issues' associated with the implementation of the debate process, and the extent to which this might be regarded as effective and fair.

Chapter 5 turns to the issue of representativeness: first examining socio-demographic, and then, attitudinal, bases for evaluating performance. It then discusses wider public views towards GM food and associated matters, and the extent to which the debate findings might be said to have captured this profile of perspectives. This chapter raises the question of different modes of reasoning about GM-related issues, and the implications of this factor for the data collected, and the overall findings.

Chapter 6 turns to participants' expectations, and their assessment of debate events in terms of their own framings. This chapter notes the overlap between participants' criteria and some of the normative and sponsors' criteria. It also identifies two criteria elicited from participants that seem to relate to the experience of *participation*, in itself, rather than as a measure of a fair and just process of deliberation and decision-making.

Chapter 7 examines the debate's performance in terms of its capacity to manage information and knowledge effectively. A new evaluation criterion, *translation quality*, which emerged from the process of evaluation, is identified and discussed.

Chapter 8 considers wider perspectives on the debate; first, the views of the disengaged lay public; second, the ways in which the issues in question and the debate itself were portrayed in the media; and third, the ways in which organisations that were actively engaged in the issues – environmental and consumer pressure groups, and biotechnology industry bodies – viewed the idea of the public debate, and the way in which *GM Nation?* was implemented.

Finally, Chapter 9 attempts to synthesise, with as much clarity as possible, the main findings of the book. It examines the evidence we have assembled to provide an overall assessment of the effectiveness of the debate. A number of practical and methodological lessons are considered, which we suggest have a bearing on how best to design and implement future such initiatives, and to evaluate them. The chapter concludes by returning to some of the wider issues raised at the end of Chapter 1 in order to engage with the question of the practicability of a 'deliberative future'.

2   Our approach to evaluating the debate

An evaluation process seeks to determine some aspect of the *quality* of an exercise. The *GM Nation?* public debate has generally been considered an example of an exercise in 'public participation'. In practice, however, it was a broader programme of activity, including a number of distinct component parts, some of which may, indeed, be described as 'participation', though others might be better described as 'elicitation', 'consultation' or 'communication' processes (e.g. Fiorino, 1990). The collective term 'engagement' has been used to cover all such communication, consultation and participation processes (see e.g. Rowe and Frewer, 2005). The essential difference we draw between these modes of engagement is that in consultation exercises information is simply elicited from participants without any sponsor input, whereas in participation processes, information flows to and from both parties. It is important to draw this distinction because relevant effectiveness criteria will differ depending upon the fundamental type of process, and hence purpose of the engagement being considered.

As a case in point, the role of consultation is generally to attain a comprehensive and accurate survey of opinions of relevant stakeholders, whereas the role of participation may be to allow interaction between sponsors and other stakeholders, allowing dialogue and the emergence of novel, negotiated solutions. In the latter case, the process of interaction (not present in the former case) is a factor that needs additional evaluative consideration, while concepts such as 'fairness' are also implicated as important. In this way, the *GM Nation?* debate comprised a variety of processes of different types. In our evaluation, we address this diversity by providing commentary upon each of the different aspects, as well as an overall appraisal of the initiative as a whole.

Evaluation principles

Conducting an evaluation of a major public engagement initiative is not a straightforward process. The first question we need to ask is: what do we *mean* by the 'quality' of the exercise? In other words, how will we know if the exercise is 'successful' or not? Assessing quality, or success, requires the stipulation of clear attributes or criteria against which the performance of the initiative, and its various component parts, may be compared and judged. Unfortunately, there are no such easily measurable, and objective, attributes; none, that is, that are obvious and un-contentious. In practice, those attributes that contribute to success or failure are often multi-dimensional, subjective or in some way intangible, such as the notion of 'fairness', which is often identified as an appropriate evaluation criterion. Indeed, there is considerable disagreement within the research community as to what a 'good', 'effective' or 'successful' engagement activity should involve (Munton, 2003).

We view with some concern the tendency among those involved in conducting engagement processes to have no clear a priori ideas about what it means for their exercise to be a success. As a result, evaluations are not infrequently ad hoc affairs, which are conducted almost as an afterthought to the organisation of the exercise. As such, they may simply involve asking various participants to indicate somehow (e.g. via a simple questionnaire or during a largely unstructured interview) whether they thought the event was worthwhile (discussed in Rowe and Frewer, 2004).

It is important to note at this point that the adoption of a rather unstructured approach to evaluation may be a purposeful choice. There is a school of thought that regards selecting evaluation criteria *prior* to an exercise taking place as impossible, or at least problematic. The inductive research tradition seeks to first collect data and *then* to induce hypotheses/theories (and, indeed, definitions). Here, stating what is meant by 'effectiveness' a priori is seen as constraining the data one will collect, and so imposing a framework upon the data that might not be appropriate. This approach, which typically uses qualitative rather than quantitative research techniques, is particularly apt in new environments where little is previously known, where quantitative data are difficult to obtain, and where hypotheses are difficult to generate (e.g. Joss, 1995). This position generally leads to 'evaluations' that take the form of case studies, in which results are inevitably strongly related to the evaluators' subjective interpretations of what went on. Such evaluations have limitations in the extent to which their results may be replicated or generalised, and are open to serious questions about the reliability and validity of their findings (e.g. Clarke with Dawson, 1999).

We have suggested that such inductive exercises should be termed *assessments* rather than *evaluations* (Rowe *et al.*, 2005). Although in some respects conducting *assessments* (as defined here) would seem appropriate in a complex participation environment, there are a number of difficulties involved in taking this approach, which tend to be exacerbated by the often highly charged political nature of public engagement. Perhaps the greatest of these problems is the different values and perspectives of those involved (from the sponsors and organisers to the various participants themselves) each of whom may have different rationales for involvement. Although differing perspectives are problematic for defining effectiveness a priori, these make ascertaining effectiveness after an event a hugely fraught exercise, in which any party disagreeing with the assessment may (perhaps justifiably) question the conclusions. Clearly if effectiveness is defined beforehand then there can be less in the way of grounds for complaint after the event.

If we accept the desirability of pre-specifying evaluation criteria, what should these be? Evaluation criteria are often discussed in terms of whether they refer to event *processes or outcomes* (e.g. Chess and Purcell, 1999). Ultimately, most sponsors are interested in *outcomes*, that is, whether the activity delivered something positive, such as a notable increase in public trust in themselves, reduced public resistance to their initial plans, or a better decision (or indeed, any decision at all). Unfortunately, outcomes are often difficult to establish: the final outcomes from any particular event may be temporally distant and intangible (e.g. public trust in a sponsor may be a slow-growing and nebulous phenomenon), and practically, evaluation reports are generally required soon after the conclusion of engagement events and long before all eventualities have been played out – and indeed, long after any evaluation process has come to an end (Rowe *et al.*, 2005).

Consequently, evaluation of event *processes* may have to serve as some form of surrogate evaluation for the entire endeavour. Arguably, if the processes are poor, then the outcomes are liable to be poor; if an exercise is full of rancour between the parties involved, incompetent handling of the issues, incomplete and biased representation of the facts in a rushed and untimely manner (as examples), then one might anticipate that little positive will subsequently emerge. Of course, this will not always be the case: sometimes good results can emerge from bad decisions as the world is an inherently unpredictable place. Ideally, an evaluation will consider both process and outcome aspects.

In our initial evaluation of the *GM Nation?* debate, our focus was on processes, as we were aware of a need to provide timely commentary on matters, and indeed our focus in this book is also largely on processes. However, we have also used the subsequent months since the conclusion of the event to gather information on outcomes, and we return to this matter in the final chapter.

Other complexities in evaluation revolve around the question of *who?* (the evaluation of *processes* essentially addresses the issue of *how?*, and evaluation of *outcomes* addresses *what?*, while consideration of the *process/outcome* tension addresses the question of *when?*). There are many parties involved in any particular engagement, from the sponsors to the organisers (those running the event, who may be the same as the sponsors or may represent a consultancy or some similar organisation), and from the involved public and stakeholders to additional interested parties and commentators (e.g. political, social, academic). Each party may have a different perspective on what it means for the exercise to be a 'success', thus any evaluation needs to consider these multiple subjectivities. In the present evaluation, as will be discussed shortly, we not only consider an 'objective' or 'normative' perspective on what research in this area suggests *should* be achieved by a successful participation initiative, but we also examine alternative perspectives (namely, those of sponsors and participants), and our overall evaluation represents an attempt at balancing these perspectives.

Given these different complexities, one might reasonably ask: is it feasible, or even sensible, to talk of one set of 'normative' or ideal criteria that ought to be satisfied in order for an engagement exercise to be deemed a success? Rowe and Frewer (2004) have suggested that the answer to this question is broadly 'yes'. They have argued that although the specific aims and circumstances of engagement exercises invariably differ, they may typically be considered particular instances of more general aims, such as 'to have (some kind of) impact upon policy', or 'to increase the worth of the sponsors (in some manner) in appropriate stakeholders' eyes'. This issue of *universally generalisable* evaluation criteria has received relatively little attention in the literature, yet published evaluation reports often imply that the criteria adopted have a wider relevance than for the specific exercise they discuss. Indeed, a number of generic criteria have been identified in the academic literature, although these tend to differ in terms of their content and the ways in which they have been derived. Some have been developed on the basis of theory (e.g. Esogbue and Ahipo, 1982; Fiorino, 1990; Laird, 1993; Poisner, 1996; Webler, 1995), others through an analysis of past commentaries on the topic (e.g. Arnstein, 1969; Rosener, 1975; Rowe and Frewer, 2000; Wiedemann and Femers, 1993), and yet others through conducting surveys or interviews of those involved in participation exercises to ascertain *their* views on what constitutes an effective exercise (e.g. Carnes *et al.*, 1998; Lauber and Knuth, 1999; Moore, 1996; Shindler and Neburka, 1997; Tuler and Webler, 1999). Within this literature, a number of other researchers have presented rules-of-thumb or checklists for effective participation in which generic criteria are implicit (e.g. Desvousges and Smith, 1988; Milbraith, 1981).

Rowe and Frewer (2004) noted that the relevance, validity and utility of the various generic criteria are uncertain, as their relative merits have generally gone unchallenged (though Sewell and Phillips, 1979, did critically compare four different models for evaluation that comprised different criteria). In some cases, criteria have simply been stated and left for others to consider and apply; in other cases they have been used in the same article that introduced them as the basis for evaluating particular engagement exercises or mechanisms. Often, evaluation has been informal, based upon the researchers' subjective and theoretical assessment of a particular type of participation mechanism or comparison of several different mechanisms (e.g. Checkoway, 1981; Fiorino, 1990; Heberlein, 1976; Rowe and Frewer, 2000). The presence of validated instruments for measuring performance on specified criteria is rare.

Although there is no consensus about which set of criteria is best or most relevant, certain themes do recur (see Rowe and Frewer, 2004). The criterion of 'representativeness', for example (essentially a requirement that participants are appropriately representative of the wider affected population), has been stipulated in one form or another as an important criterion for success in many evaluations. Outcome criteria tend to include the consideration that the exercise has had some 'impact': on the decision-making or attitudes of the sponsors, or perhaps on the knowledge of the public. Process criteria have tended to consider how components of the exercise lead to 'effective' and 'fair' involvement of participants, in terms of enabling appropriate and efficient two-way communication (e.g. National Research Council, 1996; Renn *et al.*, 1995). In this respect, most of the process criteria have been related to what some would argue are certain generic aspects of the practical ethics of group interaction processes (Renn *et al.*, 1995; Webler, 1995; see also critical remarks in e.g. Bogen, 1989; Lynch, 1993; Horlick-Jones *et al.*, 2001). This perspective is closely associated with the work of the social philosopher Jürgen Habermas (Habermas, 1990; see also White, 1988), and his concepts of 'ideal speech situations' and 'communicative rationality'.

Turning to the question of what criteria we chose in order to evaluate the *GM Nation?* debate, we first recognised that despite the recurring themes mentioned above, there was no set of generic, or *normative*, criteria that could be adopted without the potential for it to be contested. As such, we decided to use an evaluation framework with which we were familiar, namely the one associated with Rowe and Frewer (2000). This framework stipulates nine different evaluation criteria, categorised as either *acceptance* criteria or *process* criteria, that ought to be met in order for a participation exercise to be seen as a success. In addition to familiarity, we chose this framework because its criteria do incorporate the main generic criteria discussed in other systems (e.g. representativeness, impact), and because it has been used before to conduct practical evaluations (e.g. Rowe *et al.*, 2004) and hence there are a number of associated measurement instruments that have in some vague sense been 'validated'. We discuss the specifics of this framework, and its limitations, in the next section.

In addition to the research literature, another important source of information regarding what should be the benchmarks of engagement exercise quality is the views of the various parties involved in the exercise, such as the sponsors and participants. In contrast to normative criteria, sponsors' and participants' criteria relate more closely to the specificity of the particular exercise in question, reflecting the details of the circumstances leading to the organisation of the exercise, and to the characteristics of surrounding issues. It is important in any evaluation to consider such criteria, as they will be more meaningful to the various participants for being recognisably expressed in their own words, and in terms of matters of importance to them. Furthermore, given the lack of widely accepted normative criteria, consideration of these additional criteria may speak to the relevance, appropriateness, validity and exhaustiveness of the chosen normative criteria. In other words, we may attempt to use different sets of criteria, expressed in different ways, to cross-validate each other.

For the evaluation exercise described in this book, we have adopted an approach that combines both sorts of effectiveness criteria: one set justified by reference to the research literature, which will enable us to comment upon the quality of the debate as an example of an engagement exercise; and the other two sets which address the quality of the exercise as a *specific* process with unique aims and objectives. The latter sets are drawn from the stated objectives of the organisers, and those criteria we infer from our research findings that could plausibly be associated with the views of the debate participants. In the following section we discuss these sets of criteria in detail.

Evaluation criteria

Normative criteria

As noted above, we decided to adopt the set of normative evaluation criteria formulated by Rowe and Frewer (2000). These authors reviewed the academic literature on public participation and identified a number of themes that constantly recur concerning the necessary requirements for a participation exercise to be successful. They expressed these themes as nine criteria that should ideally be met in order for a participation exercise to be effective (hence 'normative' framework), suggesting that the criteria fall into two types: 'Acceptance' criteria, related to whether an exercise would likely be accepted by participants as fair, and 'Process' criteria related to the effective construction and implementation of a procedure (a distinction that bears some parallel to that made by Webler (1995) between 'fairness' and 'competence'). The nine criteria as originally stated are as follows:

Acceptance criteria:

- *Representativeness*: public participants should comprise a broadly representative sample of the population of the affected public.
- *Independence*: the participation process should be conducted in an independent, unbiased way.
- *Early involvement*: the public should be involved as early as possible in the process as soon as value judgements become salient.
- *Influence*: the output of the procedure should have a genuine impact on policy.
- *Transparency*: the process should be transparent so that the public can see what is going on and how decisions are being made.

Process criteria:

- *Resource accessibility*: public participants should have access to the appropriate resources to enable them to successfully fulfil their brief.
- *Task definition*: the nature and scope of the participation task should be clearly defined.

- *Structured decision-making*: the participation exercise should use/provide appropriate mechanisms for structuring and displaying the decision-making process.
- *Cost effectiveness*: the procedure should in some sense be cost effective.

Rowe and Frewer (2000) suggested that their nine evaluation criteria might not be appropriate in every situation. Rowe *et al.* (2004), for example, used this framework to evaluate a participation exercise but omitted use of the criterion of 'Early involvement', largely because the sponsors of the deliberative conference they evaluated did not consider it appropriate. In the case of the *GM Nation?* debate, we decided to omit consideration of the 'Cost effectiveness' criterion, primarily because it did not seem sensible to ask participants to assess this aspect of the debate. In addition, we felt that 'Cost effectiveness' could not be related in any simple way to the quality of the enactment of the participation process, and therefore it would be difficult to reconcile with the 'Process criteria' concept. We did adopt and adapt the other eight criteria as evaluation benchmarks, although we relabelled 'Resource accessibility' as 'Resources', and 'Structured decision-making' as 'Structured dialogue' – the latter to account for the fact that the exercise participants did not strictly have any decision-making requirements. In the rest of the chapter, these are the criteria labels that will be used. The adapted criteria we used are set out in Box 2.1.

One important point worth noting here is that this particular evaluation framework was intended to be specifically relevant to *public participation* processes. However, the complex, multi-level aspect of the *GM Nation?* debate only became apparent as it unfolded. Consequently, we found ourselves applying this rough framework to aspects of the initiative that might be more properly termed 'consultation' or 'elicitation' exercises. In subsequent chapters we comment upon the extent to which this framework, or aspects of it, were useful or not in evaluating such exercises, and whether other criteria might have been more appropriate instead, and we discuss how we adapted our analysis consequently.

The way we operationalised these criteria is discussed in the next chapter. In the next section we discuss the sponsors' evaluation criteria.

Sponsor criteria

In structural terms the sponsor of an engagement process may be regarded as its 'owner'. In the case of the GM debate, the independent Steering Board which oversaw the implementation of the process was clearly the sponsor. The government, meaning a combination of the Westminster parliament and Whitehall executive, together with the three devolved administrations, were the debate's 'paymasters'. They were in a position to shape the form of the debate by a variety of means, including setting formal terms of reference. We have already identified the government's terms of reference for the debate,

---

Box 2.1 Normative evaluation criteria

Acceptance (fairness) criteria:

N1 *Representativeness*: participants should comprise a broadly representative sample of the affected public.

N2 *Independence*: the participation process should be conducted in an
independent, unbiased way.

N3 *Early involvement*: the public should be involved as early as possible
in the process as soon as value judgements become salient.

N4 *Transparency*: the process should be transparent so that the public
can see what is going on and how decisions are being made.

N5 *Influence*: the output of the procedure should have a genuine impact
on policy.

Process (competence) criteria:

N6 *Task definition*: the nature and scope of the task should be clearly
defined, so that participants understand what is required of them,
and why.

N7 *Resources*: participants should have access to the appropriate and
sufficient resources (e.g. in terms of time and information) to enable
them to fulfil their designated role.

N8 *Structured dialogue*: the exercise should use appropriate mechanisms
for structuring dialogue to ensure fair and accurate information
exchange.

---

and the ways in which government rationalised the process (see Chapter 1).
Here, we focus on the Steering Board's criteria for a successful debate.

At the time we submitted our proposal (Horlick-Jones *et al.*, 2002) to carry
out the independent evaluation in September 2002, the Steering Board had
still to finalise its objectives for the debate. In our proposal we observed that
while it was to be expected that the debate was likely to have multiple
objectives, this served to create some ambiguity about the nature of the process,
with a consequent tendency to create a sense of uncertainty about what was
going on. We pointed out that it was possible that a number of distinct
purposes could be served by the proposed public debate, for example:

• an exercise in communication, designed to inform (and possibly persuade)
the lay public;
• a consultation exercise or perception study, designed to chart lay views
as they stand, unaltered by sponsor information;

- an exercise in participation, designed to engage in debate with the public, with input from sponsors and public, involving a form of what has been termed 'social learning' (crucially raising the issue of whether the lay input was likely to have any effect on subsequent policy development);
- an exercise in institutional learning, designed to assist future practice and policy development.

Finally, we noted that, ideally, all parties to be involved in the process ought to agree what criteria were to be used for its evaluation. In this case, we suggested that the Steering Board should give serious consideration to identifying criteria that could reasonably be thought to be widely acceptable.

Eventually the Board agreed a statement that encapsulated its overall aim for the debate; namely:

> To promote an innovative and effective programme of public debate on issues around GM in agriculture and the environment, in the context of the possible commercial growing of GM crops in the UK. The public will frame the issues for debate. Through the debate, provide meaningful information to Government about the nature and spectrum of the public's views, particularly at grass roots level [*sic*].

A set of nine objectives were subsequently agreed by the Board, and these are set out in Box 2.2. We also note that in the Steering Board's document which detailed these objectives,[1] a subsequent section was entitled 'How will we know that the programme of debate has been successful?'. This section discussed a further *four* indicators of success that *did not* closely address the stipulated objectives – and indeed, sometimes implied *other* objectives. These indicators are set out in Box 2.3.

The nature of these objectives, and the associated 'indicators', requires some discussion. In the first place, it is notable that many of the named objectives were essentially stipulations of functional requirements (indeed, terms of reference) for the debate. For example, objectives B4 (dialogue with experts/access to evidence) and B6 (interactions with experts) essentially state that the debate will, at least in part, involve *participative* components (there *will* be sponsor/expert–lay interactions). (B6 also hints at 'learning', and we will return to this issue in Chapter 6.) These do not really represent evaluation criteria in that they do not speak to the issue of *quality* in any sense: they simply indicate the common assumption that interaction is good in its own right (an assumption that evaluation seeks to test). Similarly, objectives B9 (providing a report to government), B7 (complementing other strands of the debate), and B3 (novelty) indicate specific functional requirements without indicating any particular aspect that might be assessed for quality (they do not allow scope for *variability*, and hence cannot be evaluated along any dimension of 'goodness'). Objective B8 ('calibration' of views) is also somewhat problematic. We understood the word 'calibrate' to mean the comparison of

---

Box 2.2 Steering Board objectives

B1 To allow the *public to frame the issues* for debate so that the programme of debate focuses on what the public sees as relevant issues.

B2 To *focus on getting people at the grass roots* level whose voice has not yet been heard *to participate* in the programme (but: 'people who have expressed their views will not be excluded from participating, but neither will they be specifically targeted and will not be allowed to steer events in the programme of debate').

B3 To create *new and effective opportunities* for the deliberative debate about the issues.

B4 To enable (through dialogue with experts [B4a] and other activities) *access to the evidence* [B4b] and other balanced and substantiated information the public may want and need to debate the issues.

B5 To create widespread awareness [B5a] among the UK population of the programme of debate, even if people do not wish to participate directly in events (above 11 years), and give widespread *opportunities to register views* [B5b] (in at least the most basic way, e.g. by letter or internet).

B6 To provide occasions within the programme of debate for *interactions* between members of the public debate, and *mutual learning* between the public and experts.

B7 To seek to *complement* and inform the *economic and science strands* and, in turn, as appropriate, utilise their outputs.

B8 To *calibrate {meaning 'situate' in this context*} the views of organisations* who have already made their views known by contrasting their views with other participants in the debate (which will involve: 'capturing the dynamic of the debate between these two groups, noting areas of shared understanding and agreement (where this is apparent) and areas of remaining contention').

B9 To provide intelligent qualitative information about public views emerging from the debate in a *report to Government* by end of June 2003.

* Conclusion based on analysis of interview data.

---

views of participants in the exercise with those of key stakeholder groups in the wider debate about GM. This again seems to be a functional requirement that does not speak to a quality issue (it is also unclear who was intended to do the 'calibration', how, or to what end – perhaps this was intended to be discussed in the report indicated in B9?).

Box 2.3 Additional Steering Board indicators

BI   The extent of *public awareness* of the programme, the science and related issues. This will be gauged by media coverage, hits on the website, and direct communications that the debate is going on.

BII   The *views of participants* in the debate about what they felt should be the criteria for success – both of particular events in which they participate and the programme as a whole.

BIII   The *views of informed commentators* – the extent to which they feel that the exercise has been credible and innovative, balanced, and has moved the debate beyond the polarisation that has so far characterised much of the discussion about GM crops. Also, their views on whether the report from the debate is sensitively drawn and provides an improvement on present understandings and characterisations of public views.

BIV   The extent to which the report from the debate could reasonably be said to have had an *impact on government*. Was information about public views emerging from the debate taken into account in decision-making? Also, the extent to which government views the debate as a model for future public engagement.

It might be best to refer to these different objectives as *pseudo-evaluation* criteria. Certainly the debate might be assessed on these aspects, but only in a relatively simple 'tick-box' manner: for example, did the debate have a participative component, or did it not?; did it deliver up a report on public views to government, or did it not? Consequently, though we will comment upon the achievement of these objects in the debate in a later chapter, we will not discuss them any further in detail as they raise no particularly interesting measurement and quality issues. Put another way, their relevance as proper evaluation criteria for a participation exercise are somewhat suspect: the debate could achieve all of these aspects and yet still be seen as a complete failure by almost everyone involved (save, perhaps, for accountants who might be pleased to note that the debate did deliver the specifics promised).

The other objectives are more interesting. Objective B2 (representativeness) is clearly similar to our normative criterion N1. Specifically, the intent of the sponsors was to have a debate that was not dominated by significant pressure groups, but to access the 'quiet majority', that is, to entail representative sampling of the population as opposed to biased sampling of particular cliques. Representativeness may be ascertained in several ways: it may be determined according to the socio-economic and demographic profiles of the sample (in comparison to that of the general public), or by the attitudinal similarity of sample to population. In order to conduct the latter comparison, it is necessary to have present information on public views. Fortunately we had relevant benchmark survey data from 2002, and were subsequently successful in raising funding for a follow-up survey in 2003. We will discuss these measurement and data collection issues later. Suffice it to say here, we take B2 and N1 to be equivalent, and discuss them in a similar light.

Objective B1 (public framing) is also interesting. On the one hand it too indicated a functional requirement – that members of the public would be allowed to frame the debate – and the Foundation Discussion workshops (discussed in Chapter 3) were clearly intended to fulfil this role (in this sense we might already give this objective a 'tick' and deem it accomplished). However, there are further subtleties implicit in this objective. Though the workshops did take place, did the public output truly inform the debate, or did other perspectives intervene and dominate? The debate could be perceived as a success to the extent that public influence on issue framing was real. Consequently we discuss this criterion in more detail later in the book (in Chapter 7), particularly from the perspective of 'information translation' – whether information from the various parties was fully and correctly translated from source to receiver throughout the entire process. This 'translation criterion' was not part of our original evaluation framework but became apparent as an important consideration as we observed the conduct of the overall process.

Finally, B5 is of some interest, although it actually comprised two separate objectives. B5a stated an aim to create 'widespread awareness' among the UK population of the overall debate; B5b aimed for the public to register its 'views' (although on what was not specified). Neither objective indicated a target percentage to be reached in order for the debate to be considered a success. This is an unfortunate commonality for engagement activities: by not presenting precise figures, essentially any number achieving awareness or responding can be (and usually is) claimed a success. We nevertheless comment upon exposure/involvement issues in a later chapter.

The additional indicators are interesting in that they specify potential measures. Although BI (public awareness) loosely indicates ways of assessing objective B5a, measures BII and BIII (which implicate as important the views of participants and the views of informed commentators) are not measures attached to any particular objective (evaluation criterion). During the debate, the organisers did acquire data on website hits and via feedback questionnaires (posted on the *GM Nation?* website and collected from participants attending certain events), and these figures were described in the final report (PDSB, 2003). We also had access to these data and used them in various ways to assess different evaluation criteria. Interestingly, indicator BIV (impact) indicated a need to ascertain if the debate had any influence on government decision-making, which generally corresponds to our normative criterion N5 (influence), but not to any of the sponsors' stated objectives. We thus interpret the indicator to be another sponsor objective that essentially replicates the N5 criterion.

In summary, many of the sponsors' stated objectives (evaluation criteria) were conceptually unclear and immeasurable in any rigorous or sensible manner. We nevertheless discuss the debate's performance against these criteria as best as we are able in subsequent chapters. However, at least two objectives/criteria were similar to our normative criteria (N1 representativeness and N5 influence) and will be discussed in this light, while another indicated a criterion that we have termed 'the criterion of translation', which we will discuss in considerable detail later, in Chapter 7.

Finally, it is worth noting that we fully recognise that the debate was an experiment, and it was to be expected that slippage would occur between any given set of objectives and the emerging practice of the debate process. Nevertheless, we suggest, the exercise of setting objectives might have been better informed by the growing body of research findings in this area. The lack of clear objectives regarding the process as a whole is one area of critique to which we will return.

Participants' criteria

We have discussed two sets of evaluation criteria so far: a set of ideal or normative criteria and the sponsors' criteria. There are other parties involved in the process, however, and it is important to understand their perspectives on the debate as well (to whatever extent this is possible). Of these different parties, the one most readily accessible is that of the *participants*. Other parties are either difficult to establish or to reach (for example, the sponsors talked of 'informed commentators' in their objectives document, yet never defined who they meant by this, while the uninvolved and initially uninformed general public could not sensibly be quizzed on their criteria for success of a debate about which they knew nothing). Since the participants are one direct half of the participation equation (involving sponsor–participant interaction), they are arguably the most important other constituency to query about the *GM Nation?* debate, what it ought to have achieved, and whether it did. Therefore, an important part of our evaluation was to elicit from participants *their* evaluation criteria.

Since the potential participants were not known at the outset of the debate, we are unable to discuss their criteria here: rather, we elicited the criteria *following* certain events in the debate. Specifically, in order to elicit participants' own effectiveness criteria, questionnaires were issued to participants in the Tier 1 public events (the most visible part of the debate – detailed in Chapter 3), which included a number of open questions, two of which were aimed at eliciting reasons for positive and negative value judgements regarding the event. One asked: 'what do you personally feel were the positive aspects of the event?', and the other asked: 'what do you feel were the negative aspects of the event?'. Positive and negative statements imply evaluation criteria: for example, a statement that an event was poor because 'there was not enough time', implies that 'time' (a resource) was important to that participant (and also that the event had scored badly on this criterion). The respondents' answers were transcribed and then analysed to identify themes, which are discussed in a subsequent chapter (Chapter 6), at which point the implied evaluation criteria are detailed and assessed.

Emergent criteria

Finally, it is important to note that our evaluation approach was not entirely *closed*. That is, in spite of focusing upon a number of stipulated evaluation criteria, we were aware that there might be other relevant criteria that would only become apparent to us following our engagement with the debate process. In Chapter 3 we will describe how we adopted a multi-method approach that provided us with a capacity to *learn* from the process of evaluation, and so an ability to arrive at emergent findings (cf. Bloor, 1978; Glaser and Strauss, 1967). Thus, we recognised that the normative criteria we chose to use might not be entirely relevant or, indeed, comprehensive, and that there might well be other significant criteria worth contemplating. In practice, we found that the debate's capacity to utilise information elicited by each stage of the process had an important bearing on its overall effectiveness. This capacity was not fully captured by any of the existing criteria, although we note that one of the sponsors' criteria, namely B1, the need for the public to 'frame' the way in which the issues are to be debated, addresses a related matter. This new criterion is discussed in detail in Chapter 7.

Conclusions

In this chapter we have set out the conceptual basis of our approach to evaluating the *GM Nation?* public debate. We have drawn an important distinction between 'evaluations' that take the form of case studies (and which we term 'assessments') and evaluations that seek to measure performance against given criteria. We explained why we chose to adopt an approach closer to the second kind of evaluation, working with three sets of criteria in order to address both generic and specific features of the debate, and carrying out the work in a way that was open to emergent findings. In the following chapter, we will discuss the practical details of how we implemented the evaluation exercise as the debate process unfolded. In the final chapter of the book we will return to our evaluation approach, examining the extent to which our chosen criteria were apt, the validity of the evaluation and the implications of our approach for future such evaluations.

3 The unfolding of the debate and the implementation of the evaluation exercise

Having discussed the main conceptual and methodological aspects of our approach to evaluating the debate, we now turn to the practicalities of implementing the evaluation. When deciding how best to tell this story we were faced with a number of choices. Should we organise the account according to the chronology of the debate (at this time, X and Y were going on, and we were doing Z), across component parts of the debate (we collected data on stage S1 using methods M1 and M2), or possibly by specific methods that we used (we used method M3 when collecting data on stages S2 and S3)? In practice we have combined these approaches: first, providing a brief overview of the chronology of activities as they unfolded; second, describing the specific methods we used; and third, discussing in more detail the evaluation of key component parts of the debate. At the end of the chapter we describe the overall analytic organisation of the evaluation process, and how the three sets of evaluation criteria, identified in Chapter 2, are addressed in subsequent chapters of the book.

The chronology of events offered below captures something of the dynamic unfolding of events, and the sometimes uncertain and unpredictable character of the processes that we attempted to monitor in real time. Given the novelty and scale of the debate – organised without a clear template and body of practical experience on which to draw, and burdened with serious resource and time constraints – it is perhaps not surprising that the resulting activity was often messy and filled with tension. Indeed, in some ways it is far more surprising that the final form of the debate resembled so closely the initial proposals hurriedly put together by the AEBC in April 2002.

A chronology of the debate process

In Chapter 1 we described how the debate came into being. In this chapter, we locate the beginning of the debate in September 2002, when a PDSB was established, so providing the debate with a management structure 'at arm's length' from government. An outline chronology of the debate process is set out in Box 3.1.

Box 3.1 **The chronology of key aspects of the debate process**

Date	Key events
September 2001	10th – Publication of AEBC report *Crops on Trial*.
January 2002	17th – Responding to recommendations in *Crops on Trial*, government requests advice from AEBC on how best to organise a public debate on GM issues.
April 2002	26th – AEBC makes formal recommendations to government on the form of a public debate.
May 2002	31st – Interim response from government to AEBC.
July 2002	25th – Margaret Beckett announces that a 'GM dialogue' will take place, comprising 'science' and 'economics' strands together with a public debate.
September 2002	13th – First meeting of the PDSB.
	23rd – PDSB meeting.
October 2002	3rd – PDSB meeting.
	23rd – PDSB meeting.
November 2002	7th – PDSB meeting, including presentation of findings from the desk research.
	7th – Letter of support for the debate from Margaret Beckett.
	14th–28th – Foundation Discussion workshops.
	20th – PDSB meeting. Costed options for the debate presented by COI.
December 2002	5th – Malcolm Grant writes to government drawing attention to 'the [financial] discrepancy that we now face'.
	6th – PDSB meeting.
	17th – PDSB meeting, including presentation by Corr Willbourn on the Foundation Discussion workshop findings.
January 2003	20th – Letter from Welsh National Assembly expressing concern about the timing of the debate with respect to the regional elections.
	20th – Letters from Margaret Beckett confirming that the government will make a written response to the debate findings, and offering an additional £155,000 for the debate budget.
	21st – PDSB meeting (held in private session).

	30th – Malcolm Grant writes to government proposing a revised timetable for the debate, and alluding to the 'projected new budget'. 31st – PDSB meeting.
February 2003	1st – Public meeting, staged by Dorset County Council, and addressed by PDSB Chair Malcolm Grant. This was the first public meeting associated with the GM debate. 18th – Margaret Beckett confirms a doubling of the original debate budget, and extension of its timescale. 20th – PDSB meeting.
March 2003	18th – Malcolm Grant writes to government seeking clarification regarding the significance of the EC GM product approvals process being re-started. 20th – PDSB meeting. 24th – Statement by Margaret Beckett confirming no decision on GM cultivation in the UK had been taken, and looking forward to the 'main debate activities'.
April 2003	15th – PDSB meeting.
May 2003	27th – PDSB meeting.
June–July 2003	3rd – Official launch event of the *GM Nation?* public debate. 3rd–13th – Tier 1 public events take place in Birmingham, Swansea, Taunton, Belfast, Glasgow and Harrogate. 10 June–8 July Narrow-but-Deep group meetings. 16 June–18 July – An estimated forty Tier 2 events and over 600 Tier 3 public events take place. 26th – PDSB meeting.
August 2003	4th – First drafting meeting for the final report, including presentation by Corr Willbourn on the Narrow-but-Deep process. 28th – Second drafting meeting for the final report.
September 2003	24th – Publication of the PDSB report on the findings of the debate.
October 2003	3rd – Final meeting of the PDSB.
February 2004	19th – Publication of the *Understanding Risk* team's evaluation of the GM debate.
March 2004	9th – Publication of the government response to the GM dialogue.

The Steering Board drew on AEBC membership with four additional members (serving in a personal capacity): the Chair of an agricultural bio-technology business organisation, the Director of an anti-GM coalition, a government official with specialist knowledge of public engagement, and an official from the sponsoring government department, with the brief to ensure proper accountability of public funds.[1]

As noted above, in practice the form that the debate took was remarkably close to the initial design proposed to government by the AEBC, namely:

- a preliminary series of workshops, designed to allow a range of lay perspectives to frame the terms of the process;
- an open engagement phase, comprising public meetings, availability of information materials, a website, and the opportunity to comment on the issues or complete a questionnaire;
- a series of focus groups that were conceived as providing some degree of 'control' over possible bias arising from the public engagement perhaps only attracting participation by those with pre-existing (and fixed) views.

This design was fairly novel (see Figure 3.1). It was very different from the consensus conference on biotechnology that had taken place in Britain almost a decade earlier (Purdue, 1999). This earlier experiment in lay deliberation on GM had been modelled on approaches to public consultation pioneered in Denmark. In that process the appointed panel of lay members had been able to set their own agenda, to interrogate experts, and to draw their own conclusions. The form of the debate was also rather different from experiments with smaller scale 'citizen juries' (Coote and Lenaghan, 1997), an approach that utilises a broadly representative sample of jurors, and which typically takes place over a few days, often with less extensive exploration of technical issues than in consensus conferences. This approach had already been used in the UK to explore lay views about the role of genetic technologies with respect to health care in Wales (Dunkerley and Glasner, 1998).[2]

Despite the existence of numerous similar experiments in Britain and elsewhere (see e.g. Beierle and Konisky, 2000; Joss and Durant, 1995; National Research Council, 1996; Renn *et al.*, 1995; Walls *et al.*, 2005b), it was not possible for the planning of the *GM Nation?* debate to draw upon a systematic body of design knowledge. As we have noted elsewhere (Rowe *et al.*, 2005), this shortfall arose primarily because of the relatively small number of rigorous evaluations that were to be found within the literature (Abelson *et al.*, 2003; Rowe and Frewer, 2004).

Establishing the machinery

The first meeting of the PDSB was held on 13 September 2002, and, in common with all the subsequent meetings, was held in a central London location. The meetings of the Board were held approximately every two weeks.

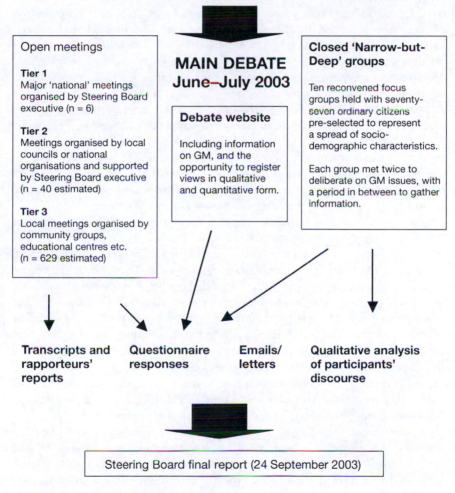

November 2002

Foundation Discussion workshops

Total of nine large 'focus groups': eight with ordinary citizens pre-seleceted to represent a spread of socio-demographic characteristics; one further meeting held with GM stakeholders.

Exploratory 'framing' of issues in preparation for the main debate process the following summer.

MAIN DEBATE June–July 2003

Open meetings

Tier 1
Major 'national' meetings organised by Steering Board executive (n = 6)

Tier 2
Meetings organised by local councils or national organisations and supported by Steering Board executive (n = 40 estimated)

Tier 3
Local meetings organised by community groups, educational centres etc. (n = 629 estimated)

Debate website

Including information on GM, and the opportunity to register views in qualitative and quantitative form.

Closed 'Narrow-but-Deep' groups

Ten reconvened focus groups held with seventy-seven ordinary citizens pre-selected to represent a spread of socio-demographic characteristics.

Each group met twice to deliberate on GM issues, with a period in between to gather information.

Transcripts and rapporteurs' reports

Questionnaire responses

Emails/ letters

Qualitative analysis of participants' discourse

Steering Board final report (24 September 2003)

Figure 3.1 The *GM Nation?* debate process

At this first meeting, COI Communications (henceforth COI) made a presentation, and some members of the Board expressed concerns that the employment of COI might send out the wrong signals to the public, potentially undermining the perceived independence of the debate. Some sympathy for these concerns was expressed by the COI personnel present, who asked the Board for advice on how best to counteract such negative impressions. Despite these concerns, the Board decided to appoint COI as the main contractor.

We are aware that among the membership of the Board, there were some misgivings about this appointment, largely because a wider choice of potential contractors was never considered. Nevertheless, it was clear that COI possessed considerable expertise in communication, event organisation and related matters. In addition, it possessed an extensive roster of suppliers, thus making possible the speedy delivery of services without going through lengthy EU procurement procedures. In the context of the time pressure on the PDSB to organise the debate, this feature appears to have been seen as a particularly important consideration. In fact, the exact circumstances that served to offer up the appointment of COI as, in essence, a fait accompli, have never become entirely clear to us. We note elsewhere in the book that COI had been consulted by central government at a very early stage to advise on the likely scale of the budget necessary to deliver a public debate; the organisation therefore had a high profile at the time when backstage discussions were taking place within Whitehall about the practicalities of holding a debate.

A further consideration regarding this appointment arises from the fact that COI was a government agency, albeit 'at arm's length'.[3] Inevitably questions were asked about COI's neutrality in the way it set about implementing the debate. Our comment on this suggestion is clear. Throughout the course of following virtually every aspect of the debate process, we found no evidence to suggest that any clear political agendas were served by COI's appointment as the main contractor. At one point it emerged that the DEFRA (Department of Environment, Food and Rural Affairs) official who was a member of the PDSB was having regular meetings with COI personnel to check that the implementation of the debate process was done in such a way as to ensure value-for-money. This revelation led to some heated exchanges at a PDSB meeting, and continued misgivings among some Board members, but no clear evidence of any possible associated manipulation ever emerged.

Also at the first meeting of the PDSB, we made a presentation on how we proposed to evaluate the debate, resulting in our appointment as the accredited evaluators. There were also presentations on the economics and science 'strands' of the GM dialogue that would be running parallel to the public debate.

The PDSB subsequently finalised its overall objectives for the debate, as we discussed in Chapter 2. The initial preparations for the debate took the form of background 'desk' research. COI undertook part of this work in-house, reviewing previous examples of public engagement exercises from around the world. A further piece of work, reviewing the research literature on public attitudes towards GM food and GM crops, was carried out by an independent researcher.[4] Work on the desk research began in mid-September, and presentations were made to the PDSB on 7 November. Interestingly, this research recognised that:

> In the light of the Steering Board's revised and full objectives, and on the basis of this study of best practice in deliberative public engagement on complex issues, *we believe that the budget of £250,000 is insufficient to achieve all of the Steering Board's objectives for the debate* (noting the dual requirements therein for both depth and breadth) in a manner consistent with best deliberative practice.
>
> (emphasis added)

During these early months concerns were expressed by members of the PDSB about the degree of government commitment to the debate, and how in practice the government would act upon the debate's findings. This led the Board Chair, Malcolm Grant, to formally request from ministers a reassurance that they would respond to the final report. In a letter dated 7 November, Secretary of State Margaret Beckett reiterated government support for the debate and commitment to the independence of the Board. She added support for the proposal to run preliminary workshops to 'identify all the questions that the public has about genetic modification and to inform how the debate process will develop'. She also made clear that the government supported the debate ranging wider than 'just crops' if this reflected the breadth of public interest in the issues.

At the meeting of the Board held on 20 November, COI presented a list of costed options for the design of the debate, and, once again, argued that the Board's objectives could not be met within the existing budget of £250,000. Soon after, on 5 December, the Chair of the Board wrote to Mrs Beckett, setting out the plans for implementing the debate, and drawing attention to the '(financial) discrepancy that we now face'.

In the meantime, the next stage of debate preparations had been put in place. During this period (14–28 November) nine 'Foundation Discussion' workshops had been run by a firm of sub-contractors to COI (Corr Willbourn Research & Development). The group sampling had been segmented across age and geographical dimensions, excluding those with a work-related or campaigning link with GM-related issues. A single group was recruited explicitly to include individuals who *were* engaged in these issues in this way (see Table 3.1). These workshops were each facilitated by two moderators, and each lasted approximately three hours.

The brief for these workshops (see Corr Willbourn, 2003a) was to:

*   establish a baseline understanding of current attitudes among the general public toward genetic modification;

Table 3.1 Sample characteristics of the participants in the Foundation Discussion workshops

Location	Sample label	Sample characteristics (age; gender; socio-economic status; geographic location)
Bromsgrove (England)	Older families/empty nesters	Age: 41–54; Gender: mixed; Status: ABC1; Suburban
London (England)	Young singles	Age: 20–27; Gender: mixed; Status: ABC1; Urban
Ludlow (England)	Teenagers	Age: 17–18; Gender: male; Status: C1C2DE; Rural
Belfast (Northern Ireland)	Young families and couples	Age: 28–40; Gender: mixed; Status: C1C2DE; Rural/suburban
Ruthin (Wales)	Older families/empty nesters	Age: 55–75; Gender: mixed; Status: C1C2DE; Rural
Edinburgh (Scotland)	Young families and couples	Age: 28–40; Gender: mixed; Status: ABC1; Urban
Altrincham (England)	Teenagers	Age: 15–16; Gender: female; Status: ABC1; Urban
Reading (England)	Young singles	Age: 20–27; Gender: mixed; Status: C1C2DE; Urban
Norwich (England)	Actively involved	Age: variable; Gender: mixed; Status: variable; Rural/suburban

Note: The workshop sampling used the standard 'social grade' form of socio-economic classification which is widely used in market research.

- discover how the public frame the issues;
- discover how the public wish best to see the debate shaped;
- ascertain how best to engage the public in debate.

Corr Willbourn presented its findings to the PDSB on 17 December. We consider these findings in Chapter 7 as part of our discussion of knowledge-handling by the debate process.

The year came to an end with considerable discontent among members of the Board over the issue of the budget. There were also concerns about the practicability of the timescale stipulated by government (reporting by the end of June 2003), and discomfort that this timescale would effectively exclude discussion of the field-scale evaluations from the debate. Matters were complicated in January by a letter from the Welsh Assembly Government, expressing concern about a possible clash between the timing of the public aspects of debate and the period of 'purdah' leading up to the regional government elections on 1 May.

On the same day (20 January), Margaret Beckett wrote two letters to the PDSB. One letter gave an undertaking that the government would make a written response to the PDSB's report on the debate. She hoped that this commitment would 'reassure the public that their participation in the debate was worthwhile'. The other letter addressed the question of funding. She offered an additional £155,000 'based on contributions from DEFRA, DTI and Northern Ireland' (omitting to mention Wales and Scotland). She added that 'we may be able to supplement' this sum, subject to discussions 'with colleagues'.

The seventh meeting of the PDSB, held on 21 January, was closed to members of the public. This was a highly charged meeting that was billed informally as an attempt to have an 'honest discussion' between key actors in the debate process. We recognise that this was a moment of real crisis for the debate. As the minutes note:

> members were dismayed that the letters (mentioned above) had only emerged on the day of the meeting but were more concerned at the situation they now faced in trying to plan the debate. Seven weeks had passed since they had written to government requesting additional funding and the amount on which they could count remained unresolved. This made final decisions impossible and posed a real threat to the credibility of the process.

Concerns had also developed about the capacity of COI to run the debate effectively. The minutes record that COI officials were presented with a list of very specific requirements to be addressed in revised advice that was to be prepared in good time for the next meeting on 31 January. These requirements included 'clear evidence' on progress made by COI in contacting local networks of organisations that would stage debate events. The mood of the exchanges is captured in the tone of this second extract from the minutes:

> The board needed to have confidence that the contractors proposed for the next phase had the capability of running a deliberative debate in line with the board's aims and objectives and not just the ability to design public friendly material.

A flurry of backstage communications ensued. Our interviews with members of the Board indicate that at this stage more than one member considered resignation. On 30 January, Malcolm Grant again wrote to Mrs Beckett. Drawing attention to the concerns over timing expressed by the Welsh and Scottish regions, he proposed that the public events should take place in June and July, thus making delivery of a final report by the end of June impossible. Interestingly, the letter alluded to the 'projected new budget'. Two weeks later, Mrs Beckett replied. She agreed both the timetable extension and a doubling of the original budget, to £500,000. DEFRA also agreed to find COI's management fee. Beckett concluded by noting that since the debate had been announced, the previous July, 'very little of it has been evident to the wider public'. She hoped that the Board would now be able to 'press ahead with designing and delivering a visible public debate programme'.

Two days later the Board issued a press release stating that 'the national GM Debate is about to get under way'. This stated that a series of public events would take place between May and July, drawing on a 'tool-kit' including a CD-ROM and a film made by the well-known documentary-maker Roger Graef. It further stated that the debate would report by the end of September. On 26 February, the PDSB announced that the name of the debate would be *GM Nation?* (following an exercise in brand-analysis by COI). The Board also announced a three-tier structure of public events, including a first tier comprising six large-scale 'national' events. The idea was that these events would act as a launch pad for local and regional meetings, as well as being genuinely 'deliberative' events themselves. The plans were outlined for a dedicated website, the CD-ROM for use at meetings, video, and a paper copy of the electronic material (we discuss these materials in Chapter 7). It should be noted that at this stage members of the Board were keen for the events to be fully participative, and to include a dimension in which there would be an opportunity for participants to question experts.

During March further concerns were raised by Board members in relation to the credibility of the debate. These arose following a presentation by a DEFRA official on the EU 'approvals process' for GM products. It emerged that the process for a case-by-case consideration of GM products for possible import and/or cultivation was re-starting under Directive EC/2001/18. Malcolm Grant wrote to Margaret Beckett noting that the public might wonder why the government was participating in this process whilst the GM debate programme was under way. He pointed out that the Scottish and Welsh administrations had both expressed concerns that any consent to applications would be premature in advance of the outcome of the debate. Beckett replied with a public statement dated 24 March to the effect that no decisions on cultivation of GM crops in the UK had been taken. The British government was simply fulfilling its legal requirements in providing comments on two applications for import (not cultivation). In her statement she took the opportunity to highlight the debate, and the government's commitment to that process.

During the weeks running up to the launch of the debate, COI engaged in a flurry of activity in an attempt to ensure all the necessary preparations were in place. A 'Technical Advisory Group' (or 'TAG team', as it was described), comprising officials and members of the Board met on an ad hoc basis to wrestle with the host of practical problems that awaited resolution.

With the launch itself scheduled for 3 June, the PDSB meeting on 27 May was, not surprisingly, a tense affair. A COI official and Richard Heller – a professional writer who had been hired to prepare the final report – together presented some ideas on how the report might be structured. A report from COI set out details on the logistics of despatch of the tool-kit to local event organisers. This report prompted expressions of dismay from the Board when

COI officials were unable to provide specific concrete details regarding the local meetings. Board members demanded an urgent status report outlining the number of people who would be attending the regional launch meetings, and the extent to which the second- and third-tier meetings were being organised, and where, precisely, they would take place.

To the best of our knowledge, COI was never able to gain such a complete picture of what was going on at a local level. In effect, the debate had 'taken on a life of its own'. Despite our status as official evaluators, we found that obtaining details of local meetings became something of an investigative process. As the level of planning by local groups escalated, COI was often unable to provide us with up-to-date information on meetings. Indeed, we found that on numerous occasions the websites of pressure groups such as Genewatch proved more helpful in this respect.

The debate goes live

On 3 June the *GM Nation?* public debate was officially launched with a press briefing in central London and the first Tier 1 meeting in Birmingham. At the press launch, Malcolm Grant faced a room full of national media correspondents. He made a short opening statement in which he described the debate as a 'high-risk experiment', and then answered questions. He stressed the transparency of the debate's organisation, and, in response to a question about whether government would listen to the feedback from the process, he referred to 'a letter from Mrs Beckett in my pocket' which confirmed the government's intention to take the debate seriously. The launch event ran very smoothly and professionally, with Pat Wilson, the debate's press officer, identifying specific journalists by name prior to inviting them to ask their question.

Grant's answers to the questions were delivered with authority and confidence. Our notes indicate two especially interesting comments he made that provide a glimpse of the underlying 'political minefield' (to use Grant's own term) that provided a backdrop to the debate process. One question referred to the constraints on the government created by EU membership. What was the point of the debate when EU obligations gave so little discretion to member states regarding GM cultivation? In response, Grant argued that recent statements along these lines by (soon to be sacked) environment minister Michael Meacher had been 'too stark'. He noted that the regional administrations in Scotland and Wales had managed to adopt 'highly precautionary positions' in comparison with Whitehall, while continuing to satisfy EU law. In response to a subsequent question, Grant took the opportunity to note the 'cultural differences' between those countries where GM crops were currently being grown and Europe. He argued that these differences had been 'thrown into sharp relief' by the US decision to take action against the EU through the WTO.

Over the next ten days, five other Tier 1 events took place: at Swansea, Belfast, Glasgow, Taunton and Harrogate, attracting around 1,000 participants in total. These public meetings, which in principle anyone could attend, were resourced by COI, and shared a number of organisational features. The events were invariably held in halls or conference venues such as the NEC in Birmingham and the Brangwyn Hall in Swansea. Admission was by ticket only, with tickets being available from COI. They were advertised on the debate website and local media, with further publicity being provided by the activities of campaigning organisations.

The seating arrangements for Tier 1 events followed a similar pattern, with clusters of tables and chairs, each allowing groups of up to a dozen people to sit together. Participants had no pre-assigned seats and sat where they liked, often with friends or acquaintances. Numbers attending each meeting ranged from around 100 in Belfast to some 240 in Harrogate. On each of the tables were placed stimulus material in the form of the 'tool-kit' booklet and materials designed to promote structured discussion. These latter materials included a 'discussion guide', which advocated the consideration of 'benefits' and 'risks and impacts' of GM, together with an index which identified where a range of issues could be found in the booklet. Pens, pencils and writing pads were also provided.

While participants were taking their seats, the 'tool-kit' video was shown on a large screen. At the end of the video, the facilitator (specially hired by COI) introduced himself and provided some background information on the debate. At some of the meetings a member of the PDSB addressed the audience. Participants were then invited to discuss the topics identified in the discussion guides provided. Each table was asked to elect a spokesperson for a later feedback session. These 'round-table' discussions between participants lasted for approximately an hour. Each table was then allocated around five to ten minutes to summarise the results of their deliberations for the entire audience.

Soon after the sequence of Tier 1 events had begun, two tiers of 'local' meetings started to take place. Tier 2 meetings, of which there were around forty, were typically hosted by town or local councils. Around thirty of these were provided by COI with technical assistance and professional facilitation. The number of attendees at these 'supported' Tier 2 meetings was extremely variable, ranging from approximately thirty in Inverness to 200 in Cambridge.

There was some variation in the format of Tier 2 meetings, which we understand reflected local needs; some councillors having received a great deal of lobbying from local stakeholder groups. Most took the form of a 'traditional' public meeting, with presentations from a number of speakers (sometimes including a member of the PDSB), followed by a question and answer session. The tool-kit booklet was made available at the majority of events, although distributed in different ways. At the Truro event, for instance, the booklets were laid out on tables near the entrance for people to pick up as they wished; while at the Gloucestershire County Council meeting in Cheltenham, they were set out with discussion guides on the participants' tables, in the manner of the Tier 1 events. At the Oxford event electronic voting pads were available, which allowed participants to register their views on a series of questions at the end of the meeting.

Some Tier 2 events – for example, the one at Truro – were run as ticket-only affairs, with people having to contact a local ticket office, and tickets being issued on a first come, first served, basis. Other events, including the Gloucestershire one, had a 'core' attendance of invited representatives of local organisations. The remaining places were advertised in the local media. Some speakers addressed a number of meetings, but the overall nature and format of information provided to the Tier 2 audiences was different for each event. There was also variation in the tone of these events: ranging from good natured, if passionate, exchanges of views, as in the well-informed debate that took place in Cambridge, to the kind of disrupted, somewhat acrimonious, event that took place in Truro, which featured constant heckling of the invited speakers.

Tier 3 meetings were mostly organised by established local voluntary bodies, although the PDSB sought to also encourage ad hoc groupings to arrange events. As the debate website and tool-kit materials put it: 'Why not hold a GM public debate meeting of your own? Perhaps you would like to get friends and colleagues together to discuss the issues.'

Events needed to be registered with COI prior to supplies of tool-kit materials and feedback questionnaires being sent to organisers. There appears to have been little enthusiasm within business organisations contacted by COI to promote local meetings for their workers, perhaps during lunch breaks. The suggestion appears to have been widely regarded as 'political' by management, and so suspect in some way. Indeed, despite COI's considerable efforts in promoting local meetings through contacting a host of public and private sector, and voluntary organisations, there seems to have been a real danger that an embarrassingly small number of Tier 3 meetings would take place. This was a pivotal moment for the credibility of the entire debate.

In practice, there seems little doubt that the debate was 'rescued' by the extensive last-minute involvement of local branches of environmental pressure groups such as Friends of the Earth (FOE). We observed one of these FOE-organised events in the small Welsh town of Abergavenny. This was staged in a hall at the back of a public house; a venue more often used for Friday-night discos. It attracted around sixty people, including a number of local farmers. The event was addressed by a GM scientist and an environmental campaigner, after which an efficiently chaired question time was held. Interestingly, although the mood of the meeting was generally anti-GM, both the main speakers and a number of contributors from the floor made a number of even-handed and nuanced points which reflected the complexity and ambiguity of the issues in question.

Overall, the Tier 3 events seem to have been highly variable in nature in terms of size, character and degree of formality. COI estimated that a figure in excess of 600 such meetings took place. However, it should be noted that the COI estimate was based on a record of expressions to hold a meeting (of thirty people or more), rather than a tally of actual confirmed meetings. In all, a total of some 20,000 individuals across the UK were estimated to have possibly taken part in the three tiers of public meetings (PDSB, 2003).

During this period, in June–July 2003, a further number of meetings were held that were not open to public participation. They involved members of the lay public, with participants specially recruited to provide a reasonable cross-section of the public, and designed deliberately to exclude people with an active interest in GM-related issues (see Table 3.2). This process was organised in response to a recognition by the PDSB that findings from the debate might be criticised for their possible bias because of the involvement in the public aspects of the debate by a self-selected sample of people. In order to attend to this difficulty, an additional closed component of the debate took the form of a series of meetings of ten discussion groups (rather like focus groups; Bloor *et al.*, 2001). These meetings were conceived as a 'control' on the findings arising from the open parts of the debate process. The process was given the name 'Narrow-but-Deep': with 'narrow' referring to the limited scope of representation, and 'deep' alluding to the anticipated extended level of engagement and deliberation in these groups, in comparison to that typically

Table 3.2 Sample characteristics of the participants in the 'Narrow-but-Deep' process

Location	Sample label	Sample characteristics (age; gender; socio-economic status; geographic location)
Sheffield (England)	Young singles	Age: 20–27; Gender: mixed; Status: ABC1; Urban, students in tertiary education
Glasgow (Scotland)	Young singles	Age: 20–27; Gender: mixed; Status: C1C2DE; Urban, non-students
Chislehurst, Kent (England)	Young families	Age: 28–40; Gender: mixed; Status: C1C2DE; Urban
Cardiff (Wales)	Young families	Age: 28–40; Gender: mixed; Status: C1C2DE; Urban
Morpeth, Northumberland (England)	Young families	Age: 28–40; Gender: mixed; Status: ABC1; Rural
Dungannon, County Tyrone (Northern Ireland)	Older families	Age: 41–59; Gender: mixed; Status: ABC1; Rural
Barnstaple, Devon (England)	Older families	Age: 41–59; Gender: mixed; Status: C1C2DE; Rural
Chislehurst (England)	Older families	Age: 41–59; Gender: mixed; Status: ABC1; Urban
Glasgow (Scotland)	Empty nesters	Age: 60–75; Gender: mixed; Status: ABC1; Urban
King's Lynn, Norfolk (England)	Empty nesters	Age: 60–75; Gender: mixed; Status: C1C2DE; Rural

possible during the open meetings. The ten groups each met on two occasions, separated by an interval of two weeks. During this intervening period, participants were invited to explore the issues concerning GM using official tool-kit materials, and any other information they could find. They were also asked to keep diaries of their findings, conversations and thoughts about GM. The Narrow-but-Deep process is discussed in more detail in Chapter 7.

By the end of July, the debate events were over. The GM science and economic reviews had both produced reports during that month. It remained for the PDSB to draw its conclusions about the findings of the public debate. A tight timescale for the production of this report had been set by Margaret Beckett's demand: 'by the end of September at the latest'.

Learning the lessons

The PDSB's final conclusions were based upon a reading of several data streams that had been generated by the different component parts of the debate process. Much of these data were qualitative, including the findings of the Foundation Discussion and Narrow-but Deep meetings, reports on the Tier 1 meetings by rapporteurs (mostly academics contacted by the Board on an ad hoc basis), and a large volume of comments that took the form of letters and emails. Much of the data was also quantitative: a total of 36,557 individuals completed the feedback questionnaire that had been developed as part of the debate tool-kit. This questionnaire had been available for participants at all the debate events, and it could also be completed on-line by accessing the debate website. This data included thirteen questions on attitudes towards GM, and seven items about the age, gender and other characteristics of the person completing the questionnaire. An additional two open-ended questions generated yet more qualitative material.

Much of the responsibility for the production of the final report lay with Richard Heller, a professional writer hired to undertake this task. The PDSB met on two occasions during August 2003 (on the 4th and 28th, from 10.30 a.m. until 3.30 p.m.) in order to consider drafts of the final report that had been prepared by Heller. At the first meeting, Corr Willbourn made a presentation on the Narrow-but-Deep findings, and there was a great deal of discussion about the interpretation of this material. Heller and COI personnel were also present, and actively involved in these discussions. These intense deliberations continued at the second meeting, which included consideration of a cluster analysis of the quantitative data that had been carried out by COI. It was clear that a considerable volume of communication by email (to which we were not privy) had taken place during the interval between the two meetings. A range of differences of opinion continued to exist among the Board members about the interpretation of the data, with matters of detail being examined over many hours of debate. The second meeting eventually came to an end with a discussion of the launch date for the report. The date agreed was 24 September, which meant that Heller needed to produce the final text by 8 September, in order to allow sufficient time for printing and binding. So he was left with just ten days to complete the task.

The considerable pressure under which Heller worked was evident. His contribution included not only drafting the report, but also significant analytic work with a considerable volume of correspondence received by the debate secretariat. The report was published at a press conference in central London on 24 September 2003. We discuss its findings in more detail in Chapter 7.

Methods used in the evaluation

We used a range of research methods in carrying out the evaluation work. The resulting multi-method approach drew upon well-developed quantitative techniques (Rossi *et al.*, 1999) and more recently developed qualitative approaches (Patton, 1990; Shaw, 1999) within the evaluation literature, and upon the evaluation team's extensive experience of social research. We have already described our conceptual stance on evaluation practice in Chapter 2. Turning now to its practical implementation, we utilised participant questionnaires, structured observation, ethnographic techniques, in-depth interviews, media analysis and a major survey of public opinion. In addition, as official evaluators, we were provided with access to a range of datasets collected for the debate Steering Board. The full range of datasets that we have used in the evaluation exercise is set out in Box 3.2, along with shorthand codes by which we will allude to the source of evidence used in our subsequent analysis.

Here, we provide a brief description of the nature of these datasets, and the methods and instruments used to collect them.

ETH, OBS(FD), OBS(T1–3) and OBS(RFG)

Across a range of debate-related events, we drew upon the tradition of ethnographic fieldwork to collect qualitative data by means of non-participant observation and informal conversations (Hammersley and Atkinson, 1995). One member of the evaluation team was present at all the Foundation Discussion workshops (with the exception of the one held in Norwich) and all the Tier 1 public meetings, at both meetings of two of the Narrow-but-Deep groups (also referred to as reconvened focus group or RFG), and at a small sample of Tier 2 and Tier 3 meetings.

Data were captured in the form of extensive written notes. In order to establish and maintain a uniformity of approach among different members of the evaluation team, we structured this observational work by means of a protocol. Rather than seeking to impose a checklist-like uniformity, our objective was simply to sensitise the observers to the analytic needs of the overall evaluation process. This protocol therefore took the form of an aide-mémoire. The topics addressed were: the clarity by which the task of the

Box 3.2 **Datasets utilised**

ETH	Observation of work of PDSB, COI and contractors, and other key actors; informal interviews; document monitoring and analysis; email traffic between secretariat, COI and PDSB.
INT	In-depth interviews with PDSB members and other key actors.
STK	Interviews with engaged stakeholders; pressure group email traffic; public statements and publications by lobbying organisations.
OBS(FD)	Observation of Foundation Discussion workshops.
OBS(T1–3)	Observation of Tier 1, 2 and 3 public meetings.
OBS(RFG)	Observation of Narrow-but-Deep groups.
QS(FD)	Short questionnaire for Foundation Discussion workshops.
QS(T1)	Short questionnaire for Tier 1 meetings.
QL(FD)	Long questionnaire for Foundation Discussion workshops.
QL(T1–3)	Long questionnaire for Tier 1, 2 and 3 public meetings.
QL(RFG)	Long questionnaire for Narrow-but-Deep groups.
MED	Media monitoring.
MORI 2002	UEA/MORI Risk survey 2002.
MORI 2003	UEA/MORI GM Food survey 2003.

Data collected for the Public Debate Steering Board

FBK(QUAN)	Data from *GM Nation?* feedback forms (quantitative).
FBK(QUAL)	Data from *GM Nation?* feedback forms (qualitative).
MISC	Miscellaneous correspondence, emails from the public.
AUD(T)	Audio tapes/transcripts from COI-supported public meetings.
AUD(FD)	Tapes from Foundation Discussion workshops.
AUD(RFG)	Tapes from Narrow-but-Deep groups.
RAP	'Official' and 'unofficial' rapporteur reports on public meetings.

meeting was defined; the apparent independence and transparency of the activity; the access to resources and decision-making enjoyed by participants; and the degree of satisfaction or disappointment evident among participants. These topics related to our normative criteria. To this list we added a section on the 'nature of the discourse', reflecting our recognition of the central roles of language and talk in processes of sense-making (Horlick-Jones, 2005c; Horlick-Jones and Walls, 2005; Horlick-Jones *et al.*, in press, b). A copy of the observation protocol is provided at Annex A, at the end of the book.

INT/STK

During the course of the debate period, in addition to informal interviews forming part of the ETH corpus of data, we conducted in-depth, semi-structured interviews with all members of the PDSB (INT), and with representatives of six engaged stakeholder groups. The STK corpus also includes attributed statements from such groups found in public statements and publications, and in email traffic to which we gained access.

QS(FD)

At the end of each Foundation Discussion workshop, two questionnaires were distributed to all participants by the organisers; the first (short) questionnaire for completion at that time (QS(FD)), and the second (long) questionnaire for completion by participants at home (QL(FD) – see below). The first questionnaire was aimed at establishing the participants' views on GM food, in order to acquire an attitudinal profile of the sample on the topic of interest. The seven questions were taken from a wider survey conducted by members of the evaluation team (see MORI below). As such, the results from these questions could be compared and contrasted with the results from the earlier survey (based upon a representative sample of the general UK population) in order to establish the degree of 'representativeness' of the participants' views. The issue of representativeness is discussed in detail in Chapter 5. This short questionnaire may be found at Annex B.

QS(T1)/QL(FD), QL(T1–3) and QL(RFG)

These questionnaires were intended first to address performance of the debate against our normative criteria and, second, to ascertain participants' own evaluation criteria through a number of open questions. The development of forerunners of these instruments has been described in detail in a series of papers and reports (see Rowe *et al.*, 2001, 2004).

The questionnaires were distributed to participants in the Tier 1 events and (by the organisers) to the Foundation Discussion events, to be completed at the end of these events and collected by the researchers (short questionnaire), or to be completed at home and returned via pre-paid envelopes we provided (long questionnaire). For those Tier 2 and Tier 3 events that we were able to observe, the questionnaires were distributed to participants and collected after the event by the researchers. In addition, questionnaires were distributed to participants in an additional twenty-six Tier 2 and Tier 3 events by the local event organisers.

Our use of two questionnaires for the Foundation Discussion workshops and Tier 1 events reflects a pragmatic choice: although we wished to collect as much data as possible, we recognised the organisers' concerns about over-taxing the participants. We also recognised that lengthy questionnaires might adversely affect response rates. In view of these considerations, we developed short questionnaires for immediate completion at the end of various events, as well as a longer one, for completion at the participants' leisure. The latter questionnaires were distributed with pre-paid envelopes allowing them to be returned to us following completion. As we discuss below, we used a single questionnaire, QL(RFG), in gathering data at the Narrow-but-Deep groups. This was very similar in form to QL(T1–3), the long questionnaire used at the Tier events.

In Chapter 4 we discuss the response rates to the various instruments, and the consistency of responses to the short and long questionnaires. The long questionnaire QL(T1–3) may be found at Annex C.

MED

During the course of the debate, and at the time of the release of the debate's final report, the following media sources were monitored: all English national daily and Sunday newspapers; the main UK news bulletins and current affairs programmes on the five terrestrial TV channels and BBC radio; selected regional and local newspapers; and internet news services and bulletin boards supported by selected newspaper and broadcasting organisations, notably the BBC, Channel 4 and *The Guardian* newspaper.

MORI

As part of the evaluation exercise we implemented a major quantitative survey of public views on GM food and crops. This was conducted for us by the research company MORI (now known as Ipsos MORI) directly after the end of the formal debate period (between 19 July and 12 September 2003). A nationally representative quota sample of 1,363 people aged 15 years and older was interviewed face-to-face in their own homes in England, Scotland and Wales. The interviews were carried out by fully trained and supervised market research personnel, and took on average around thirty minutes to complete. The overall sample comprised a core British sample of 1,017 interviews, and booster surveys in Scotland and Wales of 151 and 195 individuals respectively. All frequency data were weighted to the known profile of the British population in terms of age, gender, social class and region. The first part of our questionnaire included the statements about GM issues contained in the PDSB's 'feedback' questionnaire. This survey was directly comparable to a similar survey that we implemented in 2002, which therefore provided a benchmark for possible shifts in attitudes (Pidgeon and Poortinga, 2006; Pidgeon *et al.*, 2005; Poortinga and Pidgeon, 2003a, 2004a).

FBK(QUAN), FBK(QUAL) and MISC

The organisers provided us with access to data from over 36,000 *GM Nation?* feedback questionnaires completed by meeting participants, and by others who returned copies or who visited the debate website. Our MORI survey included a number of items which replicated those appearing in the *GM Nation?* questionnaire. This overlap is discussed in detail in Chapter 5. The organisers also provided us with a selection of qualitative material, part of which arose from responses to open questions on the feedback forms, and part of which took the form of letters and emails to the debate secretariat.

AUD

We were provided with transcripts of plenary discussions at all public (Tier 1 and Tier 2) events to which the COI provided organisational support. We were also provided with audio recording of all Foundation Discussion workshops and Narrow-but-Deep group discussions.

RAP

The organisers commissioned a number of independent rapporteur reports on the Tier 1 public events. They also received a number of unofficial reports on local (Tier 2 and Tier 3) events. We were provided with a selection of these reports.

The practical implementation of the evaluation

In this section we describe how we used the methods discussed in the previous section to collect data from the different component parts of the debate process, and some of the practicalities of the evaluation exercise.

Evaluation difficulties

Before we proceed, we first consider the extent of the practical challenges posed by the task we undertook. We have discussed the associated difficulties in detail elsewhere (Rowe *et al.*, 2005), and here we simply outline a few of them to provide a sense of the real-world context in which we operated.

It is important to note that the evaluation exercise we conducted was limited in scope in various ways. Evaluation did not emerge as a priority in the planning of the debate and, indeed, at one stage, the Chair of the PDSB stated in public that 'there was no indication of any enthusiasm on the part of government to undertake such an evaluation itself' (cited in Rowe *et al.*, 2005: 339). Limits on cash available meant that the sponsors were not able to seek contractors to bid for the evaluation, and it was therefore fortunate that we were available to do the task without payment, by allocating resources from within existing research funding. After being appointed as evaluators, we were again fortunate to be able to secure additional funds in order to carry out the survey work. Nevertheless, the relatively small scale of our overall budget precluded as elaborate an evaluation as we would have preferred to implement, and, arguably, that an initiative of this nature deserved.

As is clear from the details of the debate set out above, the scale of the evaluation task proved considerable, and involved monitoring the planning and execution of the debate process over a period of some twelve months. While it would have been desirable to receive dedicated funding in order to accomplish this task, it is difficult to imagine funding of a scale that would have made possible an evaluation team sufficiently large to allow some 600 events (as ultimately materialised) to be monitored. In practice, corners had to be cut, and to avoid over-interpretation, our findings need to be considered with these constraints in mind. We return to these qualifications in our concluding chapter. However, having noted this caveat it is also important to appreciate that the scale and complexity of the evaluation exercise that we conducted was *very* extensive in comparison with other evaluations of deliberative and participative processes that we have been able to find in the literature (e.g. for review, see Rowe and Frewer, 2004).

The circumstances that led to our appointment as evaluators led to some practical difficulties concerned with relations with the debate organisers and other parties, resulting in issues that threatened to compromise the quality of the data that we collected. The late presence of evaluators raised concerns with the recruited contractors and sub-contractors, who clearly felt a sense of disquiet at suddenly discovering that their activities would be under scrutiny. This led to some difficult negotiations that would, perhaps, not have been so difficult had the evaluation activity been built-in at the beginning.

Some difficulties arose from the structural nature of the relationship between evaluators and the sponsors (and their executive, including the secretariat, COI and sub-contractors). Given the circumstances, one might anticipate a number of such problems, for example:

- evaluators taking up a great deal of time of busy sponsors/executive by asking questions and making various other demands;
- sponsors/executive anxiety that evaluators might interpret complex issues in inaccurate or stereotypical ways;
- a potential culture clash, with evaluators' ways of behaving, talking and framing issues in ways that make sponsors/executive uncomfortable;
- the expert status of sponsors/executive being scrutinised by people who are not members of their professional 'tribe';
- a sense of vulnerability on the part of sponsors/executive, with their possible mistakes and difficulties being carefully recorded.

Therefore, it is perhaps not surprising that some examples of these difficulties did indeed occur.

We also encountered several barriers in seeking to collect a suitably high-quality corpus of data on which to base our evaluation. The experimental character of the debate gave rise to a rather untidy nexus of overlapping processes, with detailed implementation being contingent upon decisions taken at a sometimes quite advanced stage of the exercise. As the 'public' phase of the debate approached, the pace of development speeded up, and 'backstage' activity often took on a rather frenzied nature. Given these circumstances, it was not possible for us to plan our data collection schedule and associated resource demands with any degree of certainty. In response, our attempts to maintain flexibility necessitated us keeping empty diaries, and gaining the agreement of colleagues to assist us by providing data collection support at short notice.

Finally, a further limitation on data collection arose from the need for the evaluation to be conducted in as unobtrusive a manner as possible. Despite our commitment to such a style of working, limits were placed on our observational access to some closed parts of the debate process. Our lack of a formal role in the initial design of the debate meant that we were not in a position to make more strenuous requests for information access. We recognise that the PDSB was in a difficult position: caught between access requests by the evaluators and reservations expressed by their contractors. Of course, this tension points to the crucial need for an early establishment of the role, aims and scope of evaluation in the planning of such an exercise.

The Foundation Discussion workshops

We were able to gain agreement from COI and Corr Willbourn that a member of the evaluation team could be present as an observer at each of the workshops – save one. There was resistance to our presence at the single workshop in which participants would have a prior engaged interest in GM-related issues. It was anticipated that this would prove difficult to facilitate. Despite expressing concern about our exclusion, the COI view was supported by the PDSB Chair and secretariat. We were, however, provided with copies of the audio tapes of all nine workshops, including the unobserved one.

We agreed in advance with COI that our observers would behave in certain prescribed ways, namely:

- To present an unobtrusive presence (but not studiedly detached) at the workshops and be sensitive to the possibility of inadvertent non-verbal signalling to the participants.
- Not to make tape or video recordings.
- To take discreet notes by hand, and not use a laptop computer for this purpose.
- Not to interact verbally with participants unless directly addressed, or possibly informally during break times. In the latter case the observer would be careful not to ask leading or framing questions.

- Not to take photographs except for pictures of the flip-chart sheets produced during each workshop. These photographs would be taken after the event was over.
- To collect copies of stimulus material used during the workshop.

In observing the workshop we used our observational protocol whilst making contemporaneous notes. Our observers were asked to provide as much detail as possible in their workshop reports. Observers were encouraged to speak informally with workshop participants if suitable opportunities arose, bearing in mind the protocol on observers' behaviour agreed with COI.

As noted above, at the end of each workshop two questionnaires were distributed to all participants by the organisers, the first (short) questionnaire for completion at that time (QS(FD)), and the second (long) questionnaire for completion by participants at home (QL(FD)). The second questionnaire came with a pre-paid envelope for the participants to return to us their completed questionnaires.

A total of 168 completed short questionnaires were collected, which came from most, if not all, participants. A total of 62 useable long questionnaires were returned by participants. Table 3.3 summarises the responses to the two questionnaires, according to location. This reveals a wide variety in the number of responses from the different events. The overall response rate for the longer questionnaire (proportion of QS(FD) respondents who responded to QL(FD)) was 36.9 per cent. A relatively high proportion of responses was obtained from Ruthin (sample: rural Wales, C1C2DE, aged 55–75) and Norwich (informed participants), with approximately half of participants responding from Reading (sample: urban, C1C2DE), with lesser proportions from Edinburgh, Bromsgrove, Altrincham and Belfast. However, no responses at all were received from the participants attending the Ludlow (sample: rural, C1C2DE, 17–18 year old males) or London (sample: urban, ABC1) events.

Table 3.3 Responses to questionnaires from the Foundation Discussion workshops

Workshop location	Responses to QS(FD)	Responses to QL(FD) (% total respondents)	
Altrincham	20	5	(25.0)
Belfast	20	5	(25.0)
Bromsgrove	18	4	(22.2)
Edinburgh	18	6	(33.3)
London	17	0	(0.0)
Ludlow	19	0	(0.0)
Norwich	18	13	(72.2)
Reading	19	8	(42.1)
Ruthin	19	14	(73.7)
Unknown	–	7	
Total	168	62	(36.9)

Some of the response patterns in Table 3.3 are, perhaps, not surprising. Here we have in mind the stark contrast between the sample of teenage boys from Ludlow, who provided no completed questionnaires, and the good response from the well-informed participants from Norwich who attended because the topic was of interest to them. Others are more difficult to explain: for example, why none of the London respondents from higher socio-economic classes responded. Part of the reason may lie in the enthusiasm (or lack of enthusiasm) of participants for the workshops. Another factor was the instructions given by the facilitators. At the end of the Bromsgrove workshop, the facilitator in question stated: 'remember, you *don't* need to complete the questionnaires'. This matter was subsequently raised by us with the organisers, who agreed to ensure that it would not occur again.

It is thus important to recognise that the responses to the QL(FD) may represent a biased sample of participants. In any case, because the number of respondents from some workshops was so low, our subsequent analysis aggregates the data from all workshops rather than first comparing differences between these. Our wider analysis on the separate workshop data sets does suggest, however, that the trends reported in our subsequent analysis did tend to generalise across the participants in the different workshops.

The Tier 1 events

The six Tier 1 public meetings were a hybrid mix containing aspects of what have been termed 'consultation' and 'deliberation' mechanisms. Our main form of data gathering at these meetings was by means of observation and participant questionnaires. While the former allowed us to systematically evaluate the form of the meetings, and to speak informally with participants, the latter provided both formal and open questions which inquired into the experience of taking part in the debate process. We observed all six Tier 1 events, and administered questionnaires to 1,000 or so participants. The observers in each case made contemporaneous notes shaped by our observer protocol.

We gained agreement with the organisers that at each event, two of our questionnaires would be distributed to the participants; the first (short) questionnaire for completion at that time (QS(T1)), and the second (long) questionnaire for completion by participants at home (QL(T1)). The second questionnaire came with a pre-paid envelope for the participants to return their completed questionnaires to the evaluators. These questionnaires differed from those administered to participants in the Foundation Discussion workshops, but in structure, rather than in the questions per se. The first questionnaire asked a number of demographic and socio-economic questions, plus a few questions aimed at addressing our main evaluation criteria. The second questionnaire contained seven questions on attitudes to GM foods and crops, together with demographic and socio-economic questions, plus questions intended to ascertain participants' opinions on the quality and nature of the process in which they had been involved. Some were open-ended, while others were closed, requiring yes/no responses, or responses on five- or seven-point scales. Some addressed our specific evaluation criteria, while others were more general, for example asking about participant satisfaction.

Both the first and second questionnaires were coded to enable the iden-tification of each participant at each workshop location, to allow us to match responses from particular respondents across the two questionnaires. In our analysis we have considered the results from both questionnaires, combining results across them when this is appropriate, as will be discussed.

Table 3.4 shows details of the questionnaire responses from Tier 1 events. The second column indicates the number of participants who attended each event, with these figures taken from the organisers' official website. In all cases (apart from possibly the Birmingham event), the figures are estimates rather than precise counts. Therefore, the percentage figures given in the third column should only be taken as *estimates* of the percentage of *participants* who responded to the first questionnaire (QS(T1)). Otherwise, the third column indicates that we received a total of 620 completed copies of the first ques-tionnaire. The estimated percentage response rates range from just under 50 per cent (from Harrogate) to over 70 per cent (from Swansea).

The fourth column shows the number of respondents to the first ques-tionnaire who also completed the second questionnaire (QL(T1)) and returned these to us through the post, revealing that approximately two-thirds of initial respondents did so. The final column shows the number of extra responses we received from people who only completed the second question-naire (QL(T1)), but did not complete the first at the event (generally, from comments on these questionnaires, these were people from the Taunton event

Table 3.4 Responses to questionnaires from the six Tier 1 events

Debate location	Total participants according to organisers*	Responses to QS(T1) (% of participants)		Responses to QL(T1) (% of QS(T1) respondents)		Respondents completing QL(T1) but not QS(T1)
Belfast	100	63	(63.0)	35	(58.7)	2
Birmingham	126	75	(59.5)	54	(76.0)	3
Glasgow	140	89	(63.6)	56	(65.2)	2
Harrogate	250	122	(48.8)	88	(74.6)	3
Swansea	180	130	(72.2)	76	(62.3)	5
Taunton	120–210**	141		90	(68.1)	6
Total	916–1,006	620		399	(67.7)	21

Notes

* These numbers are taken from the debate organisers' website
(http://www.gmpublicdebate.org/ut_13/ut_13_25.htm).

**The Taunton number is recorded as '90 in the morning; 120 in the afternoon'. Some of those attending in the morning did not stay until the afternoon, and new participants turned up at that time. The total is likely to be much closer to 120 than to 210, and duplicate returns are possible (we have checked demographic information to confirm no repeats).

who left early, or people who had to leave quickly at the end of the event and could not spare the time to complete the first questionnaire). Adding the totals of the fourth and fifth columns yields the total number of completed copies of QL(T1) we received, namely 420.

The response rates to the second questionnaires are much higher than the rates attained for the 'take-home' questionnaire at the Foundation Discussion workshops, while the responses to the first questionnaire are also generally high (though we cannot discount the possibility of a slight response bias in our results). As with the Foundation Discussion workshop analysis, we reserve our analysis of the respondents to our questionnaire for Chapter 5, where we discuss the representativeness issue (at which place we also discuss the responses of participants to the various attitude questions about GM foods and crops). Generally in the analysis that follows, we aggregate responses over all six events. We use the responses to several of the open questions to infer participants' evaluation criteria, and these data are reported in Chapter 6.

The Tier 2 and Tier 3 events

As with the Tier 1 meetings, we set out to use a combination of protocol-structured observation and questionnaires in order to gather data at the Tier 2 and Tier 3 meetings. However, the sample of these meetings for which we were able to gather data was very small indeed. Generally, we had difficulties in learning about the existence of meetings in time to arrange for an observer to be present. As noted above, despite having the status of official evaluators, we found ourselves in the position of many would-be participants in finding out about meetings happening at some geographical distance at the last possible moment.

We were able to observe a mere twelve Tier 2 and Tier 3 events, to half of which we were able to administer questionnaires. COI provided transcripts to a further two Tier 2 meetings, and we sent questionnaires for distribution to an additional twelve meetings. In total, we were able to gather data of one form or another on seven Tier 2 meetings and nineteen Tier 3 meetings. On some occasions when it was not possible for an observer to be present, it was still possible to gain the agreement of the organisers to distribute our questionnaires.

Those events at which both our long and short questionnaires (QS(T2/T3), QL(T2/T3) were dispensed were Cambridge (T2), Ruthin (T3) and Llandudno (T3). Those events at which only the longer questionnaire (QL(T2/T3) was distributed were: Inverness (T2), Cornwall (T2), Gloucestershire (T2), Abergavenny (T3), Forest Row (T3), Norwich (held at the John Innes Centre) (T3) and Lincoln (T3). These questionnaires were identical to those presented at the Tier 1 events. As before, pre-paid envelopes were dispensed with the longer questionnaire to allow their return to us.

In our later analysis (in Chapter 4) we consider the results from both questionnaires, combining results across them when this is appropriate. Table

3.5 summarises the responses to the two questionnaires (Q1 and Q2, being the short and the long questionnaires, respectively) according to the T2/T3 event that was attended. Given that we were unable to establish the total numbers attending each event, it is not possible to calculate the overall response rates. Of the respondents who attended the three events at which both questionnaires were presented, 64.9 per cent of those completing QS(T2/T3) also completed QL(T2/T3) at Cambridge (N = 96); 57.1 per cent did so from Ruthin (N = 16); and 31.8 per cent did so from Llandudno (N = 7).

We obtained most responses from an event run by Cambridgeshire County Council, which was well attended. The small numbers from other events do not necessarily indicate extremely low response rates (some of the events were small scale) though in some cases this is likely – for example, only five responses from the event held in Lincoln – which we were unable to observe. Because of the relatively low numbers from some events it does not make much sense to split our analysis according to particular events, and so henceforth (in Chapter 4) we aggregate results across all T2 and T3 events. Table 3.5 shows that we had over 200 responses to the longer questionnaire from T2 events, and over 100 from the T3 events.

As a consequence of our limited data collection, we state our findings on these events in subsequent chapters with considerably less confidence than in a number of other areas of our evaluation work. In particular, we caution against reading too much into the questionnaire results. The limited and skewed responses to the questionnaires (e.g. most Tier 2 responses came from a single large meeting) mean that we can only provide a rough commentary on general trends from this data without providing fine-grained statistics that might imply greater validity than is merited.

Nevertheless, by bringing together a number of different sources of evidence: observation, questionnaires, conversations with the organisers of local meetings, other interviews and media reports, we arrived at a view that

Table 3.5 Responses to questionnaires from the Tier 2 and Tier 3 events

Event (Tier)	Responses to QS(T2/T3)	Responses to QL(T2/T3)
Cambridge (T2)	148	106
Inverness (T2)	–	16
Cornwall (T2)	–	65
Gloucs (T2)	–	55
Llandudno (T3)	22	10
Ruthin (T3)	28	20
Abergavenny (T3)	–	38
Forest Row (T3)	–	15
Norwich (T3)	–	25
Lincoln (T3)	–	5
Total T2 events	148	242
Total T3 events	50	113

suggested that the meetings for which we had data were not wildly different from the broad mass of meetings taking place in various locations around the UK. There are a number of other reasons that make us feel that the representativeness of our findings was at an acceptable level. The Tier 2 meetings were mostly organised by local authorities with significant input from COI. While recognising the wish of local organisers to incorporate locally specific considerations, the general structuring of the events seems to have been fairly uniform. Further uniformity was generated by the existence of a limited number of expert speakers travelling from one venue to another, presumably to say rather similar things. Turning now to the Tier 3 events, we suspect that a number of structuring features – the topic of GM, the timing, the links with COI entailed in registering the event and arranging for feedback forms and stimulus material to be sent to the organisers, and organising role of environmental and consumer pressure groups – served to lend the events a certain uniform logic, so creating similar expectations for participants.

The 'Narrow-but-Deep' process

We now turn to the series of ten closed, reconvened focus groups, involving a cross-section of participants, and which deliberately excluded people with an active interest in GM-related issues. As noted above, these groups met twice, with a gap of two weeks during which participants were invited to explore the GM issue individually, using official stimulus materials and any other information that they could access, and to keep diaries of their discoveries, thoughts, relevant conversations, and so on.

We negotiated observational access to two pairs of these groups, and audio recordings of all ten. The organisers insisted that we use the same observer for both meetings of each observed group in order to minimise possible disturbance arising from change. Our observational work was again shaped by the use of our protocol, this time in the expectation that it would be particularly relevant as these events were designed to be purposefully *deliberative* in nature.

We used questionnaires, distributed to participants by the meeting facilitator. In order to minimise disruption, the organisers specified that we should not administer questionnaires at any time other than at the *end* of the *second* meeting of each group. We were therefore unable to gather questionnaire data from participants before and after they took part in the process, as we would have liked. This time, we only used one questionnaire, which was very similar in form to the long questionnaire utilised at the Tier 1, 2 and 3 events (QL(RFG)). As before, pre-paid envelopes were dispensed with the questionnaire to allow its return to us. We received forty-two completed questionnaires from a total of seventy-seven participants, giving a response rate of 54.5 per cent. As before, our discussion of the demographic and attitudinal characteristics of this data will be included in Chapter 5.

We note in passing that the organisers invited participants to complete the debate's official 'feedback' questionnaire at the very *start* of the first meeting of each group, and at the *start* of the second meeting (rather than at the end of the second meeting). We will return to this matter in our discussion (in Chapter 7) of the interpretation of the Narrow-but-Deep process, and, in particular, of how comparisons between this process and the public activities played a central role in shaping the Steering Board's rendering of the findings of the debate.

The analytical organisation of the evaluation

As noted in Chapter 2, the evaluation we conducted was pragmatic in nature, with an emphasis on methodological plurality rather than being constrained by a commitment to either a performance-measuring, or what we have termed an *assessment*, evaluation paradigm (cf. Patton, 1990). In practice, we carried out an evaluation of performance in the sense that we were guided by criteria identified in advance (or at the start) of the engagement process, although our multi-method approach provided us with a capacity to *learn* from the process, and so an ability to arrive at emergent findings (Bloor, 1978; Glaser and Strauss, 1967).

This latter capacity proved especially important when it became increasingly clear to us that a central aspect of the debate process was not being addressed by any of the criteria with which we were working. As we discuss in detail in Chapter 7, this 'missing dimension' was the question of how effective were the processes by which each stage of the debate drew upon sources of knowledge, so informing and shaping them; a new criterion which we term *translation quality*.

The quantitative data that we collected were analysed using standard statistical techniques. Qualitative data were analysed by means of processes of analytic induction, informed by the evaluation criteria and other matters of conceptual interest (Silverman, 1993). A process of linking quantitative and qualitative data was undertaken by utilising emerging categories to interrogate other datasets (Fielding and Fielding, 1986). Finally, the expertise of the evaluation team was tapped by generating an 'analytic conversation' among members of the team about the full range of datasets and their analysis. While all parts of our findings emerge from this process of analysis, some sections draw more heavily on specific datasets. The corresponding 'analytical audit' is set out in Box 3.3.

Finally, we return to the three sets of evaluation criteria discussed in Chapter 2: the generic normative criteria, the criteria drawn up by the sponsors, and the participants' criteria that we inferred from data that we collected. In Table 3.6 we map these various criteria according to the location in the book where they are addressed.

In Chapter 4 we consider what we term 'process' issues, which correspond to normative criteria N2, N3, N4, N6, N7 and N8. Chapter 5 examines the

Box 3.3 Analytical audit

Chapter 1: The origins of the debate	ETH
Chapter 2: Our approach to evaluating the debate	the scholarly literature, ETH
Chapter 3: The unfolding of the debate and the implementation of the evaluation exercise	ETH
Chapter 4: Process issues	ETH, OBS, QS, QL, INT
Chapter 5: The issue of representativeness	ETH, QS, QL, INT, MORI, FBK, AUD(RFG)
Chapter 6: Participants' evaluation criteria	QL
Chapter 7: The management and translation of knowledge	ETH, INT, MED, MORI, FBK, AUD(RFG), MISC, RAP
Chapter 8: Other representations of the debate	ETH, INT, STK, MED, MORI
Chapter 9: Conclusions	All datasets

representativeness of the debate, arguably a particularly important dimension of the evaluation (see Rowe and Frewer, 2004), and corresponding to normative criterion N1 and sponsor criterion B2. In Chapter 6 we identify nine participant criteria (P1–P9) which we inferred from data that we collected. Participation is also addressed by sponsor criteria BII and B5b. Chapter 7 is mostly devoted to a detailed discussion of the emergent criterion that we identified, and which we named 'translation quality'. Here we also discuss the sponsor criterion B1 concerning framing. Chapter 8 considers 'other representations' of the debate, beyond the perceptions of those closely involved in the process, and, as such, addresses sponsor criterion B5a, which is concerned with the awareness of the debate that was generated. Finally, Chapter 9 includes a discussion of the debate's performance in terms of the views of 'informed commentators' (sponsor criterion BIII), and in its capacity to influence policy (normative criterion N5 and sponsor criterion BIV).

Table 3.6 Mapping the evaluation criteria

Normative criteria	Sponsor criteria	Link to evaluation
N1 Representativeness	B2 Participation	Chapter 5
N5 Influence	BIV Impact	Chapter 9 (which also includes a discussion of all the criteria)
N2 Independence N3 Early involvement N4 Transparency N6 Task definition N7 Resources N8 Structured dialogue N5 Influence (perceived)	B1 Framing	Chapter 7 Chapter 4 Process issues
	B3 Opportunities B4a Experts B4b Information B6 Mutual learning B7 Other strands B8 Situate B9 Report	Chapters 4 and 9 Pseudo criteria
	BII Participants B5b Register views	Chapter 6 Participants' criteria (listed in Box 6.1)
	B5a Awareness	Chapter 8
	BIII Informed views	Chapter 9

4 Process issues

In Chapter 2 we described our methodological approach to conducting the evaluation of the debate, and in Chapter 3 we discussed how we implemented the evaluation exercise as the debate unfolded in time. We now turn to the first part of our examination of how the debate process performed in terms of specific criteria. In this chapter we are mostly concerned with what we described in our initial mapping of the evaluation criteria (Table 3.6) as 'process issues'. Broadly speaking, these are measures of the characteristics of the debate that reflect clarity, lack of bias and fairness. In other words, they are concerned with the specific ways in which the debate was implemented. These dimensions are captured in five of our normative criteria, namely: Independence (N2), Early involvement (N3), Transparency (N4), Resources (N7) and Structured dialogue (N8). In addition to discussion of performance against these criteria, we have added an assessment of the 'nature of the discourse' at the different parts of the debate events, which draws upon our structured observation of these events. We have also added some discussion of participants' *perceptions* of the likely influence (N5) of the debate on policy.

The mapping of criteria to the various chapters of this book, which we mentioned above, also links this chapter with the set of sponsor criteria that we have collectively described as 'pseudo' criteria. We discussed the problematic nature of these criteria in Chapter 2. We will briefly consider some of these criteria in the concluding part of this chapter.

In the following section, we systematically examine how the different kinds of debate meeting – the Foundation Discussion workshops, Tier 1 'national' public meetings, Tier 2 and Tier 3 local public meetings, and the Narrow-but-Deep groups – performed according to the five process criteria. We draw on data collected by means of structured observation (OBS(FD), OBS(T1–3) and OBS(RFG)), and from the short and long questionnaires (QS(FD), QL(FD), QS(T1–3), QL(T1–3), QS(RFG) and QL(RFG)).

It is important to emphasise that the normative criteria were originally intended to be of relevance to *participation* events, rather than those that take more of an *elicitation* or *consultation* nature. As we discussed earlier in the book, the debate took on a hybrid nature, comprising a number of components that generated different kinds of process. The Foundation Discussion workshops, for example, were primarily concerned with information elicitation rather than deliberation and decision-making. We suggest that most of the criteria still have relatively high relevance across the range of event types, although there are some instances where this is not the case and so, for example, we omit any analysis of the Early involvement criterion with regards to the Foundation Discussion workshops. Elsewhere, we comment on the likely relevance or otherwise of the specific criteria, and the way in which they were operationalised, where we see this issue as notable. In some cases, in order not to distract the flow of our analysis, we simply omit discussion of clearly irrelevant items and the responses to these.

Evaluation according to select normative criteria

Independence (N2)

The first criterion related to the concept of acceptability or fairness that we consider is 'Independence'. It has been suggested by a number of commentators that a participation process should, ideally, be run in a way that is in some sense independent from the sponsors and their views and agendas.

We observed that at the end of most of the Foundation Discussion workshops the moderators *did* briefly describe their relationship with COI and the debate sponsors. However, on at least one occasion no details were provided at all. Where such details were provided, this was done in an inconsistent manner. On one occasion the moderator was explicitly asked 'who is funding this research?' to which the answer given was 'central government'. At the Tier 1 meetings, the facilitators described themselves and their role in slightly different ways in each event. In all cases the relationship they had with COI and the Steering Board was briefly discussed. The facilitators explained that they had been employed to act independently and objectively. However, a certain unease over the independence of the events was expressed among the participants, despite the 'arm's length from government' characterisation of the exercise. At the Tier 2 events we observed, there was very little in the way of explanation of the role and status of the organisers or their relationship with the sponsors of the debate. At Tier 3 events, the relationship between the local organisers and the overall debate sponsors was often vague. The facilitators at the Narrow-but-Deep events tended to describe themselves as hired investigators, with no 'axes to grind', while the sponsors were rather vaguely described.

Responses to various questionnaire items by Foundation Discussion workshop participants suggested they were not concerned about this independence issue. The great majority (93.6 per cent) either agreed or strongly agreed that 'The exercise was run in an unbiased way'. Indeed, the moderators were perceived positively: over three-quarters (77.4 per cent) of respondents *disagreed* that 'The moderators were biased by the views of the people who commissioned this workshop', and not a single respondent agreed with the negative statement that 'There was too much control by the moderator over the way the exercise was run'. Finally, approximately two-thirds agreed with the statement that 'The information that was given to participants was fair and balanced', with only 11.3 per cent disagreeing. However, we note that the relevance of this last item is somewhat suspect, as no information was given to participants, and the consultative nature of the exercise demanded only information elicitation. Nevertheless, the participants' responses do hint at the positive way in which the exercise was generally perceived.

Questionnaire responses for the Tier 1 meetings revealed that the events themselves were largely seen to be fairly and independently run. Nearly two-thirds (60.9 per cent of 613 respondents) agreed that 'The people running the event were not promoting a specific view on the issues around GM' (only 18.4 per cent disagreed). The facilitators were also generally seen to have *not* been biased 'by the views of the people who commissioned this event' (59.2 per cent concurred with this, while only 11.9 per cent thought they had been biased; total respondents 360). Further, the majority of respondents agreed with the more general statement that 'The event was run in an unbiased way' (of 397 responses, 57.5 per cent agreed, 20.1 per cent disagreed, and the remainder neither agreed nor disagreed). The only question on this criterion about which there was a high degree of equivocality was one that asked about agreement with a statement that 'The information that was given to participants was fair and balanced'. Over one-third agreed and over one-third disagreed with this (42.2 per cent versus 33.4 per cent, respectively; N = 386).

In general, questionnaire respondents from both Tier 2 and Tier 3 events seemed to rate the independence of the process and those running it to be good (e.g. they didn't think that the people running the event were promoting a specific view on the issues around GM; they thought the events were run in an unbiased way; and they thought the information given to participants was fair and balanced).

In general, questionnaire respondents from the Narrow-but-Deep groups seemed to rate the independence of the process and those running it to be very good. The facilitators were generally thought to be fair in not providing any particular view on the topic: for example, 97.6 per cent *disagreed* or *strongly disagreed* with a statement that the facilitators were 'biased by the views of the people who commissioned these discussions' (only 2.4 per cent agreed; N = 42), while 95.2 per cent agreed or strongly agreed that the events had been run in an unbiased way (only 4.8 per cent disagreed; N = 42). Furthermore, most respondents agreed that 'The information that was given to participants was fair and balanced' (85.4 per cent agreed, while 7.3 per cent disagreed and 4.9 per cent neither agreed nor disagreed; N = 41).

Early involvement (N3)

This criterion suggests that for an event to be regarded as acceptable or fair to participants, they should perceive their involvement to be taking place at a time in which actual influence is possible, without the main decisions having already been taken. Given that this criterion was not something about which we could make sensible *observations*, it was evaluated using questionnaires alone, asking to what extent participants felt they had been involved sufficiently early in the policy process to have an influence. We framed a question on this topic in two different ways in the two questionnaires (QS(T1) and QL(T1)).

Responses to these questions from those taking part in the Tier 1 meetings reveal a fair degree of participant cynicism. In other words, respondents expressed fairly strong agreement with the statement that 'I think that this event has taken place too late to allow me and the other participants to influence Government policy on GM' (79.5 per cent agreed, 9.4 per cent neither agreed nor disagreed, and 11.1 per cent disagreed; N = 614). Similarly, respondents tended to agree with the statement that 'The event has taken place too late in the policy making process to be influential' (77.3 per cent agreed, 9.6 per cent neither agreed nor disagreed, 13.1 per cent disagreed; N = 375). From these results we suggest that the debates have not convinced the participants (respondents) that they have a serious role in policy.

Responses to questionnaires from participants in Tier 2 and Tier 3 events suggested that they, too, were concerned about the timeliness of the events and their potential influence on policy matters.

In common with the public events, participants in the Narrow-but-Deep groups did not rate performance highly on this criterion. In particular, questionnaire respondents generally agreed that 'The discussions have taken place too late in the policy making process to be influential' (66.7 per cent of those expressing an opinion): only 21.2 per cent disagreed that this was so, while 12.1 per cent neither agreed nor disagreed. The level of uncertainty was highlighted, however, by the number of 'non responses': only thirty-three respondents expressed an opinion on this question (out of forty-two who returned their questionnaires).

Transparency (N4)

Another of the evaluation criteria is that of 'Transparency', which states that the acceptability of a participation exercise (related to its perceived fairness) will be partly dependent upon the process being seen as transparent and without hidden agendas.

At the very end of all the Foundation Discussion workshops, the facilitators asked whether the participants were willing to be contacted in the future by the sponsors about future events related to the debate. Otherwise, there was no mention of how the participants could follow the subsequent course of the debate, or have further involvement, save in completing the COI feedback questionnaire that was issued to them. In some groups there was also some mention that the information gathered would be used as a basis for the next stage of the debate, but this was never developed or discussed further.

At some Tier 1 events the facilitators suggested ways in which participants could take the debate forward, for example by organising their own local events. Toward the end of the events, the facilitators suggested to participants that if they wanted stimulus material forwarded to them in order to run their own local events then they should leave their name and address at the exit. The idea discussed by the Steering Board that the Tier 1 events should act as a stimulus for the organisation of local events was never made clear in either the advertising or execution of the events. If this was the real intention, then it was poorly communicated. Indeed, the discussions were not framed or discussed in relation to the overall objectives of the debate, and the objectives were never mentioned.

At a number of the Tier 1 events it was made clear that participants could access the transcripts of the event in the following week on the *GM Nation?* website, the address for which was provided in the introduction to the day. However, there was no mention of how the participants could access the report of the overall debate when completed, nor was there any discussion of how the data would be written up or presented. The main emphasis on feedback came in the form of the feedback questionnaire to be filled in and returned to the organisers. People were encouraged to complete this questionnaire, together with our independent evaluation questionnaires. There was no mention of any other form of feedback mechanism aside from a statement about the organisers guaranteeing to relay participants' views to government, although this tended to be received with scepticism from the participants.

While feedback questionnaires were distributed in all Tier 2 events, it was not clear (in the few events we attended) how the output from the meetings would be used, or how participants could follow the progress of the debate, or have further involvement in the process. Neither was it clear what would happen to the data generated by the meeting. In Tier 3 events, we understand that participants were also encouraged to complete feedback forms, however, at those events that we observed there was very little in the way of explanation of how participants could follow the course of the debate process, or have further participation.

In the case of the Narrow-but-Deep groups, participants were asked if they would be prepared to take part in future discussions, if so invited. They were not, however, provided with a mechanism for further involvement if the impetus for such involvement came from them. Generally, the facilitators provided very little information about the overall debate process, although, of course, participants were exposed to such information during the two weeks of the 'diary' process. The description of how outputs from the group would be used was rather vague.

Turning now to our questionnaire data, for the Foundation Discussion workshops these showed an even split (33.9 per cent each) of participants who agreed or disagreed that 'It was not clear how participants in the exercise were selected'. However, more disagreed than agreed with the statement that 'It is not clear to me how the results of this exercise will be used' (45.2 per cent versus 30.6 per cent, respectively), which is perhaps understandable, since the PDSB itself did not seem entirely certain of this at this stage, and hence the organisers/consultants had no such information to impart. A third question asked participants: 'Do you expect to get any feedback on the results of these workshops?', to which 38.7 per cent replied 'no', 40.3 per cent 'yes', and 21.0 per cent 'don't know'. What is clear from the answers to these questions is that participants were not clear about important aspects regarding the process: how participants would be selected, whether they would receive feedback, and how their results would be used. However, it is unclear whether this was really a problem, and indeed, this state of affairs appeared inevitable given the purpose and development of the exercise.

Questionnaire responses from the Tier 1 meetings generally confirmed that many participants were uncertain about various key features of the debate. For example, about three-quarters of respondents agreed that 'It is not clear to me how the results of this event will be used' (83.2 per cent agreed, 5.2 per cent neither agreed nor disagreed, and 11.5 per cent disagreed; N = 407). Uncertainty as to the purpose of the events was perhaps reflected in responses to a question about there being a 'hidden agenda' to the events, with 55.5 per cent suggesting there might be, and only 23.2 per cent indicating that they did not think there was a hidden agenda (the remainder neither agreed nor disagreed; N = 616). There was also no clear expectation from respondents about whether they would or would not receive any feedback from the events.

Similarly, questionnaire responses from both Tier 2 and Tier 3 confirm that respondents were not clear about how the results of the event would be used, and did not generally expect to receive any feedback from the event. Interestingly, however, and unlike those at the Tier 1 events, Tier 2 and 3 respondents did not feel there was a 'hidden agenda' behind the particular events they attended.

The Narrow-but-Deep groups scored better than the Tier events, although responses still indicated substantial uncertainty about aspects of the event, so indicating a lack of transparency. For example, 41.7 per cent agreed that 'It was not clear how participants in the discussions were selected' (against 47.2 per cent who disagreed/strongly disagreed, and 11.1 per cent who neither agreed nor disagreed; N = 36), while 42.2 per cent agreed/strongly agreed that 'It is not clear to me how the results of the discussions will be used' (against 44.7 per cent who disagreed/strongly disagreed and 13.2 per cent who neither agreed nor disagreed; N = 38). Respondents were also uncertain about whether or not they would receive any feedback from the process.

Task definition (N6)

The 'Task definition' criterion states that it is important that the task facing participants is well defined so that they are able to contribute appropriately.

In the case of the Foundation Discussion workshops, this criterion's relevance is questionable. Indeed, in seeking to avoid imposing any exterior framing upon the participants' views, the facilitators tended to say little about the purpose of the workshop. There was a balance to be struck here, however, and, as observers, we tended to feel that a little more openness may have generated a greater sense of ownership and engagement in the event.

The only workshop where the objectives for the discussion were stated at the very beginning was the Norwich workshop, which was the one composed of people who had already engaged with the issues around GM. Here, the lack of clarity about what the workshop would entail irritated some participants who would have liked to have known more of what was expected of them prior to arriving. In general, however, questionnaire responses did not indicate any particular difficulties from the lack of information – for example, over two-thirds of respondents either disagreed or strongly disagreed with the statement 'I was confused at times about what I had to do', and only 14.5 per cent agreed with it.

In all of the Tier 1 events the facilitators gave some background information to the attendees about the debate, with the events being presented as a way for public opinion to be fed back to government. At some events a member of the PDSB spoke briefly to the audience about the debate. However, a number of participants expressed confusion with the process, particularly why it was organised in the way it was, and what the government intended to do with the information when a 'public debate' of sorts had been in progress for some years. Interestingly, many participants seemed to expect an old-style public meeting with presentations from speakers and questions from the floor. However, no such opportunities to question an expert panel were provided.

At most Tier 1 events the facilitator asked the groups to focus on a number of broad topics (usually the risks/benefits of GM and whether GM crops should be commercialised). It should be noted that people in their group discussions generally did not adhere to these specific areas. No reasons were given to explain this choice of topics, save at one meeting where the facilitator mentioned that they had been derived from fifty-four questions identified by the PDSB. No mention was made of the Foundation Discussion workshops. Most participants did not appear to use the opportunity to engage in systematic deliberative processes using the stimulus material provided.

Responses to the questionnaires confirm that Tier 1 participants were not completely clear about the nature of the event at the outset: approximately two-thirds of those who expressed an opinion, across all the events, suggested they were not given a 'clear indication of what this event would involve' (68.4 per cent, versus 31.6 per cent who suggested that they were; N = 389). However, at a less macro-level, participants were fairly clear what they were supposed to be doing when in attendance; for example, about two-thirds of respondents disagreed that they were 'confused at times about what (they) had to do' (64.0 per cent of 386 responses, though 32.4 per cent agreed that they were confused at times; the remainder neither agreed nor disagreed).

In Tier 2 events, background information was provided on the debate, although there was variation in the quality of this information. Variation also existed in the extent to which the meetings were contextualised within the broader debate process. A number of objectives were sometimes identified for events – such as to learn and contribute to the discussion on GM – although it was not made clear why objectives were chosen or what constituted the overall aims of the meeting. In Tier 3 events there was a wide variation in the extent to which the nature of the meetings was explained and context-ualised, ranging from very clear to non-existent. Questionnaire respondents to both Tier 2 and 3 events tended to agree that it was clear what they had to do, and what the events would involve, and they disagreed that they were confused about what they had to do.

Our observational monitoring of the Narrow-but-Deep groups (and subsequent listening to audio recordings of those groups that we were unable to observe) indicates that the role of these group-based exercises within the overall debate process was not very clearly explained to participants. Similarly, the objectives for the groups were not set out in detail, although we appre-ciate that, as in the Foundation Discussion workshops, such notions of good practice were in tension with a wish to avoid imposing an external framing on the discussions. Nevertheless, questionnaire data suggest that the events 'scored' relatively well on this criterion. For example, 90.5 per cent of partici-pants who expressed an opinion agreed that they had been given clear indications of what the discussions would involve, against only 7.1 per cent who disagreed and 2.4 per cent who neither agreed nor disagreed (N = 41). Further, 88.1 per cent *disagreed* that they had been confused about what to do during the process, and only 7.2 per cent indicated that they had been confused (N = 42).

Resources (N7)

This criterion argues that participants should have sufficient resources available to them to enable them to complete their task. However, in a consultation/ elicitation-type task, such as the Foundation Discussion workshops, the necessary resources are much reduced, since the task was not to reach a decision on the basis of all available information adequately combined, but rather, to elicit all appropriate information from participants. From this perspective, the key resource constraint to a successful exercise is that of *time*. One of our questions was designed to address this criterion by asking respondents to address the statement: 'There was *not* enough time to fully discuss all the relevant issues.' Nearly half of respondents agreed with this statement (48.4 per cent), with just over one-third disagreeing (35.5 per cent). This suggests that many participants did feel that the available time was insufficient. In such an exercise this is a problem, as it suggests that not all available appropriate information has been elicited by the organisers. Observation suggested that on some occasions conversations were, indeed, curtailed, to enable the moderators to complete examination of their range of topics.

At the Tier 1 events, the style of facilitation was very much directed at setting the scene for participants, with the facilitator taking no role in the discussions that took place around the tables. We observed that participants rarely made reference to the information and materials provided for them in the form of the stimulus materials booklet and discussion guide. If they did so, it was only in a cursory and fleeting fashion. Among the round-table discussions we observed, we noted numerous occasions where participants raised questions for which relevant written materials had been provided, but which remained unanswered because the materials were not consulted. We also observed many occasions where people expressed a wish for more 'up-to-date' scientific information. There was no evidence to suggest that participants had received an opportunity to examine the stimulus material in advance of the meetings. A number of participants expressed regret that this had not proved possible. Time constraints provided an important resource consideration. A number of participants said that insufficient time had been provided for the round-table discussions in order to fully talk through the issues. At the final plenary session of each Tier 1 meeting, only five to ten minutes was provided for each table's spokesperson to report on the previous hour's discussion.

Questionnaire responses from Tier 1 participants provided further evidence for a number of these resource limitations. Regarding informational materials, respondents tended to disagree with the statement that 'The event provided me with all the information I wanted to enable me to contribute as I wished' (50.6 per cent disagreed, 15.8 per cent neither agreed nor disagreed, and 33.5 per cent agreed; N = 614). Similarly, there was a tendency to disagree with the statement that 'Participants had access to any information they wanted' (58.3 per cent disagreed, 19.4 per cent neither agreed nor disagreed, and 22.2 per cent agreed; N = 391). With regard to time resources, respondents tended to agree that 'There was not enough time to fully discuss all the relevant issues' (68.5 per cent agreed, 12.5 per cent neither agreed nor disagreed, and 19.0 per cent disagreed; N = 416).

In Tier 2 events, as in the Tier 1 meetings, little or no use was made of the stimulus materials. There was also considerable variation in the competence of the expert speakers. Sufficient time was allocated for these speakers to engage in question and answer sessions. As far as we are aware, in Tier 3 events, stimulus materials were generally not used, although *debate* materials were sometimes available. Speakers were usually present to articulate key arguments and answer questions. Sufficient time seemed available. Questionnaire data from both Tier 2 and Tier 3 generally indicated that participants thought that they were provided with/had access to all the information they wanted. Though respondents generally thought the events provided sufficient time for everyone who wanted to contribute to have their say, they also tended to agree that there was not enough time to fully discuss all the relevant issues. In total, these results (from observations and questionnaires) give ambiguous results on whether the participants in these events had access to sufficient resources.

Finally, turning to the Narrow-but-Deep groups, our observations suggest that the events were run in such a way as to allow all participants a chance to have their say, with plenty of time being available for ideas to be explored. Furthermore, those participants who read the stimulus materials workbook appeared to respond well to them. Our questionnaire data indicated that participants generally thought they had been provided with sufficient time and information. Thus, 59.0 per cent agreed or strongly agreed that 'Participants had access to any information they wanted', while only 15.4 per cent disagreed and 25.6 per cent neither agreed nor disagreed (N = 39), and 53.7 per cent *disagreed* or *strongly disagreed* that 'There was not enough time to fully discuss all the relevant issues' (29.3 per cent agreed or strongly agreed with this statement and 17.1 per cent neither agreed nor disagreed; N = 41).

Several questions in QL(RFG) asked about the quality of the stimulus material. One question asked 'In your opinion, did the information material cover all the relevant issues?', providing three options. None of the respondents (N = 42) thought that 'It covered very few relevant issues'; the majority thought that 'It covered most relevant issues' (69.0 per cent), and a relative minority thought that 'It covered all relevant issues' (31.0 per cent). Another question asked: 'In your opinion, was the information material understandable?', and again gave three options. No respondent (N = 42) indicated that it was 'not understandable'; the majority thought it was 'fairly understandable' (57.1 per cent) and a large minority thought it was 'highly understandable' (42.9 per cent). Finally, one question asked: 'Did you find the information material unbiased?' Three of the respondents failed to answer this question (N = 39). Of those who did respond, only one chose the highly negative option 'highly biased' (2.6 per cent), and a small proportion indicated that they thought it was 'somewhat biased' (15.4 per cent), although most (76.2 per cent) thought that it was 'completely unbiased'.

Structured dialogue (N8)

Arguably, it is important for the organisation of both participation and consultation processes to be structured so as to allow full and appropriate information to be elicited *from* participants. In other words, if one or more important topics remain un-elicited, perhaps because the format fails to encourage all to fully participate, then the exercise may be seen to have failed to some degree. This is a criterion we have termed 'Structured dialogue'.

Observation of the Foundation Discussion workshops suggested that the moderators were professional and courteous to the participants, and largely successful in engendering a thoughtful and convivial atmosphere. This encouraged a high level of participation, including contributions from everyone who wished to contribute. The various 'games' and other devices used by the moderators were effective in prompting participants to reflect upon 'what they already knew', and made possible quite sophisticated exchanges about matters for which little formal knowledge was in evidence. However, participants were not allowed to shape the overall direction of the process, and this meant that on some occasions the moderators curtailed conversations in order to introduce new topics for discussion. A number of questionnaire items attempted to assess participants' views regarding these general issues. One question asked to what extent participants agreed that 'All relevant issues were covered': 43.4 per cent agreed that they had been, though only slightly fewer, namely 35 per cent, thought that they had not. Another question also attempted to get at this concept of coverage of all appropriate issues, asking participants the extent of their agreement with the statement 'I didn't get the chance to say all that I wanted to say'. Over half of respondents indicated that they *did* get the chance to say all that they wanted to say (53.2 per cent), while only 16.1 per cent indicated that they did not.

One question attempted to look at the moderators as *the* possible source of inefficiency in eliciting full information. In response to the statement 'The moderator encouraged everyone to have their say, no matter how little or how much they knew about the subject' not a single respondent disagreed. Further evidence for the effectiveness of the moderators came in response to a question that asked respondent agreement with the statement 'The workshop was well moderated'. Not a single respondent disagreed with this statement. Similarly, respondents were in general agreement (91.9 per cent) with the statement that 'The workshop was well organised and structured', and only two respondents (3.2 per cent) disagreed.

From the answers to these questions we might suggest that the participants felt that the process was an effective one, in the sense of being well moderated and well structured, though some felt that not all issues were covered.

In their report on Foundation Discussion workshops (Corr Willbourn, 2003a), the organisers discuss their methodology, and their attempt to avoid pre-framing the discussions. We are broadly supportive of this approach, but have mentioned how it could be seen to be in tension with other possible objectives of the process. The organisers also report that 'clean language' was used in order to develop questions. We feel that this claim should be met with considerable caution as it appears to be in tension with an appreciation of the inherently situated nature of accounts (see e.g. Dingwall, 1997). We also note that the organisers seemed content for participants to gloss the nature of trust (or more accurately 'distrust'). We feel that participants could have usefully been pressed to expand and 'unpack' these expressions of 'distrust' in the individuals and institutions involved in GM issues.

While the Tier 1 events were not designed to come to a decision as such, participants in a number of the 'table-based' discussions that formed part of these events indicated that they had learnt something from the discussions, and that these discussions had moved 'beyond polarisation'. In this sense, there was evidence that some degree of deliberative engagement had taken place. Sadly, the process of inviting each table's spokesperson to provide a summary of the discussion while under time pressure resulted in a radical loss of the subtlety of many of the points that people were making. This served to reduce much of the feedback discussion to rather predictable (and repetitive) 'sound-bites'. While there were some tables in which individuals tended to dominate the discussion, on the whole, participants seemed to be able to have their say. We noted that these conversations were largely good natured and respectful. We could detect no clear signs of any frustration with the discussions at the tables, and there was very little evidence of any disruptive behaviour. Across all of the tables there was at best tentative articulation of the potential benefits of GM crops. We feel that this feature did not reflect the active suppression of such views, but rather the overwhelming predominance of participants who had a pre-existing 'anti-GM' position.

Questionnaire responses tended to support a number of our observational findings on positive and negative aspects of the Tier 1 meetings. For example, respondents tended to agree that 'The way the event was run allowed [them] to have [their] say' (77.7 per cent agreed, 7.5 per cent neither agreed nor disagreed, and 14.9 per cent disagreed; N = 615). There was also general agreement that 'The event was well facilitated' (63.4 per cent agreed, 23.8 per cent neither agreed nor disagreed, and 12.8 per cent disagreed; N = 404). However, respondents tended to disagree that 'All relevant issues were covered' (66.6 per cent disagreed, 9.6 per cent neither agreed nor disagreed, and 23.8 per cent agreed; N = 407). With regard to the general question of the event being 'well organised' there was a significant effect of location (F (5,403) = 8.80, p < 0.01). Respondents from Belfast and Birmingham were, on average, in disagreement with the statement, while those from the other locations were, on average, in agreement with it. A fair proportion of those from these two events, in particular, were unhappy with how they were run, including over half of those from Birmingham, and over a third of those from Belfast.

None of the Tier 2 events we observed could be described as *deliberative* in nature. Rather, they were modified 'traditional' public meetings. While the purpose of the events was not to come to a decision as such, there was limited use of a voting system in most events. In all of the events we observed the facilitation was highly professional and competent. For most of the Tier 3 meetings from which we were able to collect data, interactions tended to focus on exchanges between the participants and the speakers, rather than between participants, although some meetings included small round-table discussions as used in the Tier 1 and Tier 2 events. Tier 3 meetings tended to be well facilitated, with facilitator interventions occupying a very small proportion of the meetings, and with most participants having an opportunity to have their say. Our data indicate that all views were given sufficient time to be aired. These meetings were not decision-making fora, and votes were not taken in any that we observed. Questionnaire responses suggest that participants in Tier 2 and Tier 3 events thought that the way the events were run allowed them to have their say, with strong agreement that events were well facilitated. Generally, respondents thought that the events were well organised and structured, however there was some concern (expressed by a majority of respondents) that not all relevant issues were addressed by the meetings.

As with the Foundation Discussion meetings, the Narrow-but-Deep groups were not, of course, established to come to a decision, although the outputs included individuals taking a view on the issues. In many ways the group exchanges took a deliberative form, in the sense that there was careful consideration of evidence and of different views concerning GM. Respondents to our questions generally confirmed a positive assessment of the Narrow-but-Deep meetings with regard to this criterion. For example, most felt the events were well facilitated (97.6 per cent agreed to some extent; and 2.4 per cent neither agreed nor disagreed – while no one disagreed; N = 42); and were 'well organised and structured' (again, 97.6 per cent agreed to some extent, while 2.4 per cent disagreed; N = 42). They also tended to agree that all relevant issues were covered (87.5 per cent agreed or strongly agreed, versus 10.0 per cent who disagreed, and 2.5 per cent who neither agreed nor disagreed; N = 40). If there was any concern here, it was that there was *too much* information to consider (57.1 per cent agreed or strongly agreed that this was the case; 28.6 per cent disagreed/strongly disagreed and 14.3 per cent neither agreed nor disagreed; N = 42).

Nature of the discourse

In view of our recognition of the central role of talk in processes of sense-making about issues such as GM (see e.g. Horlick-Jones, 2005c, 2007; Horlick-Jones and Walls, 2005; Petts *et al.*, 2001) we included in our observational protocol an item that sought to examine in some detail the dynamics of such exchanges at the various debate events. In particular, we agreed that observational work should, wherever possible, record instances of the form of disagreements, and how they were resolved. We also identified for special attention the ways that moderators achieved consensus; the ways that participants warranted the views they expressed; and the degree to which such warrants drew on personal and anecdotal material, or on scientific information.

These considerations are not directly linked to our normative criteria, but they do convey a sense of the kinds of participant interactions, and engagements with the issues about GM, that were made possible by the various parts of the debate. For the purposes of preparing this book we have restricted our accounts to fairly concise descriptions. However, it should be noted that at the time of writing some members of the evaluation team are engaged in further detailed analyses of the dynamics of 'GM talk' (Horlick-Jones *et al.*, 2006a, in press, b).

At the Foundation Discussion workshops, we noted that those disagreements that occurred between participants tended to be easily resolved, because the views expressed were often highly tentative. Such views were often qualified by expressions of a lack of relevant knowledge. The facilitators were at pains to avoid any disagreements becoming unpleasant or disruptive. There were often moments of light-hearted humour, especially during many of the 'games' used to elicit information from participants. This often functioned to create an informal atmosphere, although some participants did express doubts as to how they should 'play' them. In reasoning about GM in the absence of firm knowledge, participants tended to use various forms of analogy: for example, by reference to previous food scares or by means of examples of past technological failures such as BSE and Thalidomide. We observed few references to expert or technical sources of knowledge, with the notable exception being the Norwich group comprising 'engaged' individuals. We noted that some participants, particularly in rural areas, sometimes displayed a greater awareness of technical issues. Many arguments were warranted on the basis of rather vague recollections of information drawn from a range of media-based sources, primarily TV and newspapers. An important feature of these discussions was a pervasive sense of distrust of government and industry, and their statements on GM-related matters.

We were also interested in how the discourse reflected what participants felt about the Foundation Discussion workshops. Our observations indicated no expressions of discontent in the way the workshops were run, in fact, quite the reverse. On the whole, participants seemed pleased to have had the opportunity to discuss the issues, and, along these lines, were on occasions very complimentary to the moderators. When asked by the moderators what they had learnt from the evening, many participants suggested it was more a question of realising 'how much they didn't know' about GM. Most participants expressed broad support for the idea of a debate about GM crops, particularly if it was inclusive of a range of opinions. There was near to universal approval for a televised debate or programme that would examine the issues. Responses to a number of questionnaire items confirmed these positive views. Over nine-tenths (90.3 per cent) agreed that they 'enjoyed taking part in the workshop', and over three-quarters (77.4 per cent) indicated that they were either 'very' or 'fairly satisfied' with the workshop. Consequently, it is perhaps unsurprising that 80.6 per cent of respondents thought it would be useful to have similar workshops in the future, and 98.4 per cent would be willing to participate in a similar activity again.

At the Tier 1 meetings, we noted that the discussions around the tables were mostly good natured and conducive to a fair exchange of views. Light-hearted humour was very much in evidence. Much of the talk that we observed was characteristic of those who possessed some familiarity with the issues, and many participants adopted an engaged, and predominantly 'anti', position on GM. There were many instances where scientific information was deployed to warrant expressions of concern about various aspects of GM technology. We noted few examples of disagreements, or the sort of tensions that would characterise what one might call 'truly deliberative' engagement. Rather, the talk tended to take the form of a working-through, and refinement, of arguments against GM. We recognised that many of the arguments deployed by participants chimed with claims typical of the literature produced by environmental pressure groups. Feedback from the tables was dominated by detailed expressions of concern about GM crops, typically concerning threats to health and environment. Interestingly, spokespeople often took the opportunity to make linkages with a wider set of arguments that were critical of the role of governments (in particular the US), of multinational companies and their profit motives, and of claims that GM crops might provide a means to feed the world. In this way, much of the talk at the Tier 1 meetings seemed to reflect an 'anti-GM' position that was set within an underlying *weltanschauung* encompassing such wider perspectives.

Our questionnaire items asked about a number of more general issues concerning participant satisfaction (not specifically related to the evaluation criteria). These tended to result in a positive assessment of the meetings. A total of 91.7 per cent 'found the event interesting', with only 4.1 per cent disagreeing (N = 615). Similarly, the majority of respondents claimed they 'enjoyed taking part in the event' (78.6 per cent agreed, 14.1 per cent neither agreed nor disagreed, 7.3 per cent disagreed; N = 411). As a consequence, it is no surprise, perhaps, that most felt it would be 'useful to have other events like this in the future?' (74.3 per cent replied 'yes', 7.9 per cent replied 'no', 17.8 per cent replied 'don't know'; N = 404), and most 'would . . . be willing to participate in a similar activity again' (84.2 per cent replied 'yes', 4.7 per cent replied 'no', 11.1 per cent replied 'don't know'; N = 404). At least from these perspectives, there is some support that such events may have a place in the future.

In line with the Tier 1 meetings, we noted that the views of those participating in the Tier 2 meetings were dominated by critical perspectives on GM. Much of the questioning of speakers, and discussions among participants, reflected an engaged anti-GM position. We noted evidence of participants using pressure group and technical literature to inform their contributions. While some with more even-handed positions, and a few pro-GM people were present, their voices were largely drowned out. Once again, there were few disagreements between participants, although some disagreements did occur between participants and ('pro-GM') speakers. Speakers representing organisations critical of GM crops received warm applause, and we noted the opposite response for those speakers expressing a cautious welcome for the technology.

While many of those participating in the Tier 2 events seemed to be pleased to have had the opportunity to listen to the debate and exchange views, there were a number of criticisms and concerns expressed that were similar to those articulated at the Tier 1 events. These were concerned, in particular, with the perceived lack of advertising and shortness of notice for the event, cynicism over whether the government would take any notice of the outcome, and a recognition (by some) that the participants were not 'ordinary members of the public'.

A broadly anti-GM mood characterised the Tier 3 events that we observed. However, importantly, we recorded numerous instances where a genuine exploration of some of the nuances of the arguments about GM took place.

There were few outright disagreements. Contributions by participants often took the form of a practiced engagement with the issues, deploying 'standard' arguments and technical warrants (albeit sometimes in a rather tentative way). The speakers tended to ensure that the exchanges were enriched by much technical material. The limited data that we were able to collect suggests that participants in the Tier 3 events were mostly happy with the format of the meeting, but fairly cynical about government motivation behind having the debate, with a belief that the decision about GM cultivation was a foregone conclusion.

As with the Tier 1 events, respondents to the questionnaires from both Tier 2 and Tier 3 meetings were generally positive about the experience of taking part in the events. Most agreed that the meetings were 'interesting' and that they 'enjoyed taking part'. They also largely agreed that it would be useful to have other events like this in the future, and most expressed willingness to participate in similar activities again.

Turning finally to the Narrow-but-Deep process, here we observed that the talk was structured mostly in the form of a facilitator-led group discussion. Only during the second meeting of each group did a much greater density of inter-participant exchange take place. This shift may have reflected participants' greater awareness of the issues after the 'diary' period between meetings, and partly the facilitators' willingness to relax control over the discussion. Most participants had extremely rudimentary understandings of GM at the start of the process, such that much of the first meetings of each group tended to be dominated by attempts to capture the nature of the 'thing' that they were being invited to discuss. The participants' positions accordingly shifted as different topics were introduced in the groups' attempt to make sense of the issues in question. However, identifiable positions did finally emerge. We noted that mild disagreements were explored with great courteousness and without frustration, reflecting perhaps a lack of political engagement with the issues. As the groups became more familiar with the issues, the discussion shifted from early attempts to categorise and make sense of things to explorations of the relative merits of arguments about GM. In this sense the discourse was very different from the 'engaged talk' that could typically be observed at the Tier 1–3 events.

We noted that participants of those groups to which we gained observational access all seemed reasonably happy with their involvement. Indeed, most appeared quite animated and content throughout the process. This positive view was confirmed by participants' responses to our questionnaire: 95.3 per cent found the event enjoyable (only 4.8 per cent disagreed that it was so; N = 42); and every participant who responded (100 per cent) indicated that they were either very or fairly satisfied with the discussions (N = 42). All but one participant agreed that they would be willing to take part in such events again (N = 40). The Narrow-but-Deep groups were therefore perceived even more positively than the other processes that formed part of the *GM Nation?* debate. In addition, response to a number of open questions (not discussed here) revealed a wish to *learn* something. In other words, many respondents praised the workshops *because* they had learnt something about GM and/or the views of others on the topic, while others discussing negative aspects focused on *not* having learnt very much. Clearly, in a consultation exercise, the main objective of sponsors, and organisers, is to *gain* information from the target sample and sometimes it may be forgotten that the participants have an expectation of gaining something themselves.

Influence (N5)

Strictly speaking, this criterion it is not one of our 'process issues'. It suggests that for a participation exercise to be successful it should have an influence on subsequent policy-making, and that it should also be *perceived* by participants to have (or be expected to have) such an effect. Here we address this question of *perception*.

As the nature of the Foundation Discussion workshops was somewhat in doubt (were they participation or consultation exercises?), the relevance of this criterion is uncertain here. We recognise that observation could not address this aspect specifically, though some participants were observed to express scepticism of the intentions of government and industry. Responses to a number of questions, however, did shed some light upon the matter. One question asked participants to respond to the statement: 'The people who commissioned this workshop will not take any action on the views and recommendations made by participants.' Approximately half of respondents thought that sponsors *would* act on their views (48.4 per cent disagreed or strongly disagreed with the statement), though nearly a third (29.5 per cent) were uncertain – neither agreeing nor disagreeing – and only 8.2 per cent thought their views would *not* be influential. A second question asked, more broadly, participants' agreement with the statement that 'The results of this workshop will be influential in the future'. Again, a substantial amount of uncertainty was evident (33.9 per cent neither agreed nor disagreed), though over a third thought results would be influential and only one respondent thought the results would not be influential in the future.

Turning now to the Tier 1 events, we note similarities with the 'Early involvement' criterion. Again, we found that participants were generally sceptical about the place of the meetings in policy-making. Respondents generally disagreed that 'feedback from this event will be taken seriously by the Government', with 71.7 per cent disagreeing, 12.3 per cent neither agreeing nor disagreeing, and 15.9 per cent agreeing (N = 616). Similarly, respondents tended to agree that 'The people who commissioned this event *will not* take any action on the views and recommendations made by participants'. Here, 59 per cent agreed with this negative appraisal, with 23.9 per cent neither agreeing nor disagreeing, and 17.1 per cent disagreeing (N = 327). Furthermore, respondents tended to disagree that 'Feedback from this event will be influential on the future of GM foods and crops in the UK'.

Here, 64.7 per cent disagreed, 19.6 per cent neither agreed nor disagreed, and 15.7 per cent agreed (N = 306). What was notable in responses to these questions was also the extent to which uncertainty was manifest in terms of 'no responses' – for example, in the case of the last question, 114 respondents expressed no opinion (did not answer the question).

At the Tier 2 and Tier 3 meetings, questionnaire responses again revealed scepticism about the influence that the events would have on wider policy. Respondents from both types of events generally disagreed that 'Feedback from this event will be taken seriously by the Government', and that 'Feedback from this event will be influential on the future of GM foods and crops in the UK'. They generally agreed that 'The people who commissioned this event will not take any action on the views and recommendations made by participants'.

Finally, participants in the Narrow-but-Deep process felt much uncertainty about the potential influence of these groups, emphasised by the number of 'don't know' or non-responses to the relevant questions in QL(RFG). Of respondents who did express an opinion, there was evidence that a majority believed they *would* be influential. That is, 55.1 per cent disagreed/strongly disagreed with the statement that 'The people who commissioned these discussions will *not* take any action on the views and recommendations made by participants' (13.8 per cent neither agreed nor disagreed, while 31.0 per cent agreed/strongly agreed – though only 29 of 42 respondents answered this question). Furthermore, 49.4 per cent agreed/strongly agreed with the statement that 'Feedback from the discussions will be influential on the future of GM foods and crops in the UK' (while 22.6 per cent neither agreed nor disagreed, and 29.1 per cent disagreed/strongly disagreed, though only 31 of 42 respondents answered this question). In this respect, the RFG respondents appeared considerably less cynical than those from other events in the GM debate about their likely impact on wider events.

Summary of findings

Having discussed in detail the performance of the four types of debate events according to 'process' considerations, we now summarise our findings. In Table 4.1 we set out comparative details of the performance of the various component parts of the debate process against the normative process criteria.

The Foundation Discussion workshops

Here the methodology used was very sound and, in general, the exercise was perceived positively by participants. As an exercise concerned primarily with information gathering, the organisers were able to capture most of the data required by the PDSB. However, on occasion some of the participants were unsure how to 'play' the games utilised as part of the workshops, and this may have hindered the expression of views and opinions. We would also caution

Table 4.1 Summary of performance of component parts of the debate against normative process criteria

Criterion	Foundation Discussion workshops	Tier 1 meetings	Tier 2 and Tier 3 meetings	Narrow-but-Deep groups
Independence	Good performance. Overall, the participants thought the events were fair and unbiased.	Moderately successful. Facilitation regarded as fair and unbiased, although some concern about the fairness and balance of the information provided.	Quite successful. Facilitation and information provided generally perceived as fair and unbiased.	Very good performance. Strong support for the fairness and lack of bias of the events.
Early involvement	In principle, good. Participants had the opportunity to shape subsequent events, however see discussion in Chapter 7.	Fairly poor. Participants not convinced that the events had been held early enough to be influential.	Fairly poor. Participants not convinced the events had been held early enough to be influential.	Fairly poor. Participants not convinced that the events had been held early enough to be influential (but highly uncertain about this).
Transparency	Fairly poor. Participants not clear about aspects such as how participants were selected and how the results would be used. However, unclear whether this was a problem with an exercise of this nature.	Quite poor. Participants not clear how results from events would be used. It was generally thought that there was a 'hidden agenda' behind the events.	Quite poor. Although respondents did not think there was a 'hidden agenda', they were unclear about aspects such as how participants had been selected and how the results would be used.	Better than the Tier events, but still substantial uncertainty about selection, use and feedback aspects of transparency.
Task definition	Organisers' wish to avoid imposing framing means that the relevance of this criterion is questionable here.	Events scored moderately well. Participants generally unclear what the events would involve, although fairly clear about what to do when taking part in the events.	Events scored moderately well. Participants generally clear about what events would involve etc., but there was variation in information provided by organisers across different events.	Relevance of criterion questionable. Nevertheless, strong participant support for a view that the tasks and their implementation were both explained clearly.

Table 4.1 continued

Criterion	Foundation Discussion workshops	Tier 1 meetings	Tier 2 and Tier 3 meetings	Narrow-but-Deep groups
Resources	Fairly poor. Many participants felt too little time was available.	Events scored poorly. Participants thought they had insufficient information, and they needed more time.	Mixed results. Participants generally thought they had sufficient information, but unclear whether they felt they had enough time.	Good performance. Participants felt they had sufficient time and information.
Structured dialogue	Good performance. Professional and competent facilitation: most participants had the opportunity to have their say, and most felt the events were well run. However, on occasions, moderators curtailed discussions, and some participants felt that not all issues were covered.	Uncertain performance. Participants agreed that facilitators tried to involve people, but disagreed over whether the events were well run.	Mixed results. Events were generally regarded as well run and organised, with facilitators trying to involve people. Participants less convinced that all relevant issues were covered. These events were essentially public meetings' rather than 'truly' deliberative events.	Strong performance, featuring elements of deliberative engagement. Participants regarded the meetings as well run, and that all relevant issues had been addressed. If there was any concern it was that there was too much information to consider.
Influence	Relevance of criterion in doubt here. Participants uncertain about likely influence on policy.	Much scepticism expressed about likely impact on policy.	Much scepticism expressed about likely impact on policy.	Participants uncertain about likely influence on policy, but less cynical than those from other debate events.

against accepting the claim made in the organisers' report that 'clean language' was used to develop questions.

One area of *potential* concern relates to the criterion of 'Transparency'. Participants were not clear about important aspects regarding the process: such as how participants were selected, whether they would receive feedback, and how their results would be used. Given the consultation nature of the workshops, however, the relevance of this criterion is less certain and hence we do not believe that the workshops should be criticised on this ground. We suggest that the underlying purpose of the workshops might have been given greater emphasis, thereby enabling participants to understand the importance of their discussions with regard to subsequent stages of the debate. This could have encouraged a greater engagement and ownership of the event. While the organisers were highly effective with regard to most elements of the exercise brief, they were less successful in ascertaining what would encourage members of the public to engage with the overall GM debate.

The Tier 1 meetings

In organisational terms, these public meetings were regarded by those attending as poorly advertised, with participants tending to find out about them at the last moment. This is not surprising given the relatively small amount spent on direct advertising, and the restricted time available for conducting the main debate. Although it was the PDSB's intention to provide stimulus material to participants in advance of the meetings, very often the late notice appears to have militated against this happening. Accordingly, participants were generally unclear about what the events would involve until discussion began.

Our respondents generally felt that the events were well facilitated, and that they had had an opportunity to have their say. They also found the events enjoyable. However, they also reported that they had insufficient information and needed more time to complete the process of deliberation. Many participants expected that they would be able to engage directly with experts on both sides of the GM debate, although the Tier 1 events did not provide this facility. The events were often dominated by discussions characteristic of a knowledgeable and experienced engagement with GM issues. The discussions were not, however, truly deliberative, and they made little use of the stimulus materials that were provided. Time constraints were an important resource consideration, both in terms of being seen to curtail the round-table discussion and reduce the summaries of these discussions to a series of often rhetorical 'sound bites'. Finally, participants were not convinced that their views would be taken seriously by government.

The Tier 2 and Tier 3 meetings

Again, a fairly consistent picture emerges as to how the participants perceived these meetings in terms of our normative criteria. Overall, they appeared to be viewed more positively than the Tier 1 events: for example, participants on average did not think there was a 'hidden agenda' as they did for the Tier 1 events. They also seemed to perceive the events as being better run, with participants seen as being representative of the affected population (see Chapter 5 for discussion of the representativeness issue), and with a greater proportion of participants rating time and information resources as being sufficient. In line with the Tier 1 events, the Tier 2 and Tier 3 events were generally thought to be enjoyable and satisfying, and participants thought it could be useful to run similar events in the future.

The Narrow-but-Deep groups

Here our findings were broadly positive. The facilitation of the groups was professional and independent, with participants being able to have their say, and sufficient time being available to complete the exercise. Although the process tended not to be very clearly explained, participants expressed no confusion about what they needed to do. The group discussions contained serious examination of the issues around GM, they were courteous in manner, and featured a high density of inter-participant interaction during the second meetings. Participants found the process enjoyable.

Unlike participants in the other events, participants tended to think that their views *would* be influential in some way. Although most participants felt that the process was being held rather too late in the day to influence the issue of the debate, many (a greater proportion than for the other events) disagreed with this view. Hence, participants were typically less cynical about the debate process than those from the other events forming part of the debate process.

Despite this good performance, we are wary about giving too high an endorsement of the Narrow-but-Deep process. We have certain misgivings about the methodology used, in particular, about the extent to which the process might be regarded as truly 'deliberative'. We return to this matter in our discussion of knowledge-handling by the debate in Chapter 7.

Concluding remarks

Our central conclusion is that the practical implementation of the debate was flawed in a number of important respects. Our analysis of the 'process' aspects of the debate has raised a great many matters of detail, and we hope that these will contribute to a process of learning about how best to implement future such initiatives.

We have only mentioned in passing the extent to which participants felt that the outcome of the debate would be taken seriously by government, and would have some concrete influence on GM policy. This matter is addressed by the normative criterion N5, and this matter is discussed in the final chapter of the book. At this stage we simply note that the three tiers of public meetings all scored poorly in this respect.

Earlier in the chapter we mentioned the seven sponsor objectives that we labelled 'pseudo' criteria. According to the data reported here, the criterion B3 ('to create new and effective opportunities for deliberative debate about the issues') might be said to have been addressed to some extent, although it is not clear what 'new and effective' means, and, as we have seen, there is doubt about the extent to which any component parts of the debate could reasonably be described as truly 'deliberative'. Criteria B4a and B4b ('dialogue with experts' and 'access to evidence') were also addressed to some extent. Expert speakers were, of course, only involved in some of the Tier 2 and Tier 3 meetings. Participants were dissatisfied with the stimulus materials, and our observational work indicated that they were little used. We have nothing further to say regarding the pseudo criteria at this stage. We will return to this matter in Chapter 9.

5   The issue of representativeness

One important criterion for the success of a process of engagement is that the participants are typical, or 'representative', of the wider population affected by the issue under consideration. Clearly, this criterion is of central relevance to the GM debate. It would be very difficult for the sponsors and organisers to justify the title of a 'national' debate if the sample of those taking part were in some way biased and unrepresentative of the range of views present within the 'nation'. Indeed, the issue of 'representativeness' is an evaluation criterion identified in all our sets of criteria – including that of the debate sponsors.

There are two main approaches for judging such representativeness. The first is by comparing the demographic and socio-economic profiles of the samples involved in the engagement process with known national distributions of these characteristics. If the respondents were predominantly of one gender, for example, the event could be open to charges of being 'sexist'. Similarly, if participants were predominantly of a certain age, or particularly well educated or financially well-off, the event might be regarded as 'ageist' or 'elitist'. The second approach is to consider attitudinal distribution, which in many ways is an equally (if not more) important aspect as socio-demographic spread. That is, people with particular or extreme attitudes may come in all shapes and forms, and hence a demographic profile of the event sample that matches the national profile does not necessarily preclude attitudinal bias. It is clearly just as important for a 'national' debate to involve participants who match the 'attitudinal profile' of the national population as well as its socio-demographic profile.

In practical terms, we used two main methods to examine the representativeness of the debate process:

- First, we collected basic socio-demographic and attitudinal data from various samples of participants of the *GM Nation?* events (the Foundation Discussion workshops, Tier 1, 2 and 3 events, and Narrow-but-Deep meetings). These data were then compared with the socio-demographic profile of the UK population and comparable attitude data from our two nationally representative British surveys conducted by MORI in 2002 and 2003 respectively.

- Second, the *GM Nation?* organisers had collected over 36,000 feedback questionnaires from people participating in *GM Nation?* events and via the *GM Nation?* interactive website. The quantitative items on this feedback form were then compared with data from equivalent questions included on our national survey (the MORI data) which was completed just after the conclusion of the public debate.

In addition, our survey data provided important insights into the degree of understanding of, and attitudes towards, issues concerning GM food and crops among the lay public. If the findings of the debate were very different from this wider profile of public attitudes, then it could be suggested that the debate in some sense did not acquire views representative of the public. We will discuss this matter in more detail at the end of the chapter.

The chapter is organised as follows. First, we examine the two key statistical measures of representativeness mentioned above. Second, we consider the degree to which data collected by means of the debate's feedback questionnaires might reasonably be regarded as providing views that were representative of those of the general public. Third, we consider evidence of widespread awareness of the debate, and of the regional distribution of debate-related activity. Fourth, drawing on our MORI data, we examine the profile of a number of aspects of wider public views about GM food and related matters. Finally, we bring the chapter to a close with discussion of the implications of these findings, prior to drawing some conclusions.

Statistical measures of representativeness

Socio-demographic

Using various questionnaires, we collected details on the socio-demographic profiles of participants who attended the Tier 1, Tier 2, Tier 3 and the Narrow-but-Deep meetings. Practical constraints on data gathering precluded the collection of such details from participants in the Foundation Discussion workshops. We were also unable to collect many responses from the Tier 2 and Tier 3 events participants. The figures for these latter events are presented mainly for reader interest, and we do not intend to over-generalise our conclusions from these. Table 5.1 shows a summary of selected findings; these are concerned with the ages, male–female ratios and educational levels of respondents.

In the Tier 1 events, the gender balance, averaged over all six meetings, was almost 50:50 between males and females. This ratio is not greatly dissimilar to that in the national UK population (48.6 per cent male to 51.4 per cent female, according to data taken from UK 2001 Census.[1] Respondents from the other events generally showed a greater proportion of female to male respondents. This ratio was considerably dissimilar to the UK population; although, because of possible response bias, we should not read too much into

Table 5.1 Socio-demographic characteristics of respondents from various events

	Tier 1	Tier 2	Tier 3	Reconvened focus groups
Total N	618	148	50	42
Male	51.0%	38.8%	39.0%	38.1%
Female	49.0%	61.2%	61.0%	61.9%
[N]	[549]	[139]	[41]	[42]
Mean age	49.6	46.5	54.1	4.95*
(SD)	(15.0)	(18.1)	(12.2)	(2.05)
[N]	[510]	[134]	[35]	[42]
Proportion with at least a degree [N]	66.3% [525]	82.1% [134]	48.6% [35]	23.8% [42]
Proportion with a higher degree [N]	33.3% [525]	48.5% [134]	20.0% [35]	0% [0]

Note: * Measured on different scale: a value of '4' indicates a range between 35 and 44, and a value of '5' indicates a range between 45 and 54.

these figures. Regarding the age profile, the average of respondents across these different events was between 45 and 55 for the three 'Tier' events, but slightly younger for the Narrow-but-Deep meetings. Overall, they were rather older than the median age of the UK population.

The most interesting results are concerned with educational level. In this case a fairly clear bias does emerge, in particular in response to a question asking the respondents for their 'highest qualification'. We also asked, for example, about number of years in education after the age of 11, the results from which are not shown here, although they do appear to validate the 'highest qualifications' claims. Table 5.1 shows the proportion of respondents who claimed to have a degree (BSc, BA, or equivalent), and the proportion who claimed to have a higher degree (Masters, PhD, etc.). Notable is that approximately two-thirds of Tier 1 respondents claimed to have a degree, and that about one-third of all respondents to the questionnaires claimed to have a higher degree. The figure is even higher for the Tier 2 respondents, but this is not entirely surprising, given that this data was derived from a meeting in Cambridge. The figure is slightly lower for the Tier 3 participants while the Narrow-but-Deep sample is much closer to the national profile in this regard; as would be expected, given that these participants were recruited to be broadly representative of the UK population, rather than being self-selected.

According to the UK 2001 Census, 19.6 per cent of the population between the ages of 16 and 74 have qualifications at degree level or higher. This suggests that the participants in the Tier 1 events were *highly atypical* of the national population with regard to educational level. Indeed, even if we assumed our sample of respondents was *completely* biased (i.e. all people with degrees responded, and none of those who failed to respond had a degree), this would still not account for all of the difference. Formal estimates of the numbers who attended the Tier 1 events suggest that approximately two-thirds of all participants responded to our questionnaires. So if we assume that none of those who failed to respond (the other one-third) had a degree, then our figures still imply that 44 per cent of the sample held a degree: twice as high as the national population. Indeed, this figure is liable to be an under-estimate, and the actual proportion with a degree is likely to have been higher.

Attitudinal

Assessing representativeness in terms of attitudes is not as easy as using socio-demographic evidence. There exists no national profile information on attitudes equivalent to that provided, for example, by the latest National Census. However, in the survey conducted for us in 2002 by MORI, we were able to gain a representative sub-sample of about 300 respondents that had answered a number of questions on attitudes to GM foods. We subsequently incorporated seven of these questions into various questionnaires given to participants at the various events forming part of the GM debate. The 2003 survey, also conducted for us by MORI, gained a much larger representative sample answering the same questions soon after the main public debate events took place.

Of course, the 2002 survey sample is not the ideal baseline, primarily because it took place one year prior to the *GM Nation?* events, and so attitudes might have changed in that year. The 2003 survey addressed this concern by allowing us to see whether views had changed since that first polling. Now one could also argue that, given the apparent demographic/socio-economic representativeness of the event samples (despite being clearly biased in terms of educational achievements), the results from the debate events are just as likely to be attitudinally representative as our survey samples. However, this is unlikely to be the case. In the first place, for those events where participant recruitment was intended to be diverse (if not representative per se; notably in the Foundation Discussion workshops and the Narrow-but-Deep meetings), the numbers recruited were small in comparison to our 'control' samples. Second, in the case of other events, where participants were largely self-selected (the 'Tier' events) it is not unreasonable to suppose that they might have held an unusual degree of interest in the topic. Therefore, though we accept that the results from the two national surveys should not be taken unequivocally as a 'gold standard' of public GM attitudes, we suggest they are more likely to be representative of baseline attitudes than any comparative sample from the GM Debate events. It follows that any systematic bias in attitudes for participants at these events are likely to represent a genuine difference.

In Table 5.2 we present the mean scores on the seven different questions about GM asked in the original 2002 survey. The first question, entitled 'Benefits', asked: 'How would you assess the benefits, if any, of genetically modified food for British society as a whole?' The scale ranged from 1 ('Very low') to 7 ('Very high'), with 4 ('Some') being the mid-point value.[2] Although the mean from each event was below the mid-point value, one can see some differences between the seven samples. Respondents of the three 'Tier' events perceived the lowest benefits, while respondents of the two national surveys, as well as of the Foundation Discussion workshops, perceived the highest benefits for society as a whole. The scores of the respondents from the Narrow-but-Deep meetings fell in between.

This general pattern is repeated for the other questions. The second question, on 'health risks', asked: 'How would you assess the risks, if any, to human health from genetically modified food for British society as a whole?'

Table 5.2 Mean scores on seven GM questions for seven different samples

Event	Benefits (1–7)	Health Risks (1–7)	Environment Risks (1–7)	Concern (1–5)	Importance (1–5)	Regulations (1–5)	Accept-ability (1–5)
Foundation Workshops							
Mean	3.72	4.46	4.45	3.41	3.26	2.45	2.74
(SD)	(1.64)	(1.54)	(1.75)	(1.17)	(1.14)	(1.17)	(1.17)
N	166	164	165	164	159	166	168
Tier 1 events							
Mean	1.86	5.51	6.18	4.48	3.92	1.59	1.59
(SD)	(1.62)	(1.96)	(1.61)	(1.16)	(1.53)	(1.14)	(1.18)
N	392	395	403	405	354	399	407
Tier 2 events							
Mean	1.91	5.20	6.00	4.39	3.62	1.70	1.68
(SD)	(1.57)	(1.88)	(1.51)	(1.11)	(1.55)	(1.10)	(1.18)
N	237	231	239	240	224	235	241
Tier 3 events							
Mean	2.19	4.88	5.85	4.29	3.63	1.74	1.92
(SD)	(1.79)	(2.11)	(1.70)	(1.11)	(1.53)	(1.22)	(1.43)
N	108	108	109	110	103	110	111
Narrow-but-Deep							
Mean	2.86	4.90	5.60	4.10	3.02	2.10	2.10
(SD)	(1.75)	(1.72)	(1.61)	(1.01)	(1.46)	(0.93)	(1.08)
N	42	42	42	42	41	42	42
MORI 2002							
Mean	3.45	4.54	4.89	3.14	3.29	2.61	2.64
(SD)	(1.54)	(1.44)	(1.39)	(1.31)	(1.23)	(1.10)	(1.17)
N	254	246	245	285	285	258	272
MORI 2003							
Mean	3.24	4.43	4.60	3.48	3.45	2.35	2.69
(SD)	(1.62)	(1.61)	(1.62)	(1.23)	(1.19)	(1.17)	(1.18)
N	1161	1149	1154	1332	1317	1275	1294

Sources: UEA/MORI Risk Survey 2002 (*Unweighted* dataset, N = 296) and UEA/MORI GM Food Survey 2003 (*Weighted* dataset, N = 1,363).

This time, all mean values were above the scale mid-point. It appeared that the respondents of the two national surveys and the Foundation Discussion workshops perceived the lowest risks, while the respondents of the Tier 1 and Tier 2 events perceived the highest risks for British society as a whole. Respondents from the Tier 3 events and the Narrow-but-Deep groups could be found in between. However, the differences here were small.

The third question, on 'environmental risks', asked: 'How would you assess the risks, if any, to the environment from genetically modified food?' All mean ratings were above the mid-point value. In line with the previous question, respondents from the two national surveys and the Foundation Discussion workshops perceived the lowest risks to the environment, while respondents of the Tier 1 and Tier 2 events perceived the highest risks to the environment.

The fourth question, on 'concern', asked: 'How concerned or not are you about genetically modified food?' On this occasion, the scale ranged from 1 ('Not at all concerned') to 5 ('Very concerned') with 3 ('Neither/Nor') as the scale mid-point. All means were above the mid-point of the scale. It appeared that respondents of the Tier 1, Tier 2 and Tier 3 events, as well as the Narrow-but-Deep meetings were the most concerned about GM food, while respondents of the two national surveys and the Foundation Discussion workshops were the least concerned.

The fifth question, on 'importance', asked: 'How important is genetically modified food for you?' Again a 5-point scale was used. All respondents found the issue of GM food to some extent important, as the means for all seven samples were above the scale mid-point. The respondents from the three 'Tier' events found the issue of GM food more important than the respondents from the other events (especially the Narrow-but-Deep respondents). However, these differences were small.

The sixth question, on 'regulations', stated: 'I feel that current rules and regulations in the UK are sufficient to control genetically modified food.'[3] A 5-point scale was used. All mean ratings fell below the mid-point value, suggesting widespread distrust in the regulation of GM food. Respondents of the three 'Tier' events indicated less trust in the regulation of GM food than respondents from the other events.

Finally, the question on 'acceptability' asked: 'On the whole, how acceptable or unacceptable is genetically modified food to you?' A 5-point scale was used. Respondents from the Tier 1 and Tier 2 events found GM food the least acceptable, while respondents from the Foundation Discussion workshops and the two national surveys found it the most acceptable. The Tier 3 events and the Narrow-but-Deep groups could be found in between. However, *all* mean scores were below the scale mid-point.

In summary:

- The attitudes of respondents from the 2003 and 2002 surveys were fairly similar. The benefits of GM food were rated slightly lower in the 2003 survey than in the previous 2002 survey, as were general and environmental risks. Concern and importance were slightly up in 2003, while the acceptability of GM food was roughly the same. The question on regulations is difficult to interpret.

- It would seem that the GM debate events that were attitudinally most like the 2002/3 surveys were the Foundation Discussion workshops. Importantly, at these events respondents were *selected* to attend with no prior knowledge about GM foods and crops, and they completed the questionnaires after an evening of discussion of the issues.
- Those from the Narrow-but-Deep groups were intermediate in the level of their general opposition to GM foods. In other words they reported higher perceived risks, lower benefits, greater concern and lower acceptability than respondents from the surveys.[4] These respondents had also been recruited as having no prior knowledge. In contrast to the Foundation Discussion and survey respondents, they had been provided with the *GM Nation?* debate 'tool-kit' materials, had collected further information about the topic, and taken part in two discussion sessions prior to completing our questionnaire.
- The respondents who were most negative about GM foods across all of the measures were those from the Tier 1, Tier 2 and Tier 3 events. It should be noted that our restricted sampling means that the Tier 2 and 3 findings should be interpreted with caution. All these participants were, of course, largely self-selected.

Our general conclusion is that, at least attitudinally, many of the participants who attended the open GM debate events (the 'Tier' events) were *significantly more negative* about GM foods than either the closed group participants or respondents to the two 'representative' national surveys. Of course, the question arises as to whether these participants held such views *prior to* the event, or whether they became more negative as a consequence of what they had learned at the event. We have some evidence that indicates they did hold negative views before the event (here we have in mind the responses of participants to the open questions on our questionnaires, and the data generated by our observation of a range of events). Nevertheless, it is certainly possible that participants became more negative, to a greater or lesser degree, as each event proceeded. Restrictions on our evaluation work precluded us being able to administer questionnaires both before *and* after events in order to assess any such possible attitudinal change.

The voice of the people? The *GM Nation?* 'feedback' data

The quantitative findings from over 36,000 'feedback' questionnaires, completed by meeting participants, and by others who returned copies or who visited the *GM Nation?* interactive website, formed an important component of the evidence discussed in the PDSB's final report. As we note in Chapter 8, these findings also played a significant part in the media commentary on the debate's outcomes. Indeed, much of the British media presented these numerical findings as if they had been the result of a national opinion poll or even a referendum. It should be stressed that the PDSB report offered a more nuanced set of conclusions, which drew on both quantitative and qualitative data. We discuss the production of that report in more detail in Chapter 7, and consider the extent to which its main findings might be regarded as broadly 'representative' at the end of this chapter. In this section we consider the degree to which the data collected by means of the feedback questionnaires might reasonably be regarded as representative of the view of the general public.

As noted above, our national survey, conducted immediately after the end of the *GM Nation?* debate, included a number of the quantitative items replicating those appearing on the *GM Nation?* 'feedback' questionnaires. Table 5.3 shows responses to ten equivalent questions for four datasets respectively. They are as follows: in the first two columns data from the Narrow-but-Deep participants; administered first at the beginning of their first meeting (NBD-1), and second at the *start* of their second meetings (following the two-week 'diary' period) (NBD-2); then the 'feedback' questionnaire returns (Feedback); and finally our own nationally representative survey (MORI 2003). These items include five risk-oriented questions, Q1–5, and five benefit-oriented questions, Q6–10.

Inspecting Table 5.3,[5] and in particular the net agreement figures, shows that the results of our nationally representative survey (MORI 2003) are closest to the NBD-1 data. This is to be expected as both represent the views of a cross-section of people asked without any specific prior information, and without any discussion of the issues in question. The findings of our national survey are relatively similar to NBD-2 as well, although, as the PDSB final report (2003) points out, attitudes in the Narrow-but-Deep groups 'hardened' with time. In Table 5.3 we see that there is more net agreement, particularly with respect to the risk items, in NBD-2 compared to NBD-1.

Turning to consider the Feedback data, two things are evident. First, the Feedback responses to questions that explore the potential risks associated with the technology are largely in line with the other three groups, if somewhat more polarised. All four sets of respondents hold similar views regarding the potential risks associated with GM, albeit to a greater or lesser extent. However, the Feedback responses to statements that ask about the potential benefits associated with GM are exactly opposite to the other three samples. While both the Narrow-but-Deep and the MORI 2003 samples show net agreement that there could be potential benefits to GM food and crops, the Feedback respondents overwhelmingly disagree with this notion.

We conducted a principal components analysis to examine the underlying structure in people's responses to the statements. This analysis shows that the ten risk and benefit statements can be described by two main factors, which

Table 5.3 Mean scores on ten GM questions for four different samples

	NBD-1 June/July (N = 77)	NBD-2 June/July (N = 77)	Feedback June/July (N = 36,557)	MORI 2003 Jul/Aug/Sep (N = 1,363)
Q1. I am concerned about the potential negative impact of genetically modified crops on the environment				
Agree	57	85	91	63
Disagree	14	12	7	10
Unsure/Neutral	28	4	2	27
Net	+43	+73	+84	+53
Q2. I am worried that this new technology is being driven more by profit than by the public interest				
Agree	69	88	93	75
Disagree	9	9	6	7
Unsure/Neutral	22	3	1	17
Net	+60	+79	+87	+68
Q3. I think genetically modified crops would mainly benefit the producers and not ordinary people				
Agree	56	77	85	64
Disagree	24	11	8	9
Unsure/Neutral	19	10	5	25
Net	+32	+66	+77	+55
Q4. I don't think we know enough about the long-term effects of genetically modified food on our health				
Agree	80	96	93	85
Disagree	7	1	5	4
Unsure/Neutral	12	1	2	10
Net	+73	+95	+88	+81
Q5. I am worried that if genetically modified crops are introduced it will be very difficult to ensure that other crops are GM free				
Agree	64	79	93	68
Disagree	17	15	5	7
Unsure/Neutral	19	6	2	24
Net	+47	+64	+88	+61
Q6. I believe genetically modified crops could help to provide cheaper food for consumers in the UK				
Agree	43	60	14	45
Disagree	14	24	70	23
Unsure/Neutral	42	16	15	31
Net	+29	+36	−56	+22
Q7. I believe that genetically modified crops could improve the prospects of British farmers by helping them to compete with farmers around the world				
Agree	40	47	9	31
Disagree	23	39	79	26
Unsure/Neutral	37	14	11	43
Net	+17	+8	−70	+5
Q8. I think that some genetically modified crops could benefit the environment by using less pesticides and chemical fertilisers than traditional crops				
Agree	54	53	14	44
Disagree	17	29	71	20
Unsure/Neutral	32	17	13	35
Net	+37	+24	−57	+24

Table 5.3 continued

	NBD-1 June/July (N = 77)	NBD-2 June/July (N = 77)	Feedback June/July (N = 36,557)	MORI 2003 Jul/Aug/Sep (N = 1,363)
Q9. I believe that genetically modified crops could benefit people in developing countries				
Agree	50	63	13	56
Disagree	18	28	75	17
Unsure/Neutral	32	9	12	25
Net	+32	+35	−62	+39
Q10. I believe that some genetically modified non-food crops could have useful medical benefits				
Agree	32	60	23	40
Disagree	12	16	41	11
Unsure/Neutral	56	25	35	49
Net	+20	+44	−18	+29

account for 56 per cent of the variance in responses. As might be expected, the first five items of Table 5.3 loaded highly on a single factor, which can be interpreted as the *perceived risks* of GM food and crops. Similarly, the latter five items in Table 5.3 loaded highly on a second *perceived benefits* factor. An internally consistent perceived risks measure (Cronbach's α = 0.82) was then calculated for each survey respondent by averaging the scores on the first five items, and a reliable perceived benefits measure (α = 0.81) using the latter five items. In this way each individual can be assigned a combined perceived risk score and a combined perceived benefits score, scaled from 1 (low) to 5 (high) with 3 as the mid-point.

The composite perceived risk and benefit measures can be used to explore overall attitudes towards GM food and crops. In many cases, beliefs about risks and benefits will be consistent with one another. In other words, someone who believes that GM crops and food have high benefits and low risks holds a *positive* attitude towards the technology, while one who sees few benefits and high risks predominantly holds *negative* beliefs. However, some might believe that GM crops pose unknown long-term environmental risks while simultaneously taking the view that there may be potential benefits to farmers, the economy, or consumers from such crops. Such an individual can be said to be *ambivalent*.

Figure 5.1 illustrates the frequency distribution for our nationally representative survey sample of individual responses in terms of their joint risk and benefits scores. In line with previous research (Gaskell *et al.*, 2003; Marris *et al.*, 2001; Petts *et al.*, 2001), our results suggest that, rather than simply for or against, many individuals hold essentially *ambivalent* attitudes towards the risks and benefits of GM food and crops. Taking the scale mid-point as the cut-off for each axis it is immediately apparent that there are very few indifferent individuals, and only a small number who are positive. The main distribution is essentially bimodal, with a major proportion (about

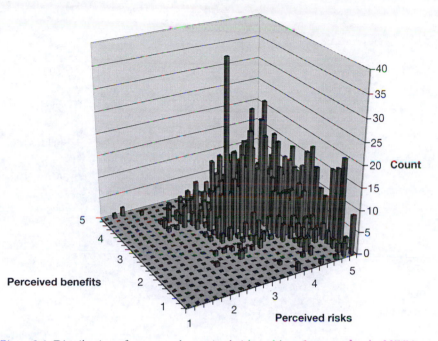

Figure 5.1 Distribution of compound perceived risk and benefit scores for the MORI study (N = 1,326)

Note: Thirty-seven of the MORI questionnaires (or 2.7 per cent) contained one or more missing values on the risk/benefit items. Accordingly, the factor analysis shown here is based on a slightly reduced sample of 1,326 repondents.

Source: Pidgeon *et al.*, 2005.

50 per cent) clustering in the top right-hand ambivalence quadrant. A further 30 per cent hold a clear negative pattern of attitudes.

In contrast, Figure 5.2 illustrates an equivalent re-analysis of the Feedback data,[6] where similar risk and benefits measures can be constructed. In contrast to the findings of our own survey, Figure 5.2 shows that the responses almost completely cluster in the lower right-hand quadrant. In other words, respondents to the Feedback questionnaires were overwhelmingly *negative* towards GM with very little endorsement of potential benefits.

While accepting that our survey data should be seen as complementary evidence, rather than in any sense 'better' than those derived from the *GM Nation?* Feedback questionnaires, our analysis set out above generates some interesting conclusions. First, that concern about the risks of GM is largely *shared* across all groups of respondents in Table 5.3. Our 2003 survey findings, therefore, corroborate one of the official overall conclusions of the debate – namely, that 'people are generally uneasy about GM' (PDSB, 2003). However, what clearly marks out the Feedback data from all others is the lack of

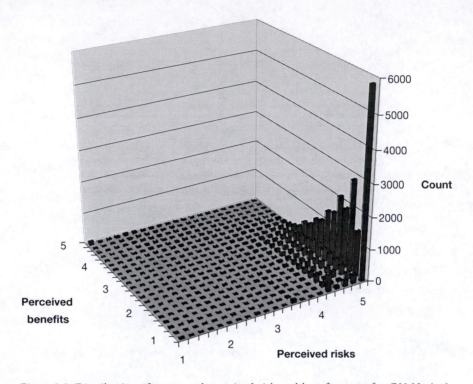

Figure 5.2 Distribution of compound perceived risk and benefit scores for *GM Nation?*
         open questionnaires (N = 35,177)

Note: 1,380 open *GM Nation?* questionnaires (3.8 per cent) contained at least one missing value.
We have therefore used a reduced sample of 35,177 for the factor analysis shown here.
Source: Pidgeon *et al.*, 2005.

endorsement of any potential benefits. Given the underlying distribution of
attitudes revealed in our own survey this latter finding is not entirely
surprising. This is consistent with engaged individuals, with existing strong
views about GM, being disproportionately represented at the open events,
and responding to the 'Feedback' questionnaire via the official debate website.

We conclude this discussion by first noting that engaged people with clear
views on an issue have a legitimate contribution to make in any significant
public policy debate. Indeed, the *GM Nation?* debate sought to explore public
views and encourage debate, rather than being an opinion poll or research
exercise. Overall, our survey findings suggest that current UK 'public opinion'
is not a unitary whole, but fragmented with considerable ambivalence co-
existing alongside outright opposition. Such ambivalence means that while
many people are prepared to endorse potential future benefits of GM food
and crops, there also exist widespread concerns about the technology.

Some measures of awareness and activity associated with the debate

A number of additional considerations may be seen to have a bearing on the overall 'representativeness' of those involved in the debate in some manner, whether as active participants or relatively passive recipients of information. To what extent, for example, were members of the general public aware that the debate was taking place? Similarly, one might reasonably ask about the geographical distribution of participation in the debate. Was it seen as predominantly a 'London' or 'English' event, or did the regions of the United Kingdom regard it as a truly 'national' event?

Visibility

One of the objectives of *GM Nation?* was to create widespread awareness among the population that the debate was taking place. According to our national survey, a majority (71 per cent) of the general public had never heard of the *GM Nation?* debate. In addition, 13 per cent had heard of the debate *but* knew nothing about it. In contrast, 15 per cent of the general public claimed some awareness of the debate. To be more specific, about 12–13 per cent indicated that they knew a little about the debate, while only 3 per cent said they knew a fair amount or a lot about the debate (see Figure 5.3).

These figures can be interpreted in a number of ways. On the one hand, the bulk of the population (seven in ten) had not heard of the debate at all. On the other hand, this finding does suggest that a sizeable minority of the British adult population had to some extent been made aware of its existence. Given the relative lack of advertising, tabloid and television coverage of the

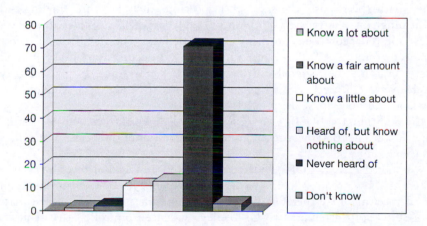

Figure 5.3 How much do you know about 'GM Nation? The Public Debate', the national debate on genetic modification of food and crops that has been going on recently? (Weighted dataset, N = 1,363)

debate (see Chapter 8), this figure might be regarded as representing a modest success, and indeed this performance could usefully be compared to data on awareness of other government initiatives in comparable areas of science and technology.

In view of the fact that interest in the issue of GM food is generally high (as indicated by our survey, and in terms of media newsworthiness), our finding that only a small minority of the general public seems to have heard of the debate suggests that the debate only partially met its objective of creating a widespread awareness of its existence. However, it should be noted that on a question of this kind one might get 'false positives'. In other words, people sometimes claim to have heard or read about something when in fact they have not done so. Indeed, our observational work at the Foundation Discussion workshops and Narrow-but-Deep meetings indicates that people often claimed a vague awareness of a 'debate' about GM going on in society, alluding to the general ongoing political debates about the issue, rather than the specific *GM Nation?* process.

Regional activity

The original design of the debate formulated by the AEBC (as contained in advice provided to government, dated 26 April 2002) recognised the need to be sensitive to, and inclusive of, views in the UK regions possessing devolved administrations. Indeed, the need to take full account of possible regional variations in perspectives was stressed in a letter to the AEBC on 19 August 2002 from Ross Finnie, writing on behalf of the Scottish Executive, the National Assembly of Wales and the Department of the Environment in Northern Ireland.

Of the 675 public meetings estimated by COI as having been associated with the debate, the six Tier 1 meetings included three in England (Birmingham, Harrogate and Taunton) and one each in Wales (Swansea), Scotland (Glasgow) and Northern Ireland (Belfast). The PDSB's final report indicates 'around 40' Tier 2 meetings, and COI documentation has allowed us to examine the regional distribution of these meetings. In practice they were overwhelmingly held in England, with three in Scotland, one in Northern Ireland and none in Wales.

In addition, the PDSB report (2003) provides a break-down of the location of an additional 630 meetings. Our regional analysis of these Tier 3 meetings is shown in Table 5.4.

As noted earlier, COI calculated the existence of a local meeting having been held by a request for 30 or more feedback forms. The total number of local meetings may therefore have diverged significantly from the estimate of 630. Despite attempts by COI to elicit evidence from callers that requests for multiple copies of feedback forms were, indeed, intended for use in public meetings, there exists uncertainty over whether this was, in fact, always the case. Clearly the potential existence of a 'grey area' of relatively informal semi-

Table 5.4 Regional analysis of debate-related activity (% shown in parentheses)

	Requests		Meetings	
England	3,866	(89.7)	545	(86.5)
Scotland	178	(4.1)	43	(6.8)
Wales	170	(3.9)	24	(3.8)
N. Ireland	31	(1.4)	9	(0.7)
Not coded	65	(1.5)	9	(0.7)

Source: COI data reported in the debate Steering Board's (2003) report *GM Nation? The Findings of the Public Debate* (DTI, London).

public meetings means that we will never know precisely the number or distribution of public meetings.

Comparing the distributions in the chart above with current figures (available from National Statistics: www.statistics.gov.uk) on the regional population distribution across the UK suggests that, per head of population, the local *GM Nation?* meetings were slightly skewed in favour of England (83.7 per cent of the population) in comparison with Wales (4.9 per cent), Scotland (8.5 per cent) and Northern Ireland (2.9 per cent).

Despite contributing financially to the cost of the debate the regional administrations in Wales and Scotland did not actively promote participation in the debate. However, the Scottish Executive had previously carried out a great deal of public consultation on the issue, and the National Assembly of Wales has a relatively well-publicised 'highly precautionary' position on GM cultivation.

Finally, it is worth noting that the name given to the debate, despite being informed by an exercise in 'branding' research by COI, failed to recognise possible regional sensitivities to the use of the word 'nation'. Indeed, it is possible to see this decision as demonstrating either an indifference towards, or a surprising ignorance of, the cultural politics of national identity (Osmond, 1988). For many people living in the Celtic regions, labelling the debate in this way may have served to reinforce an impression that the debate was very much an English, London-oriented initiative. In this sense, the branding exercise delivered a result that was inimical to the Steering Board's attempts at generating an inclusive process. This failure may go some way towards informing our understanding of the relative lack of enthusiasm for the debate in the non-English regions.

Wider public views about GM

We now turn to the findings of our survey that provide insights into some wider public views about GM food and related issues. We will consider these as a basis for asking whether the debate was 'representative' in the sense that its findings were successful in capturing this profile of public views.

GM food

In Table 5.5 it can be seen that, at the time it was carried out (the late summer of 2003), our survey indicated that GM food was unacceptable to a large proportion of our sample of the general public. It appeared that 40 per cent found GM food fairly or very unacceptable. In comparison, about one in four (27 per cent) thought that GM food was fairly or very acceptable. A similar number (27 per cent) said that GM food was neither acceptable nor unacceptable.

Comparing the results of the 2002 and 2003 surveys shows that the acceptability of GM food has largely stayed the same. In 2002, 22 per cent felt that GM food was fairly or very acceptable, 36 per cent felt that GM food was fairly or very unacceptable, and 34 per cent felt that GM food is neither acceptable nor unacceptable.

Figure 5.4 shows responses to an item that was specifically designed to measure four distinct attitudinal positions on GM food. People were asked to indicate which of four statements most closely described their opinion. The results suggest that the general public were fairly ambivalent about GM

Table 5.5 On the whole, how acceptable or unacceptable is GM food to you? (%)

	2002	2003
Very acceptable	3	4
Fairly acceptable	19	23
Neither acceptable nor unacceptable	34	27
Fairly unacceptable	16	20
Very unacceptable	20	20
No opinion	8	5

Source: UEA/MORI GM Food Survey 2003 (Weighted dataset, N = 1,363); UEA/MORI Risk Survey 2002 (Weighted dataset, N = 296).

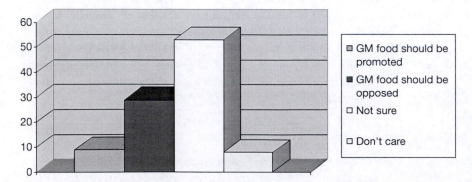

Figure 5.4 Which of the following statements most closely describes your opinion? (Weighted dataset, N = 1,363)

food. In other words, more than half of the general public were not sure whether GM food should be 'promoted or opposed'. Overall, public opinion about GM food seemed to be skewed towards opposition. While about one-third (29 per cent) indicated that GM food should be opposed, a mere 9 per cent indicated that GM food should be promoted. Moreover, 8 per cent of the public said they did not care whether GM food should be promoted or opposed.

Comparable results to the previous findings were obtained when people were asked: 'How strongly, if at all, would you say you support or oppose GM food?' This question had been used by MORI to track public support and opposition over time, as shown in Table 5.6. Whereas only 14 per cent appeared to support GM food, more than one-third opposed GM food (36 per cent). The largest part, however, neither supported nor opposed GM Food (39 per cent).

Table 5.6 shows support for GM has fallen since the issue first emerged in the media spotlight in 1996. In 1996, close to one in three (31 per cent) supported GM food. Support for GM food weakened to 22 per cent in 1998, and fell even further, reaching 14 per cent in 2003. At the same time, opposition towards GM food grew from 50 per cent in 1996 to 58 per cent in 1998. In 2003, however, opposition towards GM food dropped from 56 per cent in February 2003 to 46 per cent in June 2003, and was found to be 36 per cent in this study (July–September 2003). However, the decreased opposition to GM food does not mean that people have become more positive towards GM food. Rather, people have become more uncertain about GM food. Whereas in 1996 and 1998 about one in six (16 per cent and 15 per

Table 5.6 How strongly, if at all, would you say you support or oppose GM food? (%)

	1996[a]	1998[b]	Feb 2003[c]	Jun 2003[d]	Aug 2003[e]
Strongly support	6	6	3	3	3
Tend to support	25	16	11	11	11
Neither support nor oppose	16	15	25	33	39
Tend to oppose	24	21	26	21	19
Strongly oppose	26	37	30	25	17
Don't know	3	5	5	7	11
Support	31	22	14	14	13
Oppose	50	58	56	46	36
Net	−19	−36	−42	−32	−23

Source: (a) MORI/Greenpeace, N = 1,003, 13–15 December 1996; (b) MORI/GeneWatch, N = 950 adults, 6–8 June 1998; (c) MORI Environment Tracker, N = 2,141, 6–10 February 2003; (d) MORI Environment Tracker, N = 1,958, 19–24 June 2003; (e) UEA/MORI, N = 1,363, 19 July to 12 September 2003. Please note the question wording was slightly different in 1996 and 1998 compared to 2003. In 96/98 the question wording was as follows: 'Thinking of genetically modified food or food derived from genetic engineering, what is your opinion towards the development and introduction of such food? Would you say, support it to a great extent, support it slightly, neither support nor oppose it, oppose it slightly, oppose it to a great extent, don't know?'.

cent, respectively) neither supported nor opposed GM food, in February 2003 one in four, and in June 2003 about one in three were neutral. In the present study it was found that after the *GM Nation?* public debate (July–September 2003) about two in five (39 per cent) neither supported nor opposed GM food. This indicates that the public may have become more ambivalent towards the complex issue of GM food.

Our survey data indicates a relatively high degree of public interest in the issue of GM food. Table 5.7 shows that in 2003, although 30 per cent of the respondents were not very interested and 10 per cent were not at all interested, a majority (56 per cent) said that they were fairly or very interested in the issue of GM food. The findings displayed in Table 5.7 also show that the level of interest in the issue of GM only slightly changed between 2002 and 2003. Interest in the issue of GM food was somewhat lower in 2003 than in 2002, and the proportion of the public that has no opinion had slightly increased.

Labelling, liability and regulation

We now turn to some wider issues about GM. First, Table 5.8 shows that labelling of GM products, as well as liability of the biotechnology industry (for potential damage caused by GM products) were important issues for the general public. An overwhelming majority (94 per cent) felt that all food containing GM material should be labelled. Similarly, almost four out of five (79 per cent) agreed that biotechnology companies should be made liable for any damage caused by GM products.

Table 5.9 shows that doctors (physicians), consumer organisations, environmental organisations, and scientists working for universities were the most trusted information sources about GM food. More than three-quarters of our sample of the general population indicated they trusted these sources to be truthful about this issue. More than half of the sample said that they trusted scientists working for environmental groups, the Food Standards Agency (a British government regulatory and standard-setting agency), friends and family, the British government's Department of Environment, Food and Rural Affairs (DEFRA), 'people from your local community', and farmers to

Table 5.7 What would you say is your level of interest in the issue of GM food? (%)

	2002	2003
Very interested	22	15
Fairly interested	38	41
Not very interested	25	30
Not at all interested	14	10
No opinion	1	4

Source: UEA/MORI GM Food Survey 2003 (Weighted dataset, N = 1,363); UEA/MORI Risk Survey 2002 (Weighted dataset, N = 296).

Table 5.8 Labelling and liability (%)

	Strongly disagree	Tend to disagree	Neither/ nor	Tend to agree	Strongly agree	No opinion
Labelling						
All food containing GM material should be labelled	0*	1	3	29	65	2
Liability						
Biotechnology companies should be made liable for any damage caused by GM products	1	4	13	31	48	4

Note: * This non-empty cell (< 0.5) was rounded to 0.

Source: UEA/MORI GM Food Survey 2003 (Weighted dataset, N = 1,363).

tell the truth about GM food. The least trusted sources were scientists working for government or the biotechnology industry, local authorities, the biotechnology industry, food manufacturers, the EU, and the British government (as opposed to the Welsh or Scottish regional governments). All these sources were trusted by fewer than half of the general public. In Wales and Scotland, respondents were asked about the extent to which they trusted their regional governments to tell the truth about GM food. Responses to these questions indicated that the Welsh Assembly Government was trusted by 40 per cent of the Welsh sub-sample (N = 235), while the Scottish Parliament and Executive was trusted by 29 per cent of the Scottish sub-sample (N = 265).

These various information sources were slightly differently trusted in 2003 than in 2002. It appeared that a number of independent non-governmental and personal sources attracted even more trust in 2003 than in 2002. More people felt that people from their local community (+15 per cent), consumer organisations (+10 per cent), scientists working for environmental groups (+10 per cent), environmental organisations (+9 per cent), scientists working for universities (+9 per cent), and doctors (+9 per cent) could be trusted. Moreover, food manufacturers (+6 per cent), local authorities (+5 per cent) and scientists working for government (+5 per cent) were slightly more trusted in 2003 than in 2002. Trust in the other sources remained largely unchanged.

Two questions were used to determine people's trust in the regulation of GM food. Corresponding findings are set out in Table 5.10. The responses to both questions were largely comparable. Whereas about one in five (19 per cent and 21 per cent, respectively) agreed with the statements 'I feel confident that the British government adequately regulates GM food' and 'I am

Table 5.9 To what extent do you trust the following organisations and people to tell the truth about GM food? (%)

	Distrust a lot	Distrust a little	Neither/ nor	Trust a little	Trust a lot	No opinion
Doctors	1	2	14	42	39	2
Consumer rights organisations (e.g. Consumers' Association)	2	5	13	43	33	4
Environmental organisations	2	6	14	45	31	3
Scientists working for universities	2	4	17	46	29	2
Scientists working for environmental groups	2	7	15	48	25	2
Food Standards Agency	3	6	14	45	26	5
Friends and family	1	3	23	30	40	2
Department of Environment, Food and Rural Affairs	5	7	18	44	20	6
People from your local community	2	5	33	42	14	4
Farmers	5	10	26	36	19	3
Scientists working for government	15	21	19	34	8	3
Scientists working for the biotech industry	14	21	23	28	9	5
Local Authorities	10	17	33	31	5	3
Biotechnology industry	15	20	25	27	8	5
Food manufacturers	17	26	21	29	5	3
The European Union (EU)	20	19	25	25	7	4
The national government	23	25	19	25	5	3
The Welsh Assembly (N = 235)	15	12	27	29	11	6
The Scottish Parliament and its Executive (N = 265)	14	23	31	24	5	3

Source: UEA/MORI GM Food Survey 2003 (Weighted dataset, N = 1,363).

confident that the development of GM crops is being carefully regulated', about half of the British public disagreed (55 per cent and 45 per cent, respectively). In addition, 19 per cent neither agreed nor disagreed with the statement 'I feel confident that the British government adequately regulates GM food', while 27 per cent neither agreed nor disagreed with the statement 'I am confident that the development of GM crops is being carefully regulated'.

People were also asked to what extent they agreed or disagreed that organisations separate from government were needed to regulate GM food, and to what extent they agreed or disagreed that organisations separate from industry were needed to regulate GM food. The responses, as set out in Table 5.10, to these two statements were practically similar. Whereas a great majority (79 per cent and 80 per cent, respectively) agreed, only 6 per cent and 4 per cent disagreed that organisations were needed that are independent from government and industry, respectively. One in ten (10 per cent) neither agreed nor disagreed with both statements.

There were some discernible differences in people's responses between 2002 and 2003 to the item 'I feel confident that the British government adequately regulates GM food'. Whereas agreement with the statement remained the same (20 per cent in 2002 compared to 19 per cent in 2003), disagreement increased from 41 per cent in 2002 to 55 per cent in 2003. At the same time, the proportion of people that neither agreed nor disagreed with the statement dropped from 29 per cent in 2002 to 19 per cent in 2003. This shows a considerable drop in confidence between 2002 and 2003 in the British government to regulate GM food adequately. It appears that the need for independent organisations to regulate GM food increased from 2002 to 2003. Whereas in 2002, 59 per cent felt that organisations separate from government

Table 5.10 The regulation of GM food (%)

	Strongly disagree	Tend to disagree	Neither/ nor	Tend to agree	Strongly agree	No opinion
Trust in risk regulation						
I feel confident that the British government adequately regulates GM food	28	27	19	16	3	6
I am confident that the development of GM crops is being carefully regulated[GMN]	18	27	27	19	3	6
Independent regulatory organisations						
Organisations separate from government are needed to regulate GM food	2	4	10	39	40	5
Organisations separate from industry are needed to regulate GM food	1	3	10	38	42	6

Note:
GMN Statement taken from the *GM Nation?* Public Debate Feedback form.

Source: UEA/MORI GM Food Survey 2003 (Weighted dataset, N = 1,363).

were needed, this number grew to 79 per cent in 2003. Likewise, while in 2002 65 per cent agreed with the statement that organisations separate from industry were needed to regulate GM food, fully 80 per cent did so in 2003.

Overall, an interesting shift in public views on the *governance* of GM food seems to have taken place between 2002 and 2003. Given that many of the other items measuring more general attitudes to GM food itself remained relatively stable over the two surveys, one conclusion might be that intervening external events, for example, the involvement of the UK government in the Iraq War during the spring of 2003 and, subsequently, changed general attitudes towards the UK government and its regulatory activities over the period of the two surveys, rather than attitudes to the governance of GM food per se, were responsible for such changes.

Discussion and conclusions

A number of broad conclusions concerning the representativeness of those participating (either actively or passively) in the debate follow from the analyses reported above. First, while some socio-demographic indicators were not out of line with national profiles, there was clear evidence that the educational level of participants in the Tier 1 events was considerably higher than the actual national average. Second, among participants in debate events, the attitudinal profile of those taking part in the Foundation Discussion workshops was the closest match to our national survey results. Participants from the Tier 1, 2 and 3 events were consistently, and considerably, more negative about GM than the survey respondents.

Turning now to our re-analysis of the *GM Nation?* 'Feedback' question-naires, here our findings suggest that concern about the risks associated with GM is largely *shared* across all groups of respondents. However, respondents from the 'open' activities (Tier 1, 2 and 3 events, together with other questionnaire returns and visitors to the *GM Nation?* website) were considerably more negative than our 2003 survey respondents, and were not prepared to endorse potential future benefits of GM food and crops. Our own survey results suggest that current UK 'public opinion' is not a unitary whole, but fragmented with considerable ambivalence co-existing alongside outright opposition. It follows that most of the media reporting of the debate's findings (which was based on the 'Feedback' data) seems to have presented a misleading overestimate of the strength of outright opposition to GM food and crops in Britain.

Despite this lack of representativeness associated with the debate's 'open' activities we suggest that this component of the debate was not entirely without merit, as some researchers have implied (e.g. Campbell and Townsend, 2003). Rather, as Grove-White (2003) and others have argued, there is a need to recognise that the debate was a deliberative process, in part designed to explore and engage with lay perspectives, rather than simply a research exercise or opinion poll. In such a context, there is a need to explore the positions of those with strongly held views. Nevertheless, taking the evidence as a whole it appears that of all the component parts of the *GM Nation?* debate, the Foundation Discussion workshops and the Narrow-but-Deep groups were the *most representative* of the lay public. These considerations have important implications for the design of future such public engagement initiatives. We will return to these matters at the end of the book in Chapter 9.

We now consider the extent to which the debate was 'representative' in the sense that it successfully captured the lay public's views about GM and related matters. We have already presented some evidence on the nature of these views, as provided by our MORI survey data. The PDSB final report (2003) presents a number of 'key messages' that summarise the gist of its findings, and these are set out in Box 5.1.

Elsewhere we have examined these seven statements in detail in the light of our MORI survey data (Pidgeon and Poortinga, 2006). We conclude that the empirical comparison between the debate and survey findings is sufficiently strong to lend at least some additional corroboration to broad aspects of the PDSB's claims, specifically: in relation to the widespread concern about GM, the mistrust of government and business, people's desire for further information, and the value placed on the principles of public engagement and deliberation. Importantly, our survey findings diverge from those of the PDSB in our recognition of the widespread ambivalence about agricultural GM among the lay public across a range of measures.

A subtext to this discussion is provided by the extensive literature on the public understanding of science (and technology), a currently dominant perspective of which is provided by fierce criticisms of the so-called 'deficit model'. In essence the position which is criticised suggests that public (mis)understanding of science is largely due to public ignorance of technical facts. It is argued that lay understandings of such issues typically reflect wider

---

Box 5.1 PDSB findings from the debate: 'key messages'

1   People were generally uneasy about GM.
2   The more people engaged in GM issues, the harder their attitudes and more intense their concerns.
3   There is little support for early commercialisation.
4   There is widespread mistrust of government and multinational companies.
5   There is a broad desire to know more and for further research to be done.
6   Developing countries have special interests (in GM, to be judged on distinct arguments and values).
7   The debate was welcomed and valued.

considerations, and a range of matters of practical and personal concern. In this way the rationality associated with technical expertise may be seen as narrowly defined and, indeed, alienating in terms of its apparent disregard for issues about which people may have strong value-commitments (Irwin and Wynne, 1996; Wynne, 1995). We will return to these issues in our discussion in Chapter 7 of knowledge-handling by the debate process. However, for the purposes of this discussion, these considerations serve to raise an important question, namely: what is the relationship between familiarity with GM-related issues and the attitudinal data discussed in this chapter? Is the level of knowledge of respondents a matter of relevance?

In their critical re-evaluation of the deficit model, Sturgis and Allum (2004) have suggested that differences in levels of broadly 'political' and institutional knowledge may have an important bearing on *how* members of the lay public make sense of issues concerning science and technology. Without pursuing this argument in detail, it is important to note that it raises the possibility that different levels of background knowledge may lead to different modes of reasoning about issues in question. This suggestion chimes in interesting ways with recent work on trust in regulatory bodies, which suggests that people appear to employ different modes of reasoning about trustworthiness according to their knowledge of the regulatory body in question (Horlick-Jones *et al.*, 2003b; Walls *et al.*, 2004). Those with a rudimentary knowledge of the institution tended to reason on the basis of simple associations or 'brand' (a body might be trusted because its title included a word with positive connotations such as 'health'). As knowledge increased, a structural-calculative form of reasoning became important, in which typically the perceived interests, or 'stake', of the body with respect to the issue in question formed an important consideration. Relatively few respondents reasoned on the basis of specific personal experience of the operational effectiveness of the regulatory bodies considered. However, when this did occur, and that experience had been positive, then trust in the institution reflected this personal familiarity, sometimes despite structural features that tended to reduce trustworthiness (for instance, the regulatory body was recognised to be a part of government which, for some other reason, at that time was unpopular or widely regarded as incompetent).

Early findings from our detailed analysis of the Narrow-but-Deep groups' deliberations suggest that a not-dissimilar shift in modes of reasoning occurred as the participants were taken through a 'learning' process about GM issues (Horlick-Jones *et al.*, 2006b, in press, b; Horlick-Jones and Walls, 2005). This work, together with our observation of the Foundation Discussion workshops suggests that those without an active interest in GM-related issues had an *extremely* rudimentary grasp of such issues. These findings raise difficult matters of interpretation for the questionnaire data on attitudes towards GM issues which we considered above. Indeed, it follows that there is a need to critically examine such questionnaire data in terms of the ways in which respondents grasped the issues with which they were presented. Of central importance here is the logic of the position in which the respondents found themselves on having the questionnaire administered to them, and a recognition that resulting data in part reflected this context, rather than simply representing unmediated expressions of their 'real' opinions (Houtkoop-Steenstra, 2000; see also Garfinkel, 1967; Horlick-Jones, 2005c, 2007). It also follows that comparisons between the PDSB's findings and our survey data are complicated by the former arising from a synthesis of data derived from shifting levels of knowledge and modes of reasoning. In other words, rather than the debate seeking to 'take a snap-shot' of public views, it was a process that sought (no matter how imperfectly) to *engage dynamically* with such views.

Finally, we note that these latter considerations point to a way of understanding why the views of the Narrow-but-Deep participants 'hardened' (PDSB, 2003) as they learned more about GM. They also underline the importance of issues concerning knowledge, rationality and design in seeking to understand the nature of the *GM Nation?* debate, and importantly, in any attempt to organise such an initiative more effectively in the future. We return to some of these issues in Chapter 7.

6   Participants' evaluation criteria

Our analysis so far has concentrated upon the extent to which the various aspects of the *GM Nation?* debate succeeded against our a priori evaluation criteria. As discussed in Chapter 2, however, our intent was also to elicit evaluation criteria from the involved participants; to see to what extent these matched our normative criteria and the criteria stipulated by the event sponsors. Given the variety of different exercises incorporated in the overall event, there were several different sources from which we could elicit these criteria. We have chosen to focus on participants attending the Tier 1 conferences, as these were very much the public face of the debate process. We did not seek the opinions of those participating in the Foundation Discussion workshops (which were, in any case, essentially a consultation exercise), as they were unaware of the wider scope of the debate, and so could not have sensibly commented upon debate objectives and quality. Nor did we seek opinions from Tier 2 and Tier 3 participants, because it was logistically untenable for us to carry out. Those participating in the Narrow-but-Deep process were few in number, and they encountered a very specific process that was not common to the majority of participants; hence, their experiences and perspectives may have been unusual.

In this chapter we report the method we used to elicit participants' evaluation criteria, and discuss the key criteria that emerged. We also describe how well the Tier 1 events scored according to these criteria. We conclude by discussing the extent to which these criteria have elements in common with our predefined ones.

Method for determining the participants' criteria

In order to elicit participants' effectiveness criteria, the longer questionnaires (QL) presented at the Tier 1 events included a number of open questions, two of which were aimed at eliciting reasons for positive and negative value judgements about the events. One asked: 'What do you personally feel were the positive aspects of the event?', and the other asked: 'What do you feel were the negative aspects of the event?' Importantly, these questions occurred before the closed questions that asked about issues related to our normative criteria, so as to avoid influencing respondents' answers. The answers from these two questions were transcribed and then analysed to identify *themes*. A list of positive and negative themes was produced, combining responses from across all six Tier 1 events. The respondents' answers were then coded according to these themes. While some respondents did not answer one or both of the questions, many respondents noted two or more different positive or negative aspects to the events. In total, we received responses from over 400 participants.

In our initial debate evaluation report (Horlick-Jones *et al.*, 2004), our preliminary analysis considered the results from the two open questions separately, and then went on to discuss first the perceived positive, and then the perceived negative, aspects of the events. Whilst preparing this book, we concluded that it would be more satisfactory to combine these data. We recognised that although some revealed evaluation criteria only tended to be discussed in a positive or a negative light, other criteria were discussed according to both perspectives, so essentially reflecting ambivalence in how participants scored the exercises on those criteria. Our subsequent re-analysis produced the results that are presented in this chapter.

In the following section we identify the *key* evaluation criteria displayed by the participants, inferred from their responses. We then comment upon how well the Tier 1 events scored according to these criteria by consideration of the extent to which participants were positive or negative. As a general point, there were considerably more (and more detailed) responses to the question on event negatives than that on event positives. The criteria below are discussed in no particular order, and reflect a revision of the criteria represented in our initial report. We note the number of times that a particular theme was raised in order to give some *broad* indication of the popularity of these themes. The reader should not take the figures to reflect any high degree of accuracy, given the uncertainty associated with such attempts to interpret natural language.

Results of the analysis

Representativeness

One clear evaluation criterion concerned the representativeness of the participants in the events, and this was invariably discussed from a negative perspective. We recorded a total of sixty-five critical responses claiming that participants did *not* comprise the general public, and that there were too many participants from some specific sub-groups (mainly associated with anti-GM sentiments), and too few from other groups (for example, those holding pro-GM views). Perhaps in a related way, a number of respondents (23) criticised the events for being 'too small', and not involving enough people to truly be considered part of a 'national debate'. A number also criticised the lobbying activities of participants who used the events as an opportunity to distribute material and recruit members (10 respondents); so highlighting the rather one-sided nature of the sample of the population attending the events. Some participants suggested that the events allowed the collection of (many) diverse views, often implying inclusivity and a non-biased sampling (23 responses). However it was often unclear in these cases as to whether it was the structure of the process, or the fair representation of participants, that was being lauded. ·

Participation

Arguably, one reason for the relative paucity of evaluations of earlier participation exercises is that, for many proponents, the very act of participation is *intrinsically* good. According to this perspective, one has only to set a participation event in motion to have succeeded; to have achieved some good; and that is the end of the story. For a considerable number of participants in the Tier 1 events, this was a position they held, at least to some degree. Indeed, the most frequently cited *positive* theme (which we have translated as the *participation criterion*) was that the event was good because it provided an *opportunity* for respondents to exchange views, debate the issue, and hear both sides of the argument. Interestingly there is an emphasis here on the two-way nature of interaction as something of benefit in itself (we coded fifty-four instances that addressed this theme of *opportunity*). Similarly, a large number of respondents (41) indicated that the event was positive because it gave them and/or others a chance to air their views and opinions. A number of respondents also simply indicated that the most positive aspect of the debate was that it was happening at all (15 respondents), while a few indicated that it was good as an exercise in public participation and empowerment, allowing people to 'feel their voices are heard' (6 responses). Unsurprisingly, we recorded no negative assessments of the event on this criterion, that is, responses criticising the event for *not* allowing information exchange, the airing of views, and so on.

Learning

Another frequently discussed evaluative theme involved the learning opportunities afforded by the events. Respondents felt the events were invariably *positive* in providing an opportunity for themselves (and/or others) to *learn more*, or be *educated about* the *opinions* of others (52 instances). A number of respondents similarly praised the opportunity to learn information or *facts* (as opposed to opinions) about the topic of GM itself (19 responses). Given the ratio of time spent debating with others compared to considering the debate organisers' material which was evident at the Tier 1 events, it is, perhaps, not surprising that there was this bias in respondents' valued learning sources. There were very few instances in which participants evaluated the events negatively against this implied criterion – and these may have been associated with negative assessments of participant representativeness (in other words, with a reduced chance of learning opposing views).

Social reassurance

Participants frequently evaluated the events – invariably positively – against a criterion we have chosen to label 'social reassurance'. There were a number of identified themes that appeared to us to be associated with this more general theme of personal comfort derived from the opportunity to meet or hear others with similar views. Thus, a number of respondents suggested the event was good because it provided an opportunity to *confirm* their own beliefs, and find solidarity with others of the same view (25 respondents). Often, this aspect seemed somewhat implicit in many responses, but we separately coded responses that simply stated that the result of the event (that people did not want GM) was the most positive thing (46 responses). In other words, there was implicit satisfaction in announcing this result that confirmed their views. Again, we initially separately coded responses that declared the event to be positive for providing an opportunity to personally *meet* and speak with other (usually like-minded) people; an experience sometimes phrased as an 'opportunity to network' (45 responses). All these responses indicate something opposite to the motive of learning from the event, and suggest committed participants wanting to reinforce their pre-existing views or to campaign on the issues; indeed, two respondents baldly stated that they had attended to 'show support for the cause'.

We recognise that this criterion is potentially problematic in terms of the evaluation exercise. While it was clearly a significant and important matter for many participants, it is essentially antithetical to the concepts of learning, dialogue, negotiation and compromise, all activities that lie at the heart of the rationale for doing participation. If social reassurance is, indeed, one common purpose for people to become involved in participation exercises, then a more challenging event that achieves many normative goals may, paradoxically, also cause *more* discontent and negative evaluations from the participant community.

Influence

'Influence' is undoubtedly one, if not the most important, aim of those becoming involved in participation processes. Of course, at such an early stage of the process, participants in the Tier 1 meetings could not judge the success of the events in which they took part in terms of this characteristic. However, they could, and often did, judge the events in terms of their *likely* influence.

Unlike some of the previously discussed criteria, participants were less uniform in their evaluations here, with most of those who raised the influence issue being rather negative, but some being more positive. A considerable number of participants (41) suggested that the events were a waste of time, without any possibility of *influence*; with some suggesting that government decisions had already been made on the topic. A further set of respondents (18) described the events as 'window-dressing', a 'PR exercise', and just 'going through the motions'. Other respondents simply expressed uncertainty as to what, if anything, would come from the events (9). However, a number of respondents praised the events for raising the profile of the issue (via the media) among the wider public (15 responses). Others were positive, not just because of the higher profile, but because of the nature of the *message* that was being sent to the wider world (e.g. to the government, the debate organisers etc.), often with an expressed *hope* of influence (20 responses). In summary, influence seemed an important criterion, and participants were generally more negative in their evaluations than positive.

Fair process

One broad criterion that emerged from participant responses to the open questions was what we have termed *fair process*. This concerns the extent to which the physical processes of the events (how they were structured and run) allowed fair and appropriate exchanges of information. Participant evaluations on this criterion were both positive and negative, sometimes reflecting disagreement about particular aspects of the running of the debate, and sometimes reflecting agreement about either positives or negatives. Respondents evaluated events positively in allowing those attending to have their say (16 responses), and in doing so without hindrance from dogmatic or dominating individuals (11). Respondents also praised a lack of pressure from others (e.g. the organisers) to conform, describing the events (or the small group meetings within them) using terms such as 'polite', 'civil', 'non-confrontational' and 'adult' (19).

On the other hand, some aspects of the process were evaluated consistently negatively, in particular the small group activities (20 respondents). A number of participants noted that some self-selected groups were unbalanced, and did not include pro-GM people with whom to hold a proper debate, or suggested that these groups were poorly facilitated, or even facilitated in a biased fashion (20 respondents). It should be noted that these observations also touch upon the representativeness issue. The way in which the events were brought to a conclusion was also criticised (21): with some respondents complaining about the length and repetitiveness of the group summaries, the lack of time allocated for this activity, and the failure to tease out differences in views. Some respondents (7) suggested that the process did not lead to constructive views or consensus building but, rather, reinforced polarities and division. Other respondents expressed annoyance that they had essentially been deceived regarding the status of the event, which was 'not a debate' and 'really a workshop' (16). Furthermore, for some the events were seen as too constrained and fixed, so preventing participants from considering important issues and generally asking 'the wrong questions' (12 respondents).

There was disagreement about a couple of issues related to this evaluation criterion. A number of respondents suggested that the information available was positive in some way (13 rated it as 'fair', 'balanced', 'accessible', 'intelligent' or 'full'), although others criticised the debate documentation for being bland, pro-GM, incomplete and inaccurate (17). Meanwhile, a number of respondents suggested that the events were either *fairly* facilitated (13), *fairly* run (6), or were *well* run (9), though others criticised the events for poor organisation (16). In summary, some aspects of the debate were evaluated well, and others poorly, though on the whole there appeared to be more negative aspects than positive ones.

Resources

Resource issues were a major concern to respondents, and were invariably discussed in a highly negative way. By far the most frequently raised concern was about the *publicity* surrounding the events, or rather, the lack of this (98 respondents). Many respondents also suggested that there was simply not enough *time* to allow the proper running of the events (55), or time available beforehand to consider whatever material was available (17). Others criticised the lack of *information*, in the sense of there being no experts present to consult about the GM topic (48 respondents), or no government or biotechnology industry representatives (6). The venues themselves were also criticised by respondents (28) for being inaccessible and badly signposted. What was seen by some as the cramped nature of the venues (a problem of resource logistics) was also criticised, as was a number of matters concerned with the audibility of the proceedings (15 respondents in total). Finally, a number of respondents suggested the events were run 'on the cheap' (11), with the absence of free coffee cited as one example illustrating this perceived parsimony.

Timely involvement

A number of respondents judged the events on the basis of their timeliness with regard to the wider GM debate in society, and they did so negatively. Eleven respondents suggested that the events had occurred either prematurely or too late in the process. The implication (occasionally stated) was that these events would, therefore, have little significant impact on wider policy and, in this sense, this evaluation criterion appears related to that of 'influence'.

Enlightenment

One rather unusual criterion that emerged – which we have termed *enlightenment* – was related to participants evaluating the events on the basis of their role in providing (generally gratifying) revelations about the human condition. Thus, we coded thirty responses that praised the events because they had led participants to some form of enlightened discovery of the intelligence, thoughtfulness and passion of other participants, while a dozen more respondents discussed as positive the revelation that people (in significant numbers) were prepared to make the sacrifice (e.g. in terms of time, money, and in spite of logistic difficulties) to participate. The flip-side to this particular coin, however, was that other respondents criticised the events because they found the behaviour of some participants to be opinionated, ignorant, dishonest and narrow-minded (19 respondents).

The status of this particular evaluation criterion is difficult to judge, for it seems somewhat different from the others. In the first place, the other criteria discussed could reasonably be expected to be ones that participants might identify a priori, and consensually, as appropriate benchmarks against which participation exercise success might be judged. However, it is difficult to envisage 'enlightenment' being so identified. In the second place, achieving enlightenment as to the human condition does not seem a reasonable criterion for judging effectiveness, as success on this must rely in large part on the character of the other participants. Arguably this feature is not primarily attributable to the effectiveness of the design of the exercise, or to its satisfactory execution. In this respect, we have to attach a caution to this criterion as a relevant evaluation benchmark.

Discussion

The participants' answers to the two open questions about the quality of the events (in QL) reveal both their own evaluation criteria, and the success or otherwise of the Tier 1 events according to these criteria. Box 6.1 lists these criteria. We have added to this list an association, where clear similarities exist, to the normative and sponsor criteria we have considered, and which we discussed in detail in Chapter 2. It is probably fair to say that all eight of our normative criteria were identified by at least some respondents. Indeed, the participants' criteria that most closely matched our normative criteria seemed to be the most important to participants in their evaluations. Thus, the process of the debate – in terms of both *fair process* (similar to *structured dialogue*, N8) and availability of *resources* (criterion N7) – was described negatively by large numbers of respondents. There was also clear concern about the *representativeness* (or lack thereof) of participants (also criteria N1 and B2), and the potential *influence* of the events (N5 and BIV). The criterion of *timely involvement* (similar to N3) also appeared relevant to some, while issues related to the normative criteria of *transparency* (N4) and *independence* (N2) appeared to be incorporated within the participants' fair process criterion. The extent to which the eight normative criteria are independent, or interrelated, is a research question, and one we have considered in detail elsewhere (Rowe *et al.*, in press).

If we now compare the participants' criteria to the sponsors' criteria, we also find some similarities. We first note an overlap here with the normative criteria for the *representativeness* and *influence* participant criteria. Among the

Box 6.1 **Participants' evaluation criteria**

Similarities to normative and sponsor criteria are indicated in square brackets

P1 Representativeness	[N1, B2]
P2 Participation	[B5b]
P3 Learning	[B6]
P4 Social reassurance	
P5 Influence	[N5, BIV]
P6 Fair process	[N8]
P7 Resources	[N7]
P8 Timely involvement	[N3]
P9 Enlightenment	

rest, most notably, there is some similarity between the participants' *learning* criterion and the sponsors' criterion B6, which stipulates that there should be 'mutual learning' between experts and public. However, for the participants, the important issue was what *they* had learned. Furthermore, there is some similarity between the *participation* criterion and the sponsors' B5b criterion (concerning participants registering views), but also to some degree with B6 (stating that there should be 'interaction' as well as mutual learning) and B4 (dialogue with experts) – all of which imply that participation is a good thing in its own right.

This analysis of participants' assessment of the Tier 1 events, in terms of their own expectations and perceptions, suggests that our normative criteria have a degree of relevance to the participants' perspectives. We also need to ask whether our criteria were exhaustive, and whether they captured the most important issues, as seen by the participants. We can see that, in these terms, they were clearly *not* exhaustive. In particular, the issue of *learning* was regarded by participants as an important criterion for the success or otherwise of the Tier 1 meetings. Interestingly, this conclusion chimes with earlier research that identified a learning criterion as an important additional evaluation criterion to the list we used in this evaluation exercise (Rowe *et al.*, 2004; cf. Rowe and Frewer, 2000).

Finally, this examination of participant views identified two further bases for evaluation, which we termed *social reassurance* and *enlightenment*, and which seem to have a different character from the other criteria. We expressed some caution about both as potential evaluation benchmarks. Rather than offering a rigorous means to measure the effectiveness and fairness of a participative decision process, they appear to represent less tangible, and more subjective and context-specific, features of the experience of participation. Indeed, the act of participation *in itself* appears to have satisfied certain social needs for many of our respondents. One can find plausible ways of understanding these needs within the literatures on social movements and the nature of political engagement (e.g. Becker, 1963; Johnson, 1987; Pichardo, 1997). This finding raises important questions about the *politics* of engagement exercises, and the extent to which sponsors of such initiatives feel it necessary to address such wider societal needs. We can only speculate about such possible unspoken motivations behind the organisation of the *GM Nation?* debate. However, we can state that with respect to both social reassurance and enlightenment, participants in the Tier 1 events were generally fairly positive and, indeed, to a greater extent than they were with respect to the other criteria considered in this chapter.

In this chapter we focus on one particular aspect of the functioning of the debate; namely, how effective were the mechanisms by which it utilised and managed sources of knowledge? In particular, we focus on the ways in which conclusions drawn from one stage of the debate process became a source for its subsequent stages, informing and shaping them. We will term this characteristic of the debate process its *translation quality*.

Whilst carrying out the evaluation exercise it became increasingly clear to us that these aspects of the debate process were not being addressed by any of the evaluation criteria with which we were working, save in the sponsors' requirement that lay views should frame the terms of the debate (B1). Seen in this light, the criteria we had initially adopted seemed to offer an evaluation of the debate according to how effectively it was implemented as an *organisational process*. It was now apparent that we also needed to consider the effectiveness of the debate as an *information system* (cf. Checkland and Scholes, 1990). In this way, our evaluation work not only provided a measure of the quality of the debate process, but also identified a 'missing dimension' that would have otherwise escaped evaluation. We suggest that this capacity to learn whilst conducting an evaluation according to given criteria, and so go beyond the framework defined by these criteria, reflects positively on the nature of the methodological approach that we adopted.

Before proceeding, we first recognise that it is important to draw a distinction between our use of the term *translation* and the use that has already been made by the authors of the influential US National Research Council report *Understanding Risk: Informing Decisions in a Democratic Society* (1996: 14).[1] As we understand it, their use of the term refers to a conception of a hypothetical instrumental process that might provide scientific knowledge in a user-friendly form suitable for use by decision-makers. They are critical of this notion, and stress the need for multiple forms of knowledge, including lay perspectives, to be used in decision-making in an integrated way, as part of what they term an 'analytic-deliberative' process. Our notion of 'translation' seeks to capture how effectively various sources of knowledge are utilised in just such an interactive and integrative process.

Much of the recent literature on engagement processes (e.g. Abelson *et al.*, 2003) stresses the need for two-way communication between debate sponsors and the lay public, as well as deliberation between participants in the process. Petts (1997) draws attention to the importance of such deliberative interactions in highlighting information needs, and of the examination during such interactions of a plurality of expert sources. Despite this awareness of the importance of information, knowledge and communication in the effective functioning of engagement exercises, we are not aware of any work that has considered closely the associated management of information and knowledge, nor how these factors might be assessed. These matters will be addressed in this chapter.

Pursuing this line of inquiry drew our attention to numerous information-related processes that appeared to have an important bearing on the overall effectiveness of the debate process. We illustrate these information flows schematically in Figure 7.1. More specifically, there was a need to consider the quality of a number of activities that formed part of the debate process, as set out in Box 7.1.

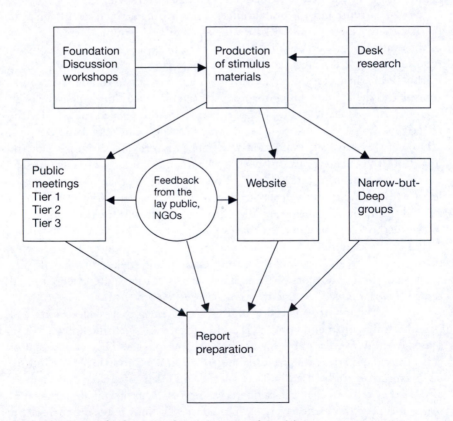

Figure 7.1 Flows of information between stages of the debate

Box 7.1 Translation processes

- The elicitation of lay perspectives, and how these were used to 'frame' the debate.
- How stimulus materials designed to inform the debate were developed.
- How the public meetings and other publicly accessible conduits were used to gather information by the organisers.
- How the 'Narrow-but-Deep' process functioned as a 'control' mechanism.
- How the Steering Board analysed all the information at its disposal, and how it drew up overall findings.

In the following sections we will discuss the relevance of the criterion of translation quality to these activities, but first, in the next section, we consider some relevant conceptual perspectives.

Knowledge, information and lay understandings

We have noted that the *GM Nation?* debate process began with a series of preliminary workshops involving members of the lay public, which were designed to elicit lay perspectives on relevant issues. The intention on the part of the debate Steering Board was that the public should be allowed to determine how the issues around GM were to be discussed. This feature of the debate's design formed a central consideration from the earliest days of its conception.[2] The notion that lay perspectives form a legitimate, and workable, basis for conducting a process of this nature – one with far-reaching policy implications – might have been regarded as radical or even dangerous in some quarters. After all, some would suggest that the lay public often display 'irrational' views towards risk issues: views that are certainly not scientific, and perhaps inappropriate to inform the making of important decisions. In this sense, the adoption of a design of this nature was, itself, an important indicator of change within the policy community.

The use of the notion of 'framing' in the initial provisional design for the debate appears to have been heavily influenced by an approach to studying the public understanding of science which is fiercely critical of the 'deficit' model mentioned above; namely, one in which public (mis)understanding of science is seen as arising from public ignorance of technical facts. This critical perspective (Irwin and Wynne, 1996; Wynne, 1995; see also Sturgis and Allum, 2004) draws on the body of scholarship known as 'science and technology studies' (Jasanoff *et al.*, 1995) which, in turn, draws on sociological (constructionist) investigations of scientific knowledge which have revealed the contingency underlying its ostensible neutrality, objectivity and certainty (e.g. Woolgar, 1988). Importantly, this perspective recognises that the lay public typically includes a wider range of considerations than technical experts do in their reasoning processes, including matters that are of relevance to their everyday lives. As noted in our discussion in Chapter 5 on public views about GM crops and food, a number of influential scholars have argued that the rationality associated with technical expertise may be seen as narrowly defined, and alienating in terms of its apparent disregard for issues about which people may have strong value-commitments.[3]

The notion of framing pre-dates the work mentioned above, and forms an expression of a tradition within the social sciences that has been concerned with the social organisation of experience and understanding (e.g. Goffman, 1975). Scientific knowledge does not escape this category-bound basis of representation and, indeed, the acquisition of such formal knowledge entails the use of everyday shared understandings as a resource (McHoul and Watson, 1984). Over thirty-five years ago the historian and philosopher of science Thomas Kuhn (1970) argued that differences between competing scientific theories could not be resolved simply by appeal to 'the facts' if these theories are differently framed. These insights have formed the basis of more recent work on apparently intractable policy controversies, in which it is recognised that technical knowledge alone rarely resolves such conflicts when competing perspectives are based upon different ways of 'looking' at the problem issue (Schön and Rein, 1994).

Recent years have seen the relative status of lay and expert knowledge becoming a matter of controversy, featuring an extended debate about the nature of what kind of 'expertise' is conferred by what has been described as 'the privilege of experience' (Williams and Popay, 1994). Advocates at one end of a spectrum of views identify such 'lay epidemiology' as a substantive form of expertise, offering a challenge to conventional science-based professional expertise. Those at the other end of this spectrum are highly critical of this position, and see the term 'lay expertise' as no more than an oxymoron (discussed in e.g. Prior, 2003). Without pursuing this debate in detail, it is possible to observe that in practice lay knowledge can make possible an enhanced utilisation of expert knowledge to address specific risk-related situations. Such knowledge offers the possibility of *contextualising*, or *re-framing*, abstract, general knowledges, in order to engage more effectively with the specifics of, for example, everyday working practices, or the details of a patient's lifestyle (Horlick-Jones, 1998; Linell, 1998; Petts, 1997).

As we will see later in the chapter, whilst preparing stimulus materials to inform the *GM Nation?* debate, the organisers encountered severe difficulties in seeking to strike some kind of balance between 'factual' knowledge and knowledge of a more ethical and political nature. Many of the issues in question in the debate were essentially about risk and its management. Arguably, decision-making about such matters necessitates processes that are not wholly technical, nor social or political, but rather something that combines these approaches (Funtowicz and Ravetz, 1992; Horlick-Jones and Sime, 2004). We note that the constructionist approach to scientific and technical knowledge, which we have identified as influential in the conception of the debate, has been subject to criticisms which argue that in corresponding accounts there is a tendency that 'the technology disappears from view' (Button, 1993: 9; see also Lynch, 1993; Horlick-Jones, 2007). Here, we suggest that it is important to recognise that technical knowledge provides an invaluable measure of the constraints and opportunities afforded by a given technology (see also Hutchby, 2001). We suggest that excluding this structuring poses a serious danger of disengaging participants in engagement processes from the real-world aspects of a decision process. We will return to this matter.

Seen according to these perspectives, engagement processes such as *GM Nation?* may be seen as attempts to incorporate and reconcile competing perspectives subject to the constraints and opportunities afforded by the character of the issue in question. The nature and roles of different knowledges emerge as matters of central importance to the effective functioning of these initiatives. Importantly, it is clear that knowledge cannot be viewed as a 'package' that can be transferred between stages of a public debate in an unproblematic way. Rather, each stage entails situated processes of interpretation, re-framing and, possibly, hybridisation of different knowledges: activities that here we generically term *translation*. Given this complexity, how is it possible to evaluate the translation quality of such processes?

Some progress towards answering this question may be made by considering part of the literature on the role of knowledge in organisational settings. Feldman's (1989) investigation of the role of information in policy-making stresses the key roles of framing, and the resulting selection or omission of matters of relevance. She also emphasises the important role played by *documents* in encapsulating such processes of categorisation. This latter focus is addressed in detail in Harper's (1998) ethnography of the functioning of a large international organisation. His notion of an 'information career' – as information is gathered, analysed, documented, transformed in various ways, and 'used' by management structures to achieve certain ends – is particularly apposite in the current discussion. The key distinction between information and knowledge is taken up by a number of writers, who conclude that the latter entails an exercise in judgement based on experience or theory (e.g. Alvesson, 2004). A recent intervention by Jensen (2005) is particularly helpful in drawing out the significance of this distinction by recognising that only *information* can be shared between members of an organisation, and that the acquisition of *knowledge* entails processes of learning, re-framing and understanding.

Processes of citizen engagement such as *GM Nation?* additionally entail the transmission of information across organisational boundaries, and between lay understandings and professional interpretations. Manning's (1988) analysis of emergency calls to the police provides some important insights into the character of such processes of sense-making and categorisation, and transformations of '"this" to "that"'. Importantly, his study serves to highlight the pivotal role of routine competencies and expectations on the part of the professionals in question. In the case of *GM Nation?*, the organisational infrastructure that implemented and supported the debate was, in effect, an ad hoc consortium of executive agencies, each with their own operational norms, which had an episodic existence. Moreover, these agencies, together, possessed a limited range of relevant competencies in order to implement the debate (Horlick-Jones *et al.*, 2004, 2006b). Both features suggest that knowledge-handling by the debate was likely to have been a complicated, potentially messy process. These are important considerations for the design of future such public debates. They present a serious challenge for the assessment of translation quality.

All these considerations highlight the pivotal, and potentially complex, roles of information and knowledge in engagement initiatives. They also show how the notion of translation applies to multiple processes of gathering, presenting, disputing, agreeing, framing and re-framing and, finally, using different kinds of information and knowledge. A further complication is presented when the engagement process in question has, itself, a number of distinct but interlocking component parts. As we have seen, the *GM Nation?* debate possessed this multi-stage character. In the following sections, we consider the relevance of the notion of translation to evaluating a number of these component processes.

Framing the debate

We have mentioned the organisers' commitment that the public should be allowed to determine how the issues around GM were to be discussed during the debate. Here we consider how this task was addressed. In order to elicit lay framings of GM-related issues, a series of discussion groups (known as 'Foundation Discussion workshops') were organised, with the objective of investigating how a cross-section of the lay public tries to make sense of these issues.

Nine discussion groups were convened, designed to involve as broad a range of members of the general public as possible. Participants were specially recruited to represent a range of demographic characteristics. Eight of the groups comprised members of the general public who were not already actively engaged with the issues, and a single workshop was composed of those who were actively involved and interested in GM issues. In methodological terms, the workshops were rather like large focus groups. They utilised a range of moderation techniques, some of them more unusual than others, but including some elements that were, indeed, novel. These included the use of a number of games that made possible the representation of contrasting participant views in graphic and amusing terms, storytelling, and the presence of a professional cartoonist to provide stimulus material in real time.

The groups were very much facilitator-centred, which meant that interaction between participants was highly mediated by the instructions and prompts of the (two) facilitators. They were also much larger than the groups typically utilised in focus group-based research. Unsurprisingly, therefore, the groups did not generate much in the way of quasi-naturalistic talk: a potentially very useful source for tapping everyday sense-making practices (Bloor *et al.*, 2001; Horlick-Jones, 2005c; Petts *et al.*, 2001). Demonstrably the facilitators sought to avoid imposing exterior frames on the group discussions, and to promote the identification of shared everyday categories. These are techniques often adopted by social researchers using focus groups (Bloor *et al.*, 2001), and our observations suggest that the facilitation practice was highly professional in this respect.

Our observational work indicated that the group facilitators made audio recordings of the entire proceedings. We gained access to these tapes. The quality of the recordings was quite poor in places, and we recognise that this could have resulted in potentially important data being lost, although we have no specific evidence to suggest that is the case. The facilitators also retained a variety of flip-charts used during the various 'games' and procedures. Finally, they also retained the work of the cartoonist who was present at each workshop, and whose work was, it seems, at least in part inspired by the unfolding discussions (see Figures P.1 and 7.3).

The facilitators' report on the group-based exercise (Corr Willbourn, 2003a) does not indicate how all these data were analysed. They describe their methodology as following 'the principles of phenomenological and process-oriented qualitative research' (ibid.: 6) with the 'specific application' of this approach being developed in-house. We conducted informal interviews with these consultants which suggested that their analytic approach was rather similar to standard textbook methods for qualitative research.

This analysis of the group sessions identified six frames which the participants used when discussing, and trying to make sense of, GM issues. These are set out in Box 7.2.

Box 7.2 **Frames identified by the Foundation Discussion workshops**

- Food
- Choice
- Information needs
- Uncertainty and trust
- Targets and intended trajectory
- Ethics

These findings also identified numerous factual areas where participants expressed a wish to know more.

The structure of lay framing of GM-related issues revealed by these workshops was in close agreement with the findings in the recent risk perception literature, for example, over the way in which people use shared categories drawn from their everyday lives – such as food, health and trust in decision-makers – in collectively 'talking into existence' some kind of understanding of GM issues (Grove-White *et al.*, 1997; Marris *et al.*, 2001; Petts *et al.*, 2001). They also identified a high degree of ambivalence in attitudes towards GM, something that figured strongly in the findings of our survey work, where we found that more than half of the lay public were not sure whether GM food should be promoted or opposed (discussed in Horlick-Jones *et al.*, 2004; Pidgeon *et al.*, 2005; see also Chapter 5).

Overall we concluded that the workshop methodology was sound as an exercise in information elicitation and gathering, and in this respect it was able to capture most of the data required by the organisers. However, while the workshops were highly effective with regard to eliciting framing information, they were less successful in their secondary task of ascertaining what would encourage members of the public to engage actively with the wider debate process. The single workshop comprised of 'engaged' people in GM-related issues agreed that the debate should disseminate 'the facts' about GM, but, unsurprisingly, disagreed over *which* facts.

Following the completion of the Foundation Discussion workshop process, the organisers had at their disposal a report that identified frames and questions, together with a set of cartoons that loosely (and amusingly) illustrated certain themes that arose during the workshop discussions. In order to assess the translation quality of the debate, we need to inquire into the effectiveness of not only how this information was elicited, but also how it was utilised to inform and shape subsequent stages of the process. We begin to consider this latter question in the following section.

The 'facts' about GM: informing the debate

The debate organisers thought it necessary to develop a range of stimulus materials to ensure participants in the debate were informed about the nature of the arguments about GM. It was envisaged that these materials would also set out a range of technical evidence regarded by most protagonists as being of relevance to these issues. As noted above, the preparation of these materials proved problematic, not least because of the need to strike a balance between the relative status of quite well-established scientific findings (albeit subject to uncertainty and so potentially fallible) and wider value-based issues, such as political and ethical considerations. We note that a recent US National Research Council (1996) report on deliberative processes recognised that there is no easy way to strike this balance.

As a first stage, background research was commissioned: a review of the literature about public attitudes in the UK to GM issues, focusing on GM crop commercialisation; and a review of the experience in the UK and elsewhere of implementing deliberative techniques in public engagement exercises. This work was carried out partly by the main debate contractor and executive (the COI), and partly by a sub-contractor. In our view this material could fairly be described as sound but unexceptional. It contained the sort of information that one might not unreasonably expect those who were appointed to implement a major exercise such as the GM debate to already possess.

The preparation of the stimulus materials entailed the assembly of an appropriate body of 'information content'. Here it was argued that given the nature of technical terms and ideas used in debates about GM, many of which may be unfamiliar to the lay public, there was a need to create an 'agreed core' of information. The sub-contractors appointed to carry out this work were advised that while the brief was concerned with creating 'objective' information, there was a case to include 'opposing views' because 'this is often how people encounter information in real life'.[4]

In practice, the sub-contractors interviewed a number of engaged stakeholders, including the members of the Debate Steering Board, drawing on a set of questions forming an output from the Foundation Discussion workshops. Here, it seems, was the first 'translation link' with the earlier stage of the debate.

The nine initial interview areas are set out in Box 7.3. These areas and their constituent questions (up to eight for each category) were identified by the Foundation Discussion workshop sub-contractors, and are contained in their report on the workshops (Corr Willbourn, 2003a). Here, questions posed by participants during the various workshop exchanges had been grouped according to common themes.[5]

Box 7.3 **Initial question areas to generate the 'information content' for the stimulus materials**

A Basic information and definitions
B Current status of GM
C Rationale
D Possible risk to health
E Other possible effects
F Regulation and monitoring of safety
G Boundaries
H Trust and confidence
I Moral and ethical issues

As they stand, the questions address matters that are largely of a technical nature: 'What is GM?'; 'How is it done?'; 'Who eats GM food?'; 'Why do it?'; 'What's in it for me?'; 'How do I know that it will be safe?'. Clearly competing voices in debates about GM would provide different answers and, indeed, the responses obtained by the sub-contractors contained a diversity of perspectives on these 'factual' matters. These were eventually organised into a series of pithy for/against statements.

The stimulus materials took the form of a video, 'workbook' and CD-ROM. The video used the device of using conversations between three small groups of people – members of the lay public, 'scientists' and farmers – to articulate the different kinds of argument typically used in debates about GM. It is not clear to us how these individuals were selected, or the extent to which the conversations were scripted. The content of the workbook (a glossy 48-page pamphlet) and CD-ROM drew on the 'information content' mentioned above, and contained a series of questions about GM, its regulation, possible impacts and so on. This material was presented in the form of a paragraph or two of 'views for' and 'views against'. The sources of these arguments, present in the initial 'information content' text, had been removed. The final form of the stimulus material went through a series of slippages from early plans; for example, the CD-ROM was originally intended to take a much more interactive form, allowing those wishing to explore the issues further to 'drill down' through the information, however this did not happen. The content of the workbook was made available on the debate website, which also provided access to a quite extensive range of documentation associated with the debate.

The activities associated with the production of the stimulus materials entailed a number of translation processes. First, a range of questions elicited by the Foundation Discussion workshops were used to shape the gathering of information that was used in those materials. Interestingly, these questions were used rather than attempting to adopt the framings identified in the workshop report. It could be argued that by substituting questions for frames, lay perspectives were being constructed in 'deficit terms', as a particular absence of expert knowledge. This observation raises a difficult technical question: namely, how might one capture such framings in a way that can be used to shape the debate process in practical ways? While one could argue that a set of questions in some way reflects the perspectives and pre-occupations of a frame, or set of frames, this would appear a rather impoverished way of embodying the totality of shared understandings, sources of relevance, symbolic linkages and uses of language that are characteristic of a socially organised 'way of seeing' (Goffman, 1975; Schön and Rein, 1994). Here, we have identified an important challenge for the concept of translation quality.

Turning now to the use of information gathered in the production of the stimulus materials, we note that the finalised materials presented for/against arguments in a way that stripped the arguments from their source information and political context. It seems to us that important doubts exist about the extent to which information decontextualised in this way from its sources can play a meaningful role in informing a debate of this nature. Presenting such information in a symmetrical way, some of which may have been derived from relatively well-established scientific knowledge, and some from a variety of other sources, obscures the framing associated with each expression of knowledge so as to rob it of meaning.

To illustrate this point, we briefly consider one of the questions contained in the *GM Nation?* 'workbook'.[6] The text poses the question: 'Is GM food safe?' Two columns of text follow this heading, labelled 'Views for' and 'Views against'. The first column contains the statement: 'The regulatory bodies that exist are independent of industry and work in the public interest.' The second column contains the statement: 'Current tests assume that GM crops are fundamentally the same as non-GM crops, which is not the case.' Neither statement is justified on the basis of any sources or reference.

An issue also arises about the inherent complexity of some relevant knowledge. The reduction of complex, multi-faceted, and context and case-dependent arguments to racy, polarised, 'sound bites', as took place in the production of the stimulus materials, arguably distorted the process of knowledge translation in a way inimical to the effectiveness of the debate process. It seemed to us that in an effort to avoid framing the debate in terms of a narrow 'techno-scientific' version of 'the facts', the organisers had, in practice, robbed the stimulus material of meaning, so destroying the value of collecting the information in the first place.

We found that the overwhelming view of participants in the debate's various public events, and of various stakeholders and key actors that we interviewed, was that the quality of the stimulus material was bland and unsatisfactory (Horlick-Jones *et al.*, 2004, 2006b). Our analysis suggests that here the debate performed poorly with respect to translation quality.

The public meetings

Here, we are concerned with the translation quality of the various public meetings that formed part of the GM debate. We have noted that participants found the stimulus materials rather bland and unhelpful. Turning our attention now to information flow to the concluding parts of the debate, we need to consider the effectiveness of processes by which information was gathered at the public events.

The organisers produced a short questionnaire, or 'feedback form' that was distributed to all participants in all component parts of the debate. It was also available on the website. This questionnaire contained thirteen items on the possible costs and benefits of GM crops, and drew, in a rather loose way, on the questions posed by the Foundation Discussion workshops. In addition, the organisers recruited observers for the six 'national' Tier 1 meetings, who, we understand, collected qualitative material describing the form and outputs of the discussions.

In the Tier 1 meetings, the plenary sessions were professionally introduced (drawing on some of the stimulus material), shaped and facilitated. However, much of these meetings was organised around small round-table discussions between participants. We noted that participants engaged in these round-table discussions made *extremely limited* use of the stimulus materials (see Chapter 4). The feedback from each table to a final plenary was delivered by an untrained volunteer, and limits on the time available resulted in a tendency for quite complex arguments to be reduced to 'standard' formulations. The Tier 1 plenary sessions were audio taped and subsequently transcripts were made which were posted on the debate website. The organisers' observers, who were free to monitor the discussions around each table, were also volunteers who, as far as we are aware, worked in a way that was not coordinated or standardised across the various meetings. We conclude that the organisers were restricted in their capacity to capture the rich detail of the discussions that formed a central part of the Tier 1 meetings.

Turning now to the Tier 2 (regional) and Tier 3 (local) meetings, perhaps the first point to make is that these took on a diversity of forms. Some of the Tier 2 meetings, which were typically hosted by local government bodies, were supported by the debate organisers and professionally facilitated. The organisation of Tier 3 meetings was determined locally by their organisers. We were only able to gather limited information on the large number of Tier 2 and Tier 3 meetings, although we understand that a number of these meetings featured reasonably good facilitation and presentations by expert speakers, with opportunities for questions and discussion. However, we have no way of measuring the typicality of this format. We understand that occasionally informal reports on local meetings were sent to the debate organisers, however these did not arise from a process of independent observation, so their quality cannot be guaranteed. The debate executive sent stocks of feedback questionnaires to all local meeting organisers, however, the process of their distribution was not monitored by independent observers.

We conclude that the organisers' feedback questionnaires provided the main conduit for information gathering on the public meetings. There was very little in the way of systematic attempts to collect information on the rich detail of discussion and deliberation that formed part of these meetings.

Those participating in the public meetings were not selected in any way, and therefore the question of representativeness among the wider public is a relevant consideration. We found that the participants in the public aspects of the debate were not representative of the general public as a whole, in terms of either demographic or attitudinal characteristics (see Chapter 5). For example, the self-reported educational level of participants in the Tier 1 meetings was considerably higher than the UK average (some two-thirds of respondents claimed to have a degree, compared to one-fifth of the population aged between 16 and 74 according to the 2001 census). Participants in the open activities, including those completing the Steering Board's questionnaire, were considerably more negative about GM food and crops than respondents in our survey (Horlick-Jones *et al.*, 2004; Pidgeon *et al.*, 2005; see also Chapter 5). We also observed that these events were often dominated by discussions characteristic of a knowledgeable and experienced engagement in the GM issue, suggesting a pre-existing engagement with GM-related issues (see Chapter 4).

The form of discourse typical of exchanges among participants in these meetings is illustrated in the extract from one of our team's fieldwork notebooks in Box 7.4.

Despite this clear bias in representation, it is not our view that the open meetings were without merit. It is important to recognise that engaged people with clear views on GM issues had a legitimate contribution to make in the debate. Moreover, the exploration of their views was important, in view of their prominence within the political dynamics of wider debates about GM. The key question from the point of view of this book is whether participants were suitably informed by the stimulus materials, and whether their views were appropriately collected by the organisers. Our analysis would generally suggest that this was *not* the case.

The 'Narrow-but-Deep' process

The debate organisers were aware that findings from the debate drawn from a self-selected sample of the lay public could be criticised for their possible bias. In order to attend to this difficulty, an additional closed component of the debate took the form of a series of focus groups, conceived as a 'control' on the findings arising from the open parts of the debate process. These ten groups were recruited to provide a representative cross-section of the public designed deliberately to exclude people with an active interest in the GM issue. These groups each met twice, with an interval of two weeks during which participants were invited to explore the issues concerning GM using official stimulus materials, and any other materials they could find, and to keep diaries of their findings, conversations, thoughts and so on. As we noted above, the title of the process, 'Narrow-but-Deep' (NBD), refers to the limited

---

Box 7.4 **Extract from fieldwork notes at one of the Tier 1 meetings**

I arrive at the second table, one participant is holding forth, telling 'the facts'. There is a lot of technical talk among the group. Pusztai is mentioned [the scientist who claimed to show that rats fed on GM food became ill as a result]. 'what about the Newcastle study', 'loads of tests are needed' . . . one clearly-frustrated participant exclaims: 'it's all a big con'.

scope of representation (only seventy-seven members of the public took part), while 'deep' refers to the anticipated extended level of engagement and deliberation in these groups, in comparison to that typically possible during the open meetings. The specific objectives of the NBD process are set out in Box 7.5 (Corr Willbourn, 2003b: 6).

As we have seen, the Foundation Discussion workshops had identified a number of frames used by lay people in making sense of the GM issues. These were grounded in everyday lived experience. Despite the stated objectives, we could find no evidence that the NBD meetings were purposefully structured according to these framings, save by virtue of the participants being exposed to the debate's stimulus materials, and to the cartoons produced during the Foundation Discussion workshops. Rather, the NBD meetings were allowed to evolve in a largely unstructured fashion. In this way, the facilitators might be said to have followed their brief by simply allowing the lay categorisations to re-emerge in a naturalistic way.

The facilitators audio recorded each of the NBD sessions, and we gained access to the corresponding tapes. In common with the Foundation Discussion workshop recording, these recordings were of quite poor quality in places, and some gaps were present. The diaries kept by participants during the two weeks between group meetings were collected at the end of the second meeting. The facilitators carried out an examination of media stories identified in a random sample of these diaries. Their report (Corr Willbourn, 2003b) does not record any other form of analysis carried out on the diaries. Neither does it state whether transcripts were prepared from the recordings, nor how, in practice, the datasets were analysed. The evidence at our disposal suggests that standard textbook techniques for qualitative data analysis were used in this process.

Box 7.5 Objectives for the Narrow-but-Deep process

- Using the frames identified by the public, to facilitate debate and deliberation that focuses on what the public see as the relevant issues surrounding GM.
- To enable access to the evidence and other balanced and substantiated information the public may want and need to debate the issues.
- Through deliberation and access to the evidence, allow people to come to a considered view on:
  (i)   the issue of GM;
  (ii) the possible commercialisation of GM crops in the UK;
  (iii) the options for proceeding with this.

Standard *GM Nation?* feedback questionnaires were issued to the participants for completion on the spot at the *start* of both the first and second meeting of each group. In other words, none of the organisers' questionnaires were issued to participants by the organisers following the experience of the second meeting of the group (participants did, however, complete our questionnaire, which was issued with a pre-paid envelope for them to take away with them). We were interested to note that the facilitators (ibid.: 38) describe the second questionnaire as the 'post-deliberation one', and go on to describe the activities undertaken by participants during the 'diary' phase as 'the deliberation process' (ibid.: 45). Our observations suggest that the second meetings of the group were, indeed, more deliberative in nature than the first meetings, although this process took place *after* the questionnaire was completed. There seems to be some confusion here over the meaning of the word 'deliberation', and we can only speculate on the implications for the data analysis.

In the facilitators' report on the NBD process (ibid.), strong claims are made about the robustness of its findings. The process is said to 'genuinely represent "grass-roots" opinions' (ibid.: 8), and while it is recognised that the sample is too small for associated feedback questionnaire data to provide robust statistical evidence, 'it is more than adequate to provide robust qualitative data'. Significantly, the facilitators claim that 'the sample is, we believe, an accurate reflection of those whose voices have not yet been heard on the issues surrounding GM' (ibid.: 18).

In response to these claims, we note that there exists no hard and fast rule about how many focus groups need to be conducted in order to make strong claims regarding the validity of the resulting findings. The NBD process is based upon a sample of ten groups, each of which met on two occasions, and we recognise that many projects have used fewer groups to establish results publishable in peer-reviewed journals. Sufficient volumes of data need to be gathered in order to achieve saturation of the categories that emerge from analysis. Ideally sampling would continue until clear saturation is achieved. In practice, of course, it is often not possible to follow this procedure as the constraints of project budgeting necessitate the numbers of groups to be used are specified in advance. Of central importance here is the recognition that despite sometimes using relatively small numbers of groups, focus group-based research can make reasonable claims about the validity of its findings because it seeks to uncover shared norms and interpretive resources present within a wider population with certain shared experiences (Bloor *et al.*, 2001).

During the two-week interval between first and second meetings of the NBD groups, the participants were asked to explore the GM issue, and at the end of the first meetings were encouraged to discuss the diverse range of possible means by which this objective might be achieved. During this two-week 'diary' exercise, the participants were therefore exposed to potentially significantly different experiences, directly relating to GM-related issues. The

diaries they kept suggested that these influences included a diversity of
knowledge claims about GM-related issues, including those posted at websites,
many of which were anti-GM in nature (Figure 7.2; see also a limited analysis
conducted by Corr Willbourne, 2003b).[7] Arguably, such differences in
experiences created the potential for discussions at the second meetings of
the groups to move off in new, perhaps idiosyncratic directions, thus calling
into question the 'accurate reflection of unheard voices' claims of the NBD
findings.[8]

A further consideration concerns the logic of the position in which
participants in the groups were placed as a result of knowing little about the
issues, and then going on a 'crash course' during which they were exposed to
an uncontrolled range of sources of knowledge and opinion about GM-related
matters. In the groups, lay people were asked to come to a view on GM. How
does one make sense of this issue? Any new technology has potential
unintended adverse consequences, and it is clearly not possible to be completely
sure that the introduction of GM will not bring with it health and
environmental problems. The recent UK experience of BSE and other food
scares strongly reinforces this caution. The participants might quite reasonably
ask, then, 'What's in it for me?', and the answer is not at all clear. In contrast,
for instance, in the case of mobile telephones, where people clearly see
themselves as gaining significant benefits, scare stories about adverse health
consequences appear to have had little impact on the widespread use of this
technology (Burgess, 2004; Walls *et al.*, 2005a). We note that some of the
NBD groups displayed considerable enthusiasm for fantasy products such as
'GM chocolate that doesn't put on weight' (see Box 7.6), suggesting that
caution about GM may similarly be swept aside if suitably attractive
commodities became available (Horlick-Jones 2007; Horlick-Jones *et al.*,
2006a, in press, a, in press, b; Horlick-Jones and Walls, 2005).

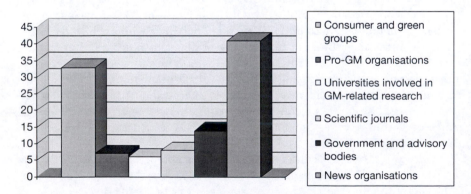

Figure 7.2 Narrow-but-Deep process: website visits recorded in participants' diaries

Source: Unpublished content analysis of the NBD diaries carried out by Tee Rogers-Hayden, then
at the University of East Anglia, provided by the author on 5 July 2005.

Box 7.6 'GM chocolate' – an example of talk during one of the 'Narrow-but-Deep' group sessions

[NBD Group 4, 53(1)] (M_i = male participants; F_j = female participants; Mod = facilitator)

1	M2	I mean you could have all sorts of food . . . I suppose you
2		don't put on any weight on, you know, you could eat as much
3		ice cream as you like cause it's got one calorie per tub
4	F3	<u>marvellous</u>
5		((laughter))
6		((data gap))
7	R	so who's up for it . . . hang on . . . it's a great question
8	F3	GM chocolate, <u>definitely</u>
9	Mod	GM chocolate, yeah
10	M2	but chocolate that had no calories . . . you could have, like,
11		six bars and be, like, that . . . it tastes the same . . . if
12		Cadbury's said 'oh we've got this little GM lab going on to
13		see' . . . you know
14	Mod	would you buy it?
15	M2	yeah, if it didn't have an adverse effect
16	F2	it's an ideal thing, isn't it?
17	Mod	quick show of hands . . . we've got F4 and F2
18	M2	<u>see, we knew we'd win over with chocolate</u>
19		((laughter))
20	Mod	it's the chocolate that does it . . . you put your hand up as
21		well didn't you ((F1)) . . . yeah
22	M2	((gap)) government . . . if they made GM chocolate, the whole
23		thing would be like a domino effect wouldn't it . . . chocolate
24		first and everything else would

A final crucial aspect of the context in which the NBD participants found themselves was being disengaged from the constraints of the decision on GM commercialisation. Our understanding of the philosophy behind the NBD methodology (based upon a presentation by the facilitators that we observed) suggests that the process design sought to avoid constraining participants with the responsibility for a decision. In our view this relaxing of constraints raises important questions about the extent to which the NBD process can truly be described as 'deliberation', in the dictionary sense of promoting the consideration and discussion of arguments for and against a measure, so as to resolve that tension. Quite simply, the structural logic of asking people who are largely ignorant of the issues, and who have no particular axe to grind or constraint to satisfy, to make up their minds about GM appears to propel them inexorably in the direction of caution.

Our discussion of the NBD process reveals a number of complicated issues for the assessment of translation quality. The shaping of group processes by external sources of knowledge appears to have been largely uncontrolled. There appears to have been some confusion in arriving at conclusions that draw on both the qualitative and quantitative data collected. We conclude that the translation quality of this stage of the debate was rather weak.

The official findings of the debate

Finally, we consider the concluding component part of the debate as an information process: namely, the drawing up by the organisers and their executive of the findings of the overall process. Members of the Steering Group met on two occasions during August 2003 in order to consider and discuss drafts of the final report that had been prepared by a professional writer hired to undertake this task. We were provided with observer status at both meetings. It is important to note that this final process of the debate – the rendering of conclusions from a voluminous range of disparate data – was the ultimate test of what we have termed translation quality.

Our first observations concern the haste with which the report was put together in order to meet the agreed deadline, and the considerable pressure under which the writer worked. His contribution included not only drafting the report, but also significant work on analysis of a considerable volume of correspondence received by the debate secretariat. We recognise that the debate executive provided a certain amount of technical support, in particular in the analysis of the quantitative feedback data. However, given the volume of data collected, and the importance of the exercise, it seems extraordinary that the analytical process was not more adequately resourced. Given these constraints, it is a credit to the writer that the final report (PDSB, 2003) is such a comprehensive and well-written document. However, and significantly, it is not at all clear what processes of data analysis were used in analysing the various sources of data collected by the debate, or how they were synthesised in order to arrive at the published findings.

We have some serious misgivings about these findings. While we concur with the debate's main conclusion, that significant levels of concern about certain aspects of GM exist among the British population, we recognise the need to qualify this finding in the light of the high levels of ambivalence about the technology in question. We are also concerned about the basis adopted by the report for suggesting that disengaged members of the lay public are not a 'completely different audience with different values and attitudes from an unrepresentative activist minority' (ibid.: paragraph 195). This suggestion, abbreviated to a slogan-like claim that the 'general population are not a "silent majority"' (ibid.) fails to appreciate both the underlying dynamics of what appears to be a superficial similarity in views, and the variation of attitudes across different populations within the lay public.

While the organisers' report does draw the important conclusion that 'attitudes hardened' as the NBD participants learned more about the issues, the report also seems to be arguing, on rather flimsy evidence, that if disengaged members of the lay public are exposed to 'the facts' then their attitudes shift such that they have rather similar views to the people who participated in the open debate process. It is important to recognise that, in statistical terms, it is incorrect to claim that apart from minor differences the attitudes of the 'post-experience' NBD groups are the same as those of participants in the public meetings (Campbell and Townsend, 2003; Pidgeon *et al.*, 2005).

Significantly, the organisers also note that an important difference between the public and NBD samples is that the NBD people are 'generally more prepared to acknowledge potential benefits of GM crops' (PDSB, 2003: paragraph 205). This final result suggests that the structure of NBD views is rather different from that part of the lay public identified in our survey which sees no benefit in GM. Rather than dismissing GM as having no possible advantages, the NBD sample seems to be able to recognise both costs and benefits. In this way, their style of reasoning is consistent with our hypothesis that it was the logic of the NBD context that tended to push them into adopting a cautionary position.

To conclude, we suggest that the translation quality of the final report production was flawed by an analysis which failed to be sufficiently sensitive to the nuances of interpretation of the various datasets. We recognise that this may have resulted from it being over-hurried and under-resourced, and appreciate the political pressures under which the organisers, their executive and consultants worked. This serious shortcoming underlines the importance of including translation quality as a generic consideration in the evaluation of engagement initiatives of this kind.

Conclusions

We have described how we concluded that what we term 'translation quality' is an important consideration in the evaluation of engagement processes. We have also provided a detailed discussion of the relevance of this issue for a number of component parts of the *GM Nation?* public debate. It is clear that considerable work is needed to develop specific instruments and procedures in order to assess translation quality in ways more systematic than the simple narrative approach that we have adopted here. Nevertheless, we suggest that the significance of this criterion for evaluation practice is evident.

Our analysis reveals that the *GM Nation?* debate was flawed in terms of this new criterion of translation quality. In essence, the gains from good initial work in identifying public framings of GM issues (in the Foundation

Discussion workshops) were steadily eroded throughout subsequent stages of the debate process. These framings were first transformed into stimulus materials that were rather bland, and which failed to capture the contextual relevance of its sources, and which, in any case, were largely ignored by participants in the debate. It was not at all clear the extent to which these materials informed the deliberations that took place in the public meetings or NBD groups, or their significance to those encountering the debate website. Attempts to capture the richness of such deliberations were largely restricted to a small number of closed questions in the 'feedback' questionnaire, which focused on ratings of a number of pre-assigned attributes of GM. Arguably, these somewhat limited data were then over-interpreted by a small number of time-pressured individuals during the process of producing the debate's final report.

We summarise these findings in Table 7.1. Here, we draw attention to how additional translation mechanisms, in particular provided by the media, politicians and pressure groups, rendered new understandings of what the debate had to say. Here it is important to note that media representations of the debate tended to portray the process as taking the form of a referendum, so indicating widespread public disapproval for GM crops and food. Such representations paid no attention to the atypical sampling which provided the basis for such a judgement. In this respect, the *GM Nation?* debate produced outcomes that might be described as 'mistranslations'. We suggest that future such attempts to implement citizen engagement should make serious efforts to attend to this source of difficulty.

It would appear that in many ways there are similarities between the measures needed to establish quality control in social research and those that appear to be needed to achieve effective translation quality in the implementation of engagement processes. This recognition suggests a need to revisit notions of reliability and validity, the need for a clear audit trail through data collection and analysis (e.g. Seale, 1999), and a critical awareness of the inherent difficulties associated with combining distinct datasets through processes of 'triangulation' (Fielding and Fielding, 1986). In view of the experimental, and sometimes unpredictable, nature of engagement initiatives, and in line with our conclusion from Chapter 5, we draw attention to the need for an enhanced attention to the social context in which data are generated, and to the logic of the position in which participants are placed (Gephart, 1988; Houtkoop-Steenstra, 2000).

To conclude, we suggest that it is difficult to conceive of any type of citizen engagement initiative in which the effectiveness of processes of information collection and transmission, which serve to shape and inform subsequent stages of the process, will not be a relevant criterion of success. Therefore, we propose that translation quality should join the list of existing normative evaluation criteria that has begun to emerge from the literature on the evaluation of engagement processes (Horlick-Jones *et al.*, in press, a).

Table 7.1 A summary of the various stages of the debate process from a translation perspective

Stage of process	Information/knowledge source	Actors/mechanisms	Outputs	Translation quality?
Foundation Discussion workshops	Workshop participants.	Sub-contractor 1 (facilitation and analysis of audio recordings of discussions and other materials). Participants (discussions and written outputs in flip-charts). Cartoonist.	Report no. 1. Cartoons.	Sound facilitation, and information elicitation and gathering.
Desk research on GM and engagement issues	The academic and grey literatures.	Contractor. Sub-contractor 2.	Report no. 2.	Basic but fairly comprehensive.
Production of stimulus material	Reports 1 and 2. Debate Steering Board members.	Contractor. Sub-contractor 3 (analysis of reports, and interviews with, and comments from, Board members)	Video. Booklet. Text for website. Questionnaire.	Was the initial framing captured adequately? Decontextualised and over-simplified information in stimulus materials.
Public meetings (Tier 1)	Stimulus materials. Participants.	Participants. Sub-contractor 4 (facilitation). Contractors (event organisation).	Reports by Steering Board observers. Transcripts of plenary discussions. Questionnaire data.	Poor quality mechanisms for capturing discussion. Stimulus materials largely ignored.
Public meetings (Tiers 2 and 3)	Stimulus materials. Participants.	Participants. Sub-contractor 4 (facilitation for some Tier 2 events). Contractors (event organisation for some Tier 2 events). Local event organisers (local government, community groups, local branches of pressure groups etc.)	Transcripts of plenary discussions for those Tier 2 events supported by contractors. Reports provided by organisers of some Tier 3 meetings. Questionnaire data.	As above.

Table 7.1 Continued

Stage of process	Information/knowledge source	Actors/mechanisms	Outputs	Translation quality?
Website	Stimulus materials.	Participants.	Comments left behind (also some emails and hard-copy letters sent by post). Questionnaire data.	Not possible to comment on participant engagement with website.
Narrow-but-Deep groups	Stimulus materials. Cartoons from Foundation Discussion workshops. Information accessed from various sources by participants during two-week 'diary' period.	Participants. Sub-contractor 1 (facilitation, and analysis of audio recordings of discussions and participant diaries).	Report no. 3. Questionnaire data.	Good quality facilitation. Implicit logic of method suspect? Diary process entailed uncontrolled exposure to a diversity of information sources. Questionnaires completed at the *start* of second meetings of the groups.
Final report production	All data collected by debate process.	Sub-contractor 5 (a professional writer). Contractors (some analytical support for the writer). Debate Steering Board (discussion of draft materials).	Report no. 4 (final report on the debate).	Severe time pressure. Methodologically worrying analysis of data.
Interpretations of final report	Report no. 4.	Media. Politicians. Industry organisations. Pressure groups.	Media coverage. Posting of material on websites. Circulation of documentation.	Worrying media coverage based largely on the questionnaire data, suggesting that the debate amounted to a simple referendum.

Figure 7.3 A cartoon produced as stimulus material during the *GM Nation?* debate

8   Other representations of
        the debate

In previous chapters we have examined the effectiveness of the debate as an organisational process and as an information system; the extent to which the debate might reasonably be described as capturing views 'representative' of the affected community; and the performance of the debate on the basis of the expectations of participants. We now consider how the debate was regarded more widely within British society.

One of the PDSB objectives (B5a) specified the need to create widespread awareness of the debate among the UK population. In Chapter 5, as part of our discussion of the representativeness of the debate's participants, we showed how our national survey provided some indication of the extent to which this was achieved. The survey also provided a sense of what the lay, uninvolved, public felt about the idea of holding a public debate of this kind. We report on these findings in the following section.

In contemporary societies the term 'public opinion' is often used in a way that reflects the extent to which an issue has been taken up by the news media. Indeed, the volume and nature of media accounts of the debate probably had a pivotal bearing on the levels of public awareness that it was taking place, and understanding of what it was about. Correspondingly, much of this chapter is taken up with a discussion of media coverage of the debate and of GM matters more generally. We also discuss evidence provided by our survey and media analysis on the relationship between media consumption and views about GM.

Media coverage of contentious issues such as GM is often prompted by, and draws upon, the lobbying activities of organisations engaged in associated political debates. In this case, such organisations include those that reflect the commercial interests of the biotechnology industry, and the campaigning agendas of the environmental and consumer movements. The third part of this chapter examines perceptions of the debate among such engaged stakeholder organisations.

Public attitudes towards the debate

We have already discussed how successful the *GM Nation?* debate was in generating 'widespread awareness among the UK population'. As we showed in Figure 5.3, our national survey indicates that over 70 per cent of the general public had never heard of the debate. Some 13 per cent reported that they had heard of the debate *but* knew nothing about it. About 12–13 per cent indicated that they knew a little about it, while only 3 per cent of the population surveyed said they knew a 'fair amount' or 'a lot' about the debate. It will be recalled that we observed that these figures could be interpreted in a number of ways; in some sense a failure to generate widespread awareness, but in others a modest success, given the lack of advertising and popular newspaper and television coverage (which we discuss below) that the debate received.

We anticipated that awareness of the debate among, at least a significant proportion of, the respondents would be low. So when we designed the survey, we arranged that respondents would be provided with some information about the background and nature of the *GM Nation?* debate, whilst being administered the final section of the questionnaire. This information is shown in Box 8.1. In this way, respondents were made aware of the character of the debate before being asked to evaluate it according to a number of measures.

Using this method, we elicited public views on the value of the debate. The results are shown in Table 8.1. A clear majority, some 66 per cent, felt that the debate was a good way for the public to get more involved in making decisions about GM foods and crops, with only 12 per cent disagreeing with this idea. However, many people, some 45 per cent, still felt that it was unclear to them what the debate was about.

When asked whether the staging of the debate demonstrated that government listened to 'normal' people's views on GM food and crops, less than a quarter (23 per cent) agreed, with almost half (45 per cent) disagreeing with this suggestion. Interestingly a sizeable minority (26 per cent) neither

---

Box 8.1 Information provided to respondents on GM Nation?

As you may know, 'GM Nation? The Public Debate' is a nationwide discussion of issues related to genetic modification (GM) of crops and food. It is sponsored by the government, and managed by an independent board of people representing diverse views on GM. During June and July 2003 a series of regional and local meetings have been organised to allow people to have their say about the role of GM in the UK. 'GM Nation? The Public Debate' is organised to involve the public in the important decision as to whether or not GM foods and crops should be grown commercially in Britain. The findings from the meetings will be fed back to the government to help inform their policy-making on GM foods and crops.

Table 8.1 GM Nation? evaluation statements (%)

	Strongly disagree	Tend to disagree	Neither/ nor	Tend to agree	Strongly agree	No opinion
Evaluation of the debate						
The debate is a good way for the public to get more involved in making decisions about GM foods and crops	3	9	16	53	13	7
It is unclear to me what the debate is about	8	23	19	31	14	6
The debate shows that the government listens to what normal people think about GM foods and crops	16	29	26	20	3	7
Organising the debate is a waste of taxpayers' money	7	30	20	25	10	8
The debate has been run fairly, without promoting any specific views on GM foods and crops	5	9	42	13	1	30
Impact of the debate						
The debate will have an influence on government's policies on GM foods and crops	11	25	27	25	3	10
Because of the debate I trust the government more to make the right decisions about GM foods and crops	18	27	25	18	3	9
The debate will make no difference, because the government has already made its mind up on GM foods and crops	2	13	19	38	21	7
It does not matter whether there is a debate on GM or not. In the end European and International laws will determine what will happen	3	8	15	43	25	5

Source: UEA/MORI GM Food Survey 2003 (Weighted dataset, N = 1,363).

agreed nor disagreed with this statement. In response to a suggestion that the debate was a waste of money, those agreeing (35 per cent) and disagreeing (37 per cent) were roughly balanced, with one-fifth neither agreeing nor disagreeing.

Despite clear support for a debate on GM foods and crops as such, there was a high level of scepticism about the impact of the debate on government policy. More than half the sample agreed with the statement: 'The debate will make no difference, because the government has already made its mind up on GM foods and crops', while only 15 per cent disagreed with this statement. Likewise, on the basis of this survey, the greater part of the British public (68 per cent) thought that European and International laws would determine what would happen.

Turning now to more general views about the idea of a public debate, our survey suggested that the British public generally felt positive about public involvement exercises such as *GM Nation?*. Interestingly, a large majority of more than three-quarters (77 per cent) felt that it is important to have public debates on other important new developments in science and technology. Only a minority of the general public thought that such debates are not very (12 per cent) or not at all (3 per cent) useful. To conclude, our respondents in the 2003 national survey held rather mixed views on the value of the GM debate, which may be summarised as follows:

- People felt that the debate was a good way for the public to get more involved in making decisions about the complex issue of commercialisation of agricultural biotechnology.
- Respondents did not have clear views either way on process issues such as the fairness of the conduct of the debate, what it was about or its value-for-money. These findings are hardly surprising given that many had never heard of the debate in the first place.
- Despite clear support for the debate, people were fairly sceptical about its likely impact on policy. Many people felt that what would happen to agricultural biotechnology was a foregone conclusion, either because the government had already made up its mind, or because European or International obligations would determine the outcome. We note with interest that these findings are entirely consistent with the views of the subset of the population which participated in the debate.
- An overwhelming majority of those surveyed felt that public debates, such as *GM Nation?* would be useful in the context of future new developments in science and technology.

Media coverage of the debate

Background

In a society bathed in mediated knowledge from print and electronic sources, one might have anticipated media coverage and representations to play an important role in shaping views on GM and creating awareness of the debate. Indeed, others have already subjected these areas to extensive investigation (e.g. Bauer, 2005; Bauer and Gaskell, 2002). We, therefore, decided to gather data both on the patterns of coverage during the debate period and on the media consumption behaviour of respondents to our 2003 survey. We monitored the following media sources:

- all UK-wide national daily and Sunday newspapers;
- the main UK national news bulletins and current affairs programmes on the five terrestrial television channels and on BBC Radio;
- selected regional and local newspapers;
- internet news services and bulletin boards supported by selected newspaper and broadcasting organisations (the BBC, Channel 4, and *The Guardian*).

The national press was analysed from hard copies. Broadcast materials were recorded off-air. Regional and local press coverage was downloaded from the Lexis-Nexis database. Internet pages were downloaded and printed.

As we noted in Chapter 1, by mid-1999, after a period of intensive debate and contention, the media coverage of GM had crystallised around four major news frames: the health and environmental risks of GM foods and crop plantings; the scale of popular opposition; distrust of government and claims that policy was more responsive to corporate interests than public concerns; and the ceding of national control over key decisions. Taken together these frames mapped out the core issues at stake in the debate and guided editorial decisions on what events to cover and how to present them.

Some UK daily newspapers underlined the centrality of the 'risk' frame by launching campaigns as with the *Daily Mail*'s 'Genetic Food Watch' and *The Independent*'s 'Stop GM foods'. We also noted how activists demonstrating against GM foods or uprooting trial GM plantings dramatised the central risk framework by dressing in costumes associated with nuclear spillages (anti-contamination suits) and with forewarnings of death (The Grim Reaper) and how photographs and cartoons of these actions were frequently used to illustrate GM stories, so reinforcing both the 'risk' and 'popular opposition' frames. As we shall see, both these strategies played an important role in organising coverage during the debate period.

During the four years between this consolidation of the GM news field and the launch of the *GM Nation?* debate, a major shift in the organisation of the media environment occurred, with the rapid growth of the internet. Major news organisations, led by the BBC and *The Guardian*, have developed websites that offer instant access to current and breaking news stories. These sites also provide the opportunity to retrieve past items from the archive and to follow links to a range of resources produced by interested organisations and groups. They also host message boards and public access areas that invite readers and viewers to post their own opinions, experiences and photographs. These web-based resources are widely used and expand a news organisation's reach well beyond the ranks of regular hard-copy readers. At the same time, by providing direct access to key news sources, such as government departments and environmental pressure groups, the Web also breaks the professional journalist's monopoly over the filtering of information.

The importance of web-based sources in providing information and ways of understanding GM-related issues was clearly illustrated by the diaries kept by participants in the Narrow-but-Deep process (see Chapter 7). Among media sources consulted and recorded in the diaries, a clear pattern of internet use emerges, with the BBC most often visited among news organisations, followed by *The Guardian*, but with the two major environmental groups Friends of the Earth and Greenpeace, and the popular science magazine *New Scientist*, also scoring a higher than average number of 'hits'.

It is important to remember, however, that access to the Web remains highly stratified, with 43 per cent of households still without home access. This figure rises to 60 per cent among those on low incomes and 72 per cent among those over 65 (OFCOM, 2006: 28). This may change as connectivity migrates to mobile phones and television sets, but at the time of the current study convenient Web access remained largely the preserve of the relatively affluent and relatively young.

Patterns of coverage

As we have discussed, soon after plans for a UK-wide debate on GM were announced, worries were expressed about both the low level of funding, and the government's willingness to take the results of the exercise fully into account when formulating policy. These concerns were addressed head-on by the then Environment Minister, Michael Meacher, in a speech to a conference in February 2003, convened by the pressure group Genewatch, and reported in *The Guardian* newspaper:

> the public generally lack trust in the Government – I think we have to recognise that – and fear the debate may be no more than a PR exercise. Therefore I am pleased, today, to be able to demonstrate the Government's commitment to this debate. We have already increased the funding in order to ensure a credible and effective programme.

However, his assurances failed to silence sceptics. On 1 May, *The Guardian* website carried a long story canvassing the opinion of key stakeholders and sub-headed: 'The government says it will not make up its mind about GM crops until after the public debate, which starts next month. But is it just spin?' Hinting that the answer might be 'yes', the article was headed with a quote from a farmer involved in one of the field-scale evaluations, who was convinced that the commercial growing of GM crops in the UK was a foregone conclusion. He was quoted as saying: 'Between you and me, it's just a matter of when.'

Misgivings about the event's organisation, and suspicions about its underlying motives, carried over into the reporting of the launch of the debate, with the result that much of the media coverage tended to be sceptical or negative. Stories pointed to the various limitations of the exercise (lack of funding, insufficient prior promotion and inappropriate timing) and high-lighted claims that the government had already made up its mind on the issue, a concern voiced most forcefully in the *Daily Mirror* headline: 'GM Debate is "PR" Stunt'. Although PDSB Chair Malcolm Grant was cited as 'believing' that 'nothing has been decided yet', the only direct quotation in the story came from the Liberal Democrat Rural Affairs spokesman, Andrew George, who asserted that: 'The Government's public consultation on GM food is little more than window dressing.' This theme surfaced periodically throughout the course of the debate. A *Daily Mail* story on 7 July, for example, pointed out that the science and economic review strands of the GM dialogue would appear too late 'to help those attending the (public) meetings'. The story quoted a 'source close to the debate's steering body' comparing it to 'holding a murder trial without hearing from expert witnesses . . . I am led to the conclusion that the government is not really interested in what the public thinks at all'.

News throughout the debate period was dominated by the war in Iraq. While this focus reduced the space available for other stories, including the *GM Nation?* debate, it also provided a new template for journalists and commentators to frame the debate. The extensive critical questioning of the government's handling of the run-up to the invasion of Iraq, and the veracity of the two dossiers claiming that Iraq had weapons of mass destruction capable of threatening British interests, offered potent comparisons. Claims that the government had exaggerated intelligence data (and plagiarised a doctoral thesis), and coupled with its perceived disregard for popular anti-war sentiments, resonated strongly with concerns about both the evidential basis of the Prime Minister's pro-GM stance and the value of the *GM Nation?* debate. Michael Meacher pointedly underlined this link in a *Times* story of 12 July: 'We don't want GM to be Iraq Mark 2 . . . where the great majority is opposed as over Iraq . . . and yet the government goes ahead in the face of all the evidence.'

The following day a Cabinet reshuffle stripped Meacher of his ministerial post, fuelling popular suspicions that the Prime Minister refused to tolerate criticism. As 'Cliffski', a regular contributor to Channel 4's message board, noted in a posting just after the news was announced: 'So Michael Meacher has been booted out of the govt for daring to hold anti-GM views. Looks like the coast is clear . . . to shovel this experimental sludge down our throats whether we like it or not.'

Such suspicions of news management were not confined to the internet. On 25 June, a local newspaper, the *Leicester Mercury* carried a humorous feature column recounting how Alastair Campbell (then the Prime Minister's Press Secretary) had visited a school in the locality, and, seeing a pile of pupils' essays putting the case for GM had: 'slipped them into his briefcase muttering "This'll stuff Meacher!"'. The piece concluded: 'Copying the work of a PhD student . . . is bad enough, but surely Downing Street can do better than the work of GCSE students? Makes you wonder if they know what they are talking about, doesn't it?'

The link to Iraq, and to the role of US corporate interests in shaping policy, was also cemented through imagery. On 10 June *The Guardian* published an opinion piece by George Monbiot, an environmental commentator, and long-standing opponent of GM. It was illustrated with a large colour cartoon showing a tank painted with the Stars and Stripes with the letters 'GM' on the gun turret.

In addition to reactivating the 'distrust' frame, coverage of the debate was also embedded securely in the 'risk' and 'opposition' frames from the outset. In the week before the launch, the BBC's main evening television news bulletin carried two stories that served to reintroduce these core framings. One focused on a mother who refused to purchase GM foods, and which showed her attending a public meeting addressed by a pro-GM spokesman from a leading research institute. The other carried interviews with two farmers, one based in Norfolk, who saw substantial benefits in GM technologies, and the other based in Inverness, who was adamantly opposed, and had been convicted of destroying a GM planting on neighbouring land. Although both stories attempted to strike a balance between pro- and anti- stances, arguably it was the figure of the mother, intent on protecting her children from avoidable harm, that most readily invited both sympathy and identification.

The centrality of the 'risk' and 'opposition' frames was confirmed in the week of the debate's launch, when BBC Breakfast News carried two further stories on consecutive days. Again there was a clear intention to provide a balanced account. However, while the story broadcast on the day prior to the debate launch detailed the generally positive stance towards GM foods and crops in the United States, the story on launch day reported on concerns among West Country residents that pollen from GM crops would 'contaminate' conventional and organic crops, and reduce the diversity of local plant and animal life. The same day, the BBC website reported the launch, but directly below the neutral headline 'GM Food: a national debate' was a photograph showing protesters dressed in 'decontamination' suits invading a GM crop field, with the caption '68 per cent of people in the West Country oppose GM crops'. The following day, the same website made a link to the 'West Country' story as one of 'This Week's Highlights', accompanied by a photograph showing a GM protester dressed as the Grim Reaper.

The press coverage of the first week of the debate was also dominated by the 'risk' frame, prompted by the publication of a report from the Royal Institution of Chartered Surveyors, which argued that 'gene drift' from GM plantings might affect land available for non-GM crops and even domestic gardens. The report argued that such 'contamination' might reduce property values. A number of newspapers seized this opportunity, with the *Daily Telegraph* story on the first public meeting, in Birmingham, headed: 'GM crop trails pose threat to property prices'. *The Times* led with the same story, under the headline: 'GM crops may blight house prices', and the *Daily Mail* coverage carried an almost identical headline; 'Blight of GM crops would hit house prices'.

Overall, the initial UK media coverage of the debate gave little sense of the intended scope of the exercise, and in volume it dropped off sharply after the Tier 1 events. Locally organised meetings did receive some coverage in the regional and local press. However, this coverage was strongly stratified by geographical location, with newspapers based in areas with substantial farming communities or in cities chosen for Tier 1 meetings (such as Birmingham) being more likely to carry stories. Conversely, coverage in many major urban centres (such as Manchester and Newcastle) was less extensive.

Towards the end of the debate period, however, the local meetings started to receive more attention in the UK national media, and the debate as a whole began to be re-evaluated. An example of this tendency is provided by *You and Yours*, a consumer programme on BBC Radio 4. The programme had covered the initial launch, and it revisited the debate process on 10 July. The latter item reported on a meeting organised in a church hall in Peterborough. Although this event only attracted some forty people, it was judged by participants to have been worthwhile. Their positive evaluation was reinforced in the later studio discussion, when a spokesperson for a consumer organisation said that she 'found it quite inspiring to see people wanting to talk about the issues', and adding that 'the whole public debate idea is really unprecedented in this country and therefore I think it's very welcome'. Coverage of the debate's Tier 3 local meetings also found their way into *The Archers*, a long-standing serial drama on BBC Radio 4, which is based in a fictional rural community, which gave over most of one episode to a GM debate staged in the 'Ambridge' village hall.

On 24 September the official report on the debate was published. With the exception of *The Sun* (the largest circulation popular British newspaper, which ignored the occasion), all the major news outlets carried stories on the debate, although as Table 8.2 shows, coverage was highly stratified. There was substantial coverage in the national broadsheet newspapers, and in the *Daily Mail* (which had run hostile campaigns about GM foods since 1999), with scant coverage appearing in the leading tabloid titles. On terrestrial television, the Channel 4 News (which tends to carry longer stories than the other channels) broadcast a substantial report. The other channels carried relatively compact coverage.

Most stories about the results of the debate highlighted the number of public meetings held, and the views expressed in the 'feedback' questionnaires. The media focus on the latter conveyed a sense that the debate had amounted to no more than a national opinion poll, or even a referendum on the topic. There was little recognition of the full complexity of the debate process. This narrow perspective resulted in banner headlines that focused on the scale of 'public rejection': '5 to 1 against GM crops in biggest ever public survey' (*The Guardian*), 'GM Crops? No thanks: Britain delivers overwhelming verdict after unprecedented public opinion survey' (*The Independent*), 'Frankenstein Food Revolt: 9 out of 10 vote NO to GM crops' (*Daily Mail*);

Table 8.2 Coverage of the *GM Nation?* official report in selected news media

Medium	Coverage	
National dailies (coverage in column cms)		
The Independent	566	Front page lead/editorial
The Guardian	279	Editorial
The Times	170	Editorial
Daily Telegraph	88	Front page
Daily Mail	235	
Daily Express	44	
Daily Mirror	34	
The Sun	0	
National Television News (coverage in mins and secs)		
BBC 1 Six o'clock news	3 mins 30 secs	
ITV1 6.30 news	3 mins 25 secs	
Channel 4 News	8 mins 6 secs	
Newsnight	No story	

'A wary public says no to GM crops' (*Daily Telegraph*); and 'Most Britons "oppose GM crops"' (BBC News website).

Similar headlines appeared in the leading regional papers, with the London *Evening Standard* proclaiming 'We don't want GM crops in Britain', and the Birmingham *Post* announcing 'UK public remains hostile to GM crops'.

Over the course of the period we monitored, the *GM Nation?* debate was referred to in just under 10 per cent (9.9 per cent) of all the GM-related UK press items coded. Given the overwhelming news focus on Iraq, and the lack of pre-publicity for the debate in major national print and broadcast media, this degree of visibility can be considered a modest success. Of course, it also means that the vast majority of items (some 90 per cent) about GM which appeared during the debate period were concerned with general issues and arguments, and did not mention the debate.

GM as news

As we have seen, the style and content of reporting of the debate was inextricably bound up with a longer-term coverage of GM-related issues. Arguably media reporting of this wider field of contention both helped to form the agenda for the debate, and to provide participants with information and ways of understanding the issues they could draw upon in arriving at their own positions. Hence, it is pertinent to ask what range of interpretative resources this general news coverage offered over the course of the debate period, and how patterns of media consumption served to expose particular groups of readers and viewers to different information and arguments.

As Table 8.3 shows, the amount of coverage devoted to GM issues during the debate period was highly uneven. While there was a considerable,

Table 8.3 Amounts of GM coverage in selected news sources over the debate period

Medium	Total coverage	Percentage of regular readers (*)
Broadsheet dailies (coverage in column cms)		
The Guardian	2,742	5
The Independent	1,386	2
The Times	826	5
Daily Telegraph	515	6
Mid-market dailies (coverage in column cms)		
Daily Mail	1,971	17
Daily Express	355	6
Tabloid dailies (total coverage in words)		
The Sun	155	20
Daily Mirror	880	NA
Web pages (coverage in cms)		
BBC News website	1,169	–

(*) Source UEA/MORI GM Food Survey 2003; Pearson Weighted Data Set (N = 1,018) Question 'Which of these daily newspapers do you read regularly? By "regularly" I mean three out of every four issues'.

although variable, amount of coverage in the more 'heavyweight' broadsheet national daily newspapers, there was virtually no coverage in the more popular tabloids. Some 20 per cent of our survey sample claimed to read *The Sun* regularly. This tabloid newspaper carried just 155 words about GM during the entire debate period. Of our sample, 17 per cent claimed to be regular readers of the *Daily Mail*, which, as we have noted, had been running a major campaign on GM since 1999, and providing extensive but partisan (anti-) coverage emphasising the risks of the technology. Substantial coverage was provided on the BBC News website, which draws on the full range of the corporation's news resources (including international and regional sources). This pattern of unequal attention is confirmed by the results of a recent study of GM coverage in three national daily newspapers during the period from January to July 2003; which logged 210 items in *The Guardian*, eighty-two in the *Daily Mail*, and just twelve in *The Sun* (Cook *et al.*, 2006).

We now consider in a little more detail how the different newspapers covered GM-related stories. The figures reported in Table 8.4 suggest that despite differences, an underlying pattern (or 'dramatic structure'; cf. Burke, 1969) existed in the ways in which press coverage of these issues was constructed: it was seen mainly as a struggle between the government and its critics in the environmental movement (in particular Friends of the Earth, which was mentioned in almost 11 per cent of stories), with farmers (as the group most immediately affected by a decision on commercial cultivation) representing the key sites on which this battle was being fought out, and the scientific community (as the principal source of verifiable knowledge about harms and benefits) acting as the principle mediators between positions.

Table 8.4 Percentage of national press items on GM referring to selected information sources

Source	Guardian	Times	Telegraph	Independent	Mail	All
Michael Meacher	5.4	12.1	14.3	3.1	34.5	13.9
Government spokespeople	27.0	6.1	14.1	18.8	34.3	21.2
Environmental groups	18.9	15.2	7.1	15.6	31.4	19.2
Farming interests	18.9	3.0	21.4	6.3	8.6	10.6
Consumer groups	8.1	3.0	7.1	3.1	5.7	5.3
Members of the scientific community	18.9	24.2	21.4	6.3	28.6	19.9

Table 8.4 also reveals that the former Environment Minister, Michael Meacher, came to play a key role in the organisation of media arguments during the debate period, acting as a 'lightning rod' for concerns about both the potential risks of GM, and the suspicions that the government had already made up its mind. As a minister, Meacher was widely seen as receptive to public concerns. His dismissal from the cabinet on 13 July left him free to speak openly about his own reservations about GM issues. As a news source he had two advantages. First, he was a former 'insider' with detailed knowledge of both the range of available research evidence on the possible risks of GM and the deliberations that had taken place 'behind closed doors' within government. Second, his reputation for moderation distanced him from the more committed activists in the environmental movements, and allowed him to take on the role of an 'honest broker' defending the public good against sectional interests. His credibility and detailed knowledge invested him with high news value and revivified news interest in the core issues around GM. As the recent study of GM coverage in three national dailies in the first half of 2003, which we mentioned above, found, his newsworthiness, both in and out of office, made him 'more visible' than the Prime Minister with 189 mentions in comparison with Tony Blair's 147 (Cook *et al.*, 2006).

The *Daily Mail*, a long-standing opponent of the government's stance on GM, was quick to capitalise on Meacher's visibility. On 19 June it carried a report on his exchange with Blair during Prime Minister's Question Time in the House of Commons. The newspaper's story was headed 'Axed Minister warns Blair to pull back from GM free-for-all'. It carried a section re-activating the paper's 'Frankenstein Food Watch' campaign, illustrated with a photograph of a protester wearing a surgical mask and a 'decontamination' suit. This logo appeared again on 7 July within a double-page spread headed 'This scandalous risk to our health', which included a story paraphrasing an interview that Meacher had given to Sky TV, which reiterated his concern about the lack of research on the potential risks posed by GM to human health, headed 'We just don't know the damage GM can cause, says Meacher'. The spread also carried an account that retold the story of the 'attempts to discredit' Arpad Pusztai's experiments with rats claiming that 'there are disturbing signs that this distinguished scientist was the victim of manoeuvring at the highest political level'. Headed 'The sinister sacking of the world's leading GM expert and the trail that leads to Tony Blair and the White House' it was illustrated with a photograph of protesters in 'decontamination' suits uprooting GM plants.

A few days later, on Sunday 22 July, GMTV's *The Sunday Progamme* and BBC1's *Breakfast* programme both broadcast interviews with Meacher and *The Independent on Sunday* newspaper carried an opinion piece by him. The following day, the *Daily Mail* once again enlisted him in support of its campaign, with yet another double-page spread, with the headline:

> Blair is blind to the risks of GM: Sacked minister delivers a searing indictment of Labour's rush to embrace 'Frankenstein Foods', whatever the cost to our health and the environment. Until the science is clear and reliable . . . STOP!

Again, the message was anchored with a reprinted news photograph, this time of the familiar figure of the protester standing in a field of corn, dressed as the Grim Reaper. It was the same image that the BBC had used on its website when the *GM Nation?* debate was launched. Indeed, this coincidence might lead one to suggest that beneath their clear presentational differences – the BBC's responsibility to maintain impartiality, against the *Daily Mail's* freedom to advance a particular position and launch a campaign – there existed an underlying communality in the way the core issues around GM were defined, constructed and anchored in a shared repertoire of repeated phrases and resonant images.

Mediated deliberations: on-air and on-line

In addition to providing an important source of information and argument for the debate, the major news media also played a role in organising deliberation about GM issues in their own right. The 'Letters to the Editor' columns in UK national newspapers, particularly the broadsheets, have traditionally offered a forum for responses to stories and comment on the issues of the day. Much of this material is provided by key stakeholders, or by those with claims to relevant expertise. In contrast, the public service project of contemporary UK broadcasting aims to be more inclusive, by involving a wider range of citizens in debates on contentious issues. This goal is pursued using variants of three main programme formats:

- Engaged individuals or experts on a particular issue are questioned by a panel drawn from the ranks of the intelligentsia, as in the BBC Radio 4 programme *The Moral Maze*.
- Politicians and public figures answer questions put to them by members of a studio audience as in the BBC 1 television programme *Question Time* and the radio programme *Any Questions*.

- An audience of the lay public is invited to engage in debate in the studio, under the direction of a host. Such programmes often include contributions from pre-arranged speakers, chosen for their expertise or involvement with the issue in question. Viewers at home are encouraged to participate by e-mailing or texting their views, or by participating in electronic opinion polls.

Over the course of the period we monitored, all three of these formats were deployed, providing broadcast audiences with opportunities to hear contending positions on GM justified and critiqued, and to contribute to deliberations around these issues. We noted that the third format appears to offer the greatest potential for public involvement in debate. However, as the edition of the daytime discussion programme, *The Wright Stuff*, broadcast on Channel 5 on the launch day of the debate, illustrates, public participation is often severely circumscribed. Although this particular programme contained an extensive segment devoted to 'The Great GM Debate', discussion was dominated by pre-arranged contributions from two stakeholders sitting in the studio audience – a spokesperson for Friends of the Earth and a scientist working at the John Innes Centre – an arrangement that reproduced the general contest of established positions outlined earlier. Lay members of the studio audience had little chance to question the speakers, and public input was mainly confined to an on-air opinion poll and a single telephone contribution from a viewer at home who was concerned about the possible impact of GM on her son's allergic condition.

Rather more inclusive options for deliberative engagement about GM issues were offered on the internet. As mentioned earlier, the websites developed by the major broadcasting organisations hosted bulletin boards that invited anyone to contribute their views on GM, and to respond to previous postings. The Channel 4 News website carried a substantial volume of such material, as did the BBC's 'Great Debate' message board. We found that the most extensively used site was the BBC Science message board. On 28 May it was announced that 'we're going to turn this topic into a GM food discussion area for a while'. This invitation generated a considerable volume of contributions across a wide range of GM-related issues.

Such 'threaded' debates are not without their problems. Whilst we were monitoring such exchanges, we noted that some threads took the form of dialogues between two participants, with other users confined to the role of eavesdroppers. On 4 June one contributor initiated a thread headed 'The future is not ours to gamble', arguing strongly for the application of the precautionary principle on the grounds that: 'Nobody knows anything about the potential long (or, for that matter, short) term effects of the introduction of GM crops, and never could have until it was too late.' This elicited a strong counter-argument from a contributor who insisted that: 'If scientists never took chances then science would never progress . . . why should we fear to break boundaries, especially when risks from GM crops are minimal to say the least.' Now, of course, neither we nor the other 'eavesdroppers' could possibly know whether these interlocutors were lay people exploring the issues or committed people using the forum to promote a particular 'line'. Nor, in a situation where a number of contributors write under aliases, and very few disclose their backgrounds, could we come to some provisional idea of either the reliability of their claims or the interests they represent.

We noted that a subsequent exchange contained contributions such as: 'I want choice as a consumer, and my vote is for more *Fairtrade* and organic produce in our shops. Keep genetic engineering in the laboratory . . . please don't unleash it on the environment via our farms' and:

> The idea of 'genetic pollution' is completely false. The only problem here is the militant nature of the organic movement . . . I can't wait for the organic balloon to burst so that everyone can see what a complete con it is. Give me tried and tested agriculture any day.

In this way, citizens are faced with increased opportunities to engage in public debate about controversial issues such as GM food and crops, yet in environments where traditional notions of expertise co-exist in uneasy ways with a diversity of knowledge-claims, rooted in the experience of activists, business and others (cf. Horlick-Jones, 2004). However, despite the limitations of these different arenas for deliberation, it is notable that the *GM Nation?* debate was one of the first major public consultation exercises where discussion and debate was taking place simultaneously in three major sites:

- face-to-face meetings forming part of the debate process;
- studio discussions and debates broadcast on UK national radio and television;
- internet message boards hosted by major media organisations.

We suggest that the question of whether such locations can be productively 'joined up' to widen public participation in future debates deserves sustained consideration. The accelerating pace of technological convergence offers new possibilities for integrating mediated materials. The migration of internet access from personal computers to mobile phones and digital televisions, and the increasing scope for 'downloading' television programming onto computers and mobile telephones is rapidly changing the communications environment in fundamental ways. In so doing it is laying the foundations for new possible forms of more inclusive, and flexible, modes of mediated access and participation. Arguably, a key challenge here for future public debates is to find creative ways of linking the information sources and argumentation available on-air and on-line with deliberations taking place off-line and live in a multiplicity of venues. Another challenge is to find ways of supporting participants in navigating and evaluating the bewildering diversity of often-competing knowledge-claims which will be advanced in such debates (Horlick-Jones, 2004; Thompson, 1995).

The views of engaged stakeholder organisations

As part of initial debate evaluation plans, we proposed that we would seek to elicit the views on the debate held by engaged stakeholder organisations. Here we conceive of such organisations as being those having relevant interests and/or value commitments in relation to GM crop technology. We conducted in-depth interviews with key individuals from a range of stakeholder organisations during July and August 2003. These organisation included biotechnology companies, environmental and consumer pressure groups and a supermarket chain. The interviews were carried out prior to the publication of the PDSB's final report on the debate.

Significantly, we found that all of the stakeholder representatives welcomed the initial proposal for a debate. However, they possessed divergent views about *why* it should take place, and *what* it should be about. The following discussion illustrates some of the nuances of those positions.

Biotechnology companies

These interviewees often supported the concept of a public debate as a process of education: imparting dispassionate scientific facts to the lay public.

One company representative put it:

> First of all we welcome the concept a lot . . . what we found in our research, and I'm sure others did as well, is that the relatively small section of the public that cares about this felt that they weren't informed . . . so we welcome the debate as a way to inform the public in those terms about the facts of GM on both sides . . . we were more than happy to engage as much as possible . . . as it progressed we had some doubts about the way it was done to start off with, at a very basic level, we were a bit worried about the title of the whole thing which was *GM Nation?* . . . almost yes or no which was never what it was going to be about.

Another observed:

> 'We don't do the stand-up town hall debates where you are just shouted at and you shout at them . . . it achieves nothing I think . . . the initial idea of the debate was to educate the public.'

Some expressed a concern with how government would reconcile the 'emotional data' generated by the debate with the 'hard' data from the science review and the economic strand. While one interviewee accepted that a decision on commercialisation could not be made solely on 'the science' alone and that ethical and broader social factors needed to be taken into account, most took the view that firm leadership was needed from government, based on rationality and science.

The reference to 'emotion' seemed to be linked with a perception that the public were unlikely to come to the debate with a great deal of relevant knowledge about GM crops. Indeed, the majority of the public were seen to be largely ignorant of agricultural issues. Such knowledge was regarded as a necessary prerequisite for a sensible and mature debate. Indeed, without a suitable 'firebreak' between what were regarded as 'opinions' and 'facts', debates of this sort were seen to have the potential to damage the standing of UK science.

The stimulus materials produced to inform the debate were seen as having been adversely affected by being insufficiently based on hard science, and including too much material that our interviewees regarded as often unsubstantiated 'mere opinion'. Some suggested it was unfortunate that data from the science review were not used to inform the stimulus material. As one interviewee commented:

> As I say that's why I go back to this opinion versus fact . . . I'm not saying all the facts are on our side, but it would have been far better if the stimulus material had generated discussion on factually tested experience . . . peer based [sic] science.

Turning to the debate process itself, a number of concerns were expressed. First, the branding of the debate as *GM Nation?* was regarded as implying a polar 'yes or no' answer to commercialisation. Some suggested that this message implied the privileging of one type of agriculture over another, so failing to convey the idea that co-existence of different kinds of agricultural production was a real possibility. Second, it was regarded as generally unlikely that 'ordinary people' would have the inclination, or feel sufficiently strongly about the issues, to attend public meetings. However, this problem was seen as being compounded by the style in which the debate was organised, and the criticisms by anti-GM pressure groups along the lines that public participation would make no difference to the final government decision. In this way the general public were seen as being discouraged from participation, thus allowing certain engaged groups to monopolise events.

The experience of a number of our interviewees who had attended some of the debate's public meetings, tended to reinforce this view that these events were dominated by people with pre-existing committed views on this issue. One company representative reflected on their sense of isolation at one of the meetings: 'I don't think I've ever felt so lonely in all my life.'

Another spoke for a number of our interviewees who had attended these meetings: 'I think my personal opinion was the anti groups were just sort of there to flood these meetings and make sure that lots of people were there saying very negative things.'

The Tier 1 events were described as a process of 'let's look at opinions and then decide which one we like'. It was suggested that far greater opportunity should have been available for participants to interact with invited speakers who held evidence-based views. All of our interviewees regarded the overwhelming majority of participants in the Tier 1 events as holding clear anti-GM views, which formed part of a wider worldview of perspectives and commitments. As one interviewee commented:

I went along expecting there to be . . . a few more people from universities or academic groups and I was really surprised by the number of people there who were obviously very anti the science, and indeed I believe the majority of people I spoke to there were anti the science full stop, and then when you talk to them about it they were actually anti big companies and globalisation and everything else so I don't think you were going to get a balanced debate from meetings like that.

However, these strong views were regarded by some as being an extreme expression of a more widespread lack of trust in industry, as indicated in the following extract:

I think we find it very difficult to do because we are very distant from the consumer basically . . . I mean our audience in the past has been regulators and farmers more than consumers . . . I think a lot of consumer trust sits in the area of supermarkets and probably less these days with scientists . . . whether it's industry scientists or academic scientists or government scientists, I think there is a leaning more to trusting the farmer but I think it's difficult for industry at the moment because industry isn't a very positive word.

Environmental and consumer pressure groups

In common with the industry interviewees, all of the environmental and consumer pressure group representatives that we interviewed welcomed the idea of direct public participation in decision-making processes. However, reservations were expressed about the particular way in which *GM Nation?* was implemented, and the extent to which government was genuine in wishing to involve the lay public in the decision-making process over possible commercialisation. One campaigner observed:

our supporters . . . I don't even think they were even aware of what the aims were or that there were aims . . . I think there was just a whole load of confusion . . . I don't even think people knew why they were being asked to get involved, so I think people got involved out of an enormous sense of frustration that there's a huge groundswell of public opinion and they feel that the government just isn't listening.

The lack of what was regarded as a clear, meaningful aim or objective for the debate gave the impression to our interviewees that the debate suffered from a mismatch between different objectives. There was considerable suspicion about government motives, because the government was perceived to be 'pro-GM' and sympathetic to the biotechnology industry. This perception led to a certain scepticism about government claims about wanting a 'full and open debate'. Two typical views are captured in the following statements:

I'm sure that's where a lot of the mistrust comes from . . . you hear Margaret Beckett saying 'we want to hear everybody's voices' and then what you actually get is the COI with a really restricted budget . . . and the reality just doesn't match the rhetoric, then people become suspicious and if you set about saying that your aim is to hear everybody in the country . . . their process designed just didn't match what they said they tried to achieve.

I don't think it's done anything to make people think that the government is . . . taking into account people's fears . . . I think they might think they're doing it to gather information, so they can manipulate policy, but I don't think people believe that the government is doing it so they . . . can do what the public want.

Interestingly, despite a general enthusiasm for public involvement, some reservations were expressed about incorporating into public policy the views of people who 'didn't care about the issues', or who had not been 'immersed in the issues'. The following interviewee seemed concerned that people would not take the opportunity to register their views seriously:

I think they also feel this thing about being asked for their opinion is a sideshow actually . . . there's no interest in their opinion . . . we already know we've had MORI polls, the supermarkets have acted, everybody knows that there's huge concern, and people are against it, and so the only sort of logical conclusion that people come to is that the government have made a choice about who they're actually listening to, so it shows how they weight the value of the arguments.

In response to suggestions (such as those advanced by the company interviewees above) that the public meetings were dominated by anti-GM voices, one campaigner commented: 'It's unfair to then say "we've only heard from the usual suspects" . . . "usual suspects" creates a perception that people who had an opinion were somehow tainted.'

Many criticisms were expressed about the practical implementation of the debate process. The timescale of the public component of the debate was seen as simply not providing enough time for community groups and individuals to organise local meetings. One campaigner commented that:

six weeks is not a lot of time for anybody really to arrange a decent meeting, and in fact we're still getting invited to meetings now . . . there are still meetings going on, where obviously the results are not going to be able to feed into the debate . . . so I think people found that very, very, frustrating.

The debate's budget was regarded as insufficient to allow an adequate number of events, and this was seen as failing to match the 'government's rhetoric'. Nonetheless, the Steering Board was commended for being able to organise a debate on the scale that it did, despite a shortage of funding.

In common with the company representatives, considerable concerns were expressed about the stimulus material. Indeed, one prominent campaigning organisation had advised its members not to use this material. It was suggested that perhaps a period of piloting the stimulus material, together with the event formats, may have enabled positive changes to be made. One campaigner observed: 'Just from talking to people who have either arranged meetings or been to meetings . . . they've not thought very much of the materials, a few people felt they were well, just not detailed enough, slightly biased even.'

There were considerable criticisms of the Steering Board's main contractors across a range of practical issues. One campaigner observed:

> we had an email from the COI came round one day . . . telling us there
> was actually going to be a meeting in London the following weekend, in
> a week's time . . . and then I just happened to phone COI about something
> else, and they said 'have you been told about the meeting in London?',
> I said 'yes it's a week on Saturday', and they said 'no it's on Saturday',
> and we'd been sent an out-of-date press release with the wrong date on
> it, so we had twenty-four hours notice . . . you know just incredible.

Despite these concerns, some campaigners felt that there was a sense that the debate had generated widespread discussion across the country among a relatively large number of lay people:

> I think it has been worthwhile, but I think one of the things it's done
> is to reignite [*sic*] a very vibrant debate . . . around the country, people
> have been debating this issue for a very long time, and it was almost as
> if *GM Nation?* hi-jacked that debate . . . you know people have been
> talking about this issue for many years.

However, interviewees were clear that the form in which *GM Nation?* was implemented did not provide a template for future such public debates:

> I personally would be horrified if this was a platform for decision-making
> in the future . . . absolutely horrified . . . completely unsustainable as a
> way of holding debates but also making decisions . . . because people
> won't engage again and again in a process like this.

The views of expert commentators

One of the PDSB's 'indicators of success' (BIII) recognised the need to take account of the views of 'informed commentators'. As we have already noted in Chapter 2, it is unfortunate that the Steering Board did not specify which individuals or organisations might constitute 'informed commentators', since any attempt to measure performance according to this indicator is clearly subject to interpretative flexibility. We recognise that a number of the representatives of stakeholder organisations, the views of whom we have reported here, could reasonably be described as 'informed'. We will therefore take these views into account when we consider in Chapter 9 how the debate performed against this criterion.

Conclusions

In this chapter we have addressed a range of themes concerned with how the *GM Nation?* debate was regarded within British society. We recognise that among the disengaged lay public, awareness of the debate was low. When informed about the debate, there was considerable support for the general notion of a public debate, yet this was tempered by scepticism about the likely impact of the GM debate on government policy. Our examination of media coverage of the debate revealed a modest and uneven level of reporting coverage. Interestingly, we found that despite ostensible differences in terms of the style of multiple media vehicles, important underlying similarities existed in the framing and 'dramatic structure' of corresponding accounts. These drew upon existing framings of GM-related issues, together with contemporaneous development, such as the Iraq war. It could be argued that the resulting patterns of coverage contained a certain hostility to the introduction of agricultural GM technologies. Our discussion of the media also addressed the rise of the internet as part of the media environment, and some of the opportunities and difficulties these changes present for the future conduct of public debates. Finally, we examined the views of a number of key stakeholder organisations, which revealed a diverse range of perspectives on the debate and associated issues, despite their apparent unanimity over the value of the initiative. We return to these themes in the final chapter.

9   Conclusions

In this final chapter we bring the story of the GM debate, and our evaluation of it, to a close. In Chapter 2 we discussed our methodological approach to carrying out this evaluation, and in Chapter 3 described how we implemented that approach, as the multi-stage process that constituted the debate unfolded in time. How well this approach to evaluation worked is, itself, something that needs to be discussed here. Chapter 3 also contained a diagram which showed how subsequent chapters would address the three sets of criteria against which we evaluated the debate's performance. Having examined these findings, it now remains for us to draw some conclusions, and to consider whether it is possible to identify a number of general lessons, or at least suggestions, for future engagement practice.

The politics of the debate

Soon after the conclusion of the debate, the British government decided to give commercialisation of GM crops in Britain a selective and tentative go-ahead. In her statement to the House of Commons on 9 March 2004, the then Secretary of State for Environment, Food and Rural Affairs, Mrs Margaret Beckett stated: 'I have concluded that [the government] should agree in principle to the commercial cultivation of GM herbicide tolerant maize, but only subject to two further important conditions.'

These conditions related to the EU food marketing conditions that such crops can only be grown as monitored trials, and that further environmental assessments need to be conducted prior to further approval. This regime emphasises that every authorisation is done on a crop-by-crop basis. Finally, there will be a liability region in place that places the burden of proof and payment upon the GM producer not to 'contaminate' non-GM crops in the vicinity.

The government rejected oilseed rape and beet species on the basis of evidence from the biodiversity field trials. However, in the light of uncertainty about the legal liability regime, the company promoting the species of maize that had gained approval withdrew the product from the market-place. At the time of writing, as we understand it, the British government does not anticipate GM crops being grown commercially in Britain until 2008 at the earliest. In political terms, it has been suggested that *GM Nation?* failed to take the political heat out of the issue (Gaskell, 2004). So it seems reasonable to ask: what was achieved by the debate?

Earlier we noted that Britain's membership of the EU imposes certain obligations regarding the licensing of crops, and that EU rulings have made clear that 'GM free zones' are illegal under EU law. We also recognised that the threatened WTO action by the US, Canada and Argentina had led to a preliminary ruling against the EU. As we completed the manuscript of this book, a final ruling was still awaited. So, given the extent to which British government action is constrained by international obligations on the issue of GM crop cultivation, serious doubts arise about whether the result of the *GM Nation?* debate could reasonably have had a substantive impact on UK domestic policy and EU regulatory practice. It will be recalled that the capacity of an engagement exercise to influence policy is one of the normative criteria of effectiveness used in our evaluation, and is one commonly identified within the evaluation literature (see Rowe and Frewer, 2004). Of course, the political and regulatory context that constrained the possible influence of the debate also provided a component of the backdrop to the UK government's decision to approve the debate in the first place. This observation raises interesting questions concerning the government's motivation for holding the debate. A full analysis of the political dynamics underlying this decision goes beyond the brief of this book (but see e.g. Toke, 2004; Walls *et al.*, 2005a). However, it is important for us to consider whether this political context had any detectable influence on the practice of the debate. We will return to this matter.

If lay opinion had been unequivocally, and overwhelmingly, hostile to GM agriculture, would the government have approved any of these crops? *Could* it have taken this decision in the absence of a basis in 'sound science'? Interestingly, as we have noted, our survey indicated that some 40 per cent of respondents tended to agree (with a quarter agreeing strongly) with the statement that, irrespective of whether a debate occurred or not, international influences would determine Britain's GM future. It therefore seems likely that many potential participants had some doubts about the credibility of the debate.

It is quite possible that the debate had some kind of impact, somewhere, on policy, but is not at all clear where this influence has occurred, or may still occur. Such doubts about the nature of *GM Nation?* take us back to our early thoughts, mentioned in Chapter 2, about the ambiguity in what the government seemed to expect of the debate in the first place. Was it, we mused, designed to be an exercise in communication, possibly seeking to persuade the lay public; or a consultation exercise that sought to chart lay views as they stood; or an attempt to engage with, and involve the lay public in a decision process; or a way of assisting government in developing future practice and policy?

Seen with the benefit of hindsight, and in view of the criticisms about credibility mentioned above, one might argue that the most valuable function that was played by the debate was as an *experiment in engagement*: a 'laboratory' with considerable learning potential about how best to organise and implement such processes in the future. As we have seen, the picture that emerges from our evaluation exercise is that, to the extent that *GM Nation?* may, indeed, be described as 'an engagement process', it was flawed in a number of important ways. We will summarise these shortcomings, together with the occasional successes of the debate, in the following section.

Before we proceed, it is important to recognise that the GM debate encountered severe difficulties that had the potential to compromise its effectiveness. First, the organisation and form of the debate were shaped by a number of external constraints, largely beyond the control of the organisers. Of prime importance here were practical challenges posed by three inter-related factors: the novelty and scale of the enterprise, the heavily constrained availability of resources and severe time pressures. Without a clear template for how best to organise such an initiative, the process of implementing the debate itself became a learning exercise. This inevitably resulted in inefficiencies and tensions. In addition, there was a failure by government at an early stage to appreciate what would be required, in terms of time and resources, in order to allow the debate to be implemented effectively. In an ironic twist, the very agency that advised government on the initial budget (namely COI) was the one appointed as the main contractor and executive body, and which went on to encounter the problems arising from its own under-estimate. This shortage of funds led to the Steering Board having to seek additional funding from government: a process that created additional tensions, and additional time and management pressures.

Second, and unsurprisingly, a great deal of politicking affected, one might say 'afflicted', the debate. It was, after all, a fairly new experiment in 'extending democracy', and about an issue that was hotly contested not only within British society but, it would appear, within the government itself. While the *realpolitik* of the process may be an inevitable part of attempts to implement engagement initiatives, this is not reflected to a significant degree within the evaluation account we have produced. Is this not an important omission? It is certainly not due to any lack of awareness on our part that this aspect of the debate took place. Neither does it reflect any wish to ignore the very real difficulties that we recognise a number of the key actors in the debate encountered. Rather, it arises from limits to the capability of evaluation instruments at our disposal, and horizons to our degree of access to 'backstage' zones where political manoeuvrings underlying the debate process were taking place. It also reflects a resolute commitment on our part to a methodological indifference to the outcome of the debate, and to a stance of neutrality with respect to the various interests involved.

Having expressed these reservations, we recognise that a number of our interview respondents made strong claims to the effect that the *realpolitik* of the debate had a concrete influence on the practicalities of its implementation. Given the nature of these claims, and the possible implications for the practicability of running effective public engagement processes in the future, we feel that we need to at least make some observations about these claims, and about the strength of evidence supporting them. As we understand it, three kinds of claims were made. In broad terms, these may be summarised as:

- the government's commitment to take the results of the debate seriously when deciding policy was a hollow one;
- there was resistance in government to provide the PDSB with a sufficiently independent role to ensure a 'genuinely deep debate' took place;
- there was day-to-day manipulation in the implementation of the debate process.

We will discuss these briefly in turn. First, we consider the suggestion that the government had no intention of allowing the debate to influence policy. As our evaluation made clear, many participants in the debate were sympathetic to this sentiment. Indeed, we used the word 'sceptical' to describe the view of most participants regarding the *Influence* criterion. We are not able to comment further, other than to report on the decisions about GM cultivation that the government made following the debate, and to observe that the extent of the debate's influence on these decisions is not known.

Regarding the second category of claim, we first recall that in Chapter 1 we reported that some members of the PDSB saw the debate as an opportunity to open up the 'sound science' basis for regulatory procedures within agricultural biotechnology to critical scrutiny. In particular, there was a commitment here to draw upon a 'social and political framing' critique of risk assessment practice. Some respondents told us that there was resistance within the government machinery to include such regulatory matters within the brief for the debate. We have no way of corroborating these claims, but recognise it as plausible that some such resistance existed, given the pivotal role of 'sound science'-based regulatory procedures within the EU and beyond.

In many ways this might be seen as a 'definitional' matter; and defining what the debate was to be about, and what was to be excluded was perhaps inevitably a political matter. However, a central aspect of the debate was that the *lay public* should define the terms in which the debate would be conducted. This was the function of the Foundation Discussion workshops. We have discussed in Chapter 7 how we assessed this process as being an effective one, but went on to recognise the shortcomings in how that framing information was incorporated into subsequent stages of the debate process. Now it seems unlikely that the lay public would identify technical aspects of the GM regulatory system as topics for discussion. So this category of claim regarding *realpolitik* would seem to be in some way either critical of the idea of the lay public framing the terms of the debate, or of the failure of subsequent stages of the debate to address these regulatory issues. This latter suggestion brings us to the third category of claim.

That third category of claim, namely a suggestion of day-to-day interference in the execution of the debate, chimes with a matter raised in Chapter 3 – namely, the regular meetings between COI and a member of the PDSB (who was also a government official), which came to light sometime during the debate process. These meetings were ostensibly concerned with ensuring value-for-money in the implementation of the debate. In Chapter 3 we made clear that we found no evidence to suggest that these meetings resulted in manipulation of the debate by government. However, we found that some members of the PDSB *did* believe that such manipulation was taking place via this mechanism. Does this make any sense? Well, in Chapter 1 we noted that the 'social and political framing' critique of 'sound science' is associated with a radical critique of the social relations of science and technology. It is, therefore, conceivable that attempts to ensure such critical perspectives were included in the debate's deliberations might themselves have been regarded in some quarters as amounting to a 'political agenda'. In such circumstances, one can imagine that various attempts to resist this perceived agenda might be made.

We have no way of verifying any of these claims. In such circumstances it is important to examine the evidence that we have, and to compare the support to be found within that evidence for different interpretations of what went on. On balance, we find much more compelling evidence for the shortcomings of the debate being primarily attributable to a 'mess' model rather than a 'conspiracy' one. In circumstances where the debate was starved of resources and under huge time pressure, and where its executive were at the time struggling to cope with a set of unfamiliar and challenging practical problems, it is hardly surprising that things went awry. Of course politicking went on, and in ways that involved people on all 'sides' of the debate. In the real world such things do happen. Indeed, initiatives such as public debates will tend to be concerned with contentious matters, and the presence of politicking will be inevitable. Arguably, in such circumstances, there is an even more urgent need for rigorous evaluation of the debate process.

In the following sections, we first summarise our findings on the performance of the debate. We then discuss some lessons of a methodological nature about the evaluation of engagement processes. Finally, we draw on the experience of evaluating the *GM Nation?* debate in order to address a number of practical considerations regarding the implementation of future engagement initiatives.

The effectiveness of the debate

In this section we summarise our findings from the evaluation exercise according to the three sets of criteria we adopted: normative, sponsors' and participants'. We also outline the debate's performance against the emergent criterion of 'translation quality'.

Performance against normative criteria

Generally speaking, the debate's performance in terms of 'universal' criteria of the fairness and competence of an engagement exercise was mixed, combining some good features with areas of considerable weakness.

The debate's degree of *representativeness* (N1), which we discussed in Chapter 5, was one of the weaker areas of performance. Those participating in the open debate events were significantly different from the lay public in terms of both their demographic and socio-economic profiles, and their range of attitudes about GM crops and food. In terms of the debate's capacity to reflect wider views about GM crops and food, a number of the key conclusions of the debate, particularly regarding the widespread levels of concern about the risks of this technology and the need for independent regulation, were broadly mirrored by our survey findings. However, our analysis also suggests that the extent of outright opposition to GM food and crops among the UK population is probably lower than indicated in the *GM Nation?* findings.

The debate's *influence* (N5) on policy, which we discussed briefly in the previous section, is not fully known. We also noted the extent to which the central issue being debated, namely the possible commercialisation of GM crops in the UK, was a matter in which government policy is heavily constrained by international obligations. In this sense, there were severe limits on the debate's capacity to perform well against this criterion. Although the government gave a firm commitment about taking the results of the debate into account when making a decision on possible GM commercialisation, many debate participants expressed cynicism about the government's position. Of course, the debate took place in a political context that had resulted in relatively low trust in the Prime Minister and the government. We found strong evidence that participants were not convinced that the debate would have an impact on policy. The message for government here appears to be fairly clear: people need to feel that the exercise is a meaningful one.

In Chapter 4, we considered the remaining six normative criteria. In terms of *independence* (N2) the debate performed well, however, some qualifications are necessary. The management of the debate was indeed independent, or perhaps more accurately, at 'arm's length' from government. However, the behaviour of government was possibly quite important in shaping the perception of the debate. Therefore, government 'body language' as well as its 'bottom line' role as paymaster provides an important consideration here. The timing of the debate with regard to the farm-scale evaluations was one example of a possible insensitivity to public perceptions. The ambiguity in government statements about the debate's overall purpose was another such potential source of influence on how the debate was regarded by potential participants. We concur with two key conclusions found by the Select Committee inquiry into the conduct of the debate: namely, that it was underfunded and too rushed. Both these important factors point to the role of government as the ultimate sponsor, and 'owner' of the debate, and raises the question of what lessons can be learned by government about its role in influencing such initiatives.

The criterion of *early involvement* (N3) was an area where the debate performed poorly. Respondents to our questionnaires indicated that they were fairly cynical about whether government had organised the debate in time to influence policy. A clear majority of participants in all component parts of the debate took the view that the debate had been held too late to have such an influence. This criterion is concerned with the perceptions of participants regarding their involvement. We might add that the design of the debate process as a whole, including as it did the *Foundation Discussion workshops*, provided an early opportunity for lay views to shape the terms in which the issues in question would be considered. While this feature of the debate process was an innovative one, and excellent in principle, we found that it was rather less satisfactory in practice. Our discussion in Chapter 7 of the debate's handling of information and knowledge is of particular relevance here.

Turning now to the question of *transparency* (N4), we conclude that the debate was generally poor in providing participants with a sense of what was going on, or how decisions were being made. There is a connection here with the issue of knowledge management, mentioned above. Participants in debate events (and those interacting with its website) were encouraged to provide views and comments, but it was rarely clear what would be done with this information. Similarly, against the criterion of *resources* (N7) the debate performed poorly. We have discussed the shortcomings of the stimulus materials in detail. In addition, the public events, in particular Tier 1, were characterised by a shortage of time necessary to fully deliberate on all the issues in question, and for the organisers to collect the corresponding views and arguments. As already noted, it is questionable whether the financial resources supplied by government, even after the PDSB's appeal for additional funding, were sufficient to run the debate effectively.

Performance against the two remaining criteria, *task definition* (N6), and *structured dialogue* (N8), varied from poor to good, according to the specific component part of the debate being considered. The Foundation Discussion workshops presented a difficulty for the former criterion, as there was a methodological wish to avoid 'pre-framing' in order for them to be effective. In these events participants sometimes were a little confused over what they were expected to do, whereas with the three open tiers of public meetings, and with the 'Narrow-but-Deep' process, participants were clear about their immediate tasks, but sometimes vague about the wider relevance of these activities. The Narrow-but-Deep process probably came closest to being 'deliberative' in the dictionary sense, however even this was quite strictly prescribed in format by the facilitators.

Performance against the sponsors' criteria

Here we consider both the debate Steering Board's *objectives*, and its subsequent list of *indicators*. There is a certain degree of overlap with the normative criteria considered above, namely with the *grassroots to participate* (B2) and *impact of government* (BIV) criteria, and the comments above apply. The question of *public framing* (B1), also mentioned above, which was a specific criterion, or rather requirement, set by the Steering Board, is considered in the discussion of knowledge-handling/*translation quality*. The criteria *views of participants* (BII) and *opportunities to register views* (B5b) overlap with our examination of participants' (implicit) criteria, discussed in Chapter 6, and summarised below.

The criterion that the debate should create *widespread awareness* (B5a) was addressed directly by the data gathered by our survey instrument. As reported in Chapter 8, we found that a clear majority (over 70 per cent) of the general public had never heard of the debate, with only 3 per cent saying they knew a 'fair amount' or 'a lot' about it. We noted that, seen in a positive light, our data suggest that a sizeable minority of the British adult population had to some extent been made aware of the debate's existence. Given the relative lack of advertising, and of tabloid and television coverage of the debate, this figure might be regarded as representing a modest success. Nevertheless, we conclude that the debate only partially met this objective.

In our discussion of the sponsors' criteria in Chapter 2, we described a number as 'pseudo' criteria in the sense that they concern 'tick-box' functional requirements rather than issues where the quality of performance can be sensibly measured. These are mostly addressed by the findings in Chapter 4 concerning process issues. We will consider them briefly here.

The first such criterion, *new opportunities for deliberation* (B3), was satisfied in some sense by virtue of the debate having taken place. However, in a more technical sense, most of the debate process was not, strictly speaking, 'deliberative' in nature. In other words, very little of the debate processes amounted to 'careful consideration with a view to decision' or 'the consideration and discussion for and against a measure' (*Shorter Oxford Dictionary*, 1973). Similarly, while the debate did indeed provide an opportunity to engage in *dialogue with experts* (B4a) (in places), to receive *access to evidence* (B4b), to allow *interactions between members of the public* (B6a) and *mutual learning* (B6b) between public and experts, therefore allowing these criteria to be satisfied in formal terms, as we have seen the associated quality of these activities was mostly low.

There were three further such 'pseudo' criteria. First, the Steering Board expressed a wish that the debate should *complement and inform the science and economics strands* (B7). While this did take place in a limited way, as we discussed in Chapter 7, the debate made practically no use of the outputs from these other strands of the 'GM dialogue'. Second, the objective that the debate should serve to *'calibrate' views* (B8) (which we understood as 'situate and compare') of hitherto engaged stakeholders against those of other participants of the debate, while good in conception, proved problematic in execution. Here, in particular, we draw attention to our analysis of the shortcomings of the analysis leading to the Steering Board's final report. The delivery of this report did, however, formally satisfy the criterion *report to government* (B9).

There is one final sponsor criterion for consideration, namely whether the *views of informed commentators* (BIII) indicate that the debate was a success. The Board envisaged such commentators advising on:

- whether the debate had been credible, innovative and balanced;
- whether the process had moved the (existing) debate beyond polarisation;
- how satisfactory had been the preparation and content of the debate report.

As we have already noted, the PDSB unfortunately did not specify which individuals or organisations might constitute 'informed commentators'. Therefore, any attempt to measure performance according to this indicator is subject to interpretative flexibility. However, on the basis of our understanding of the sentiments underlying this indicator, we suspect that 'informed commentators' might reasonably be identified as academic researchers and other independent observers, whose interest in the debate extends beyond the specific considerations of the GM issue. In other words, these are individuals who are in a position to comment intelligently and even-handedly on the implementation of the debate as a process.

In view of the fact that the PDSB appointed us as independent evaluators of the debate, we assume that what we have to say in this report will go some way towards informing a judgement on the debate's performance according to this indicator. We have already noted that when we published our evaluation report on the debate (Horlick-Jones *et al.*, 2004), we organised a workshop, at which our evaluation work formed the focus of a wide-ranging discussion. Participants in this workshop included leading academic specialists in deliberative and participation processes, members of the PDSB, and representatives of the debate's executive and of a wide range of stakeholder organisations. In preparing this book, we have done our best to take into account the views expressed at that workshop, together with other communications received, and related publications.

Performance against the participants' criteria

In Chapter 6 we discussed how we inferred a range of criteria representing participants' expectations from data gathered at Tier 1 meetings. We found a number of areas of overlap with the normative criteria. Our analysis also provided some sense of the strength of feeling expressed by participants about these criteria. We found that the process of the debate – in terms of both *fair process* (similar to *structured dialogue*, N8) and *availability of resources* (criterion N7) – was described negatively by large numbers of respondents. There was also clear concern about the *representativeness* (or lack thereof) of participants (also criteria N1 and B2), and the potential *influence* of the events (N5 and BIV). The criterion of *timely involvement* (similar to N3) also appeared relevant to some, while issues related to the normative criteria of *transparency* (N4) and *independence* (N2) appeared to be incorporated within the participants' *fair process* criterion.

In comparison with the sponsors' criteria, we also found some similarities; most notably between the participants' *learning* criterion and the sponsors' criterion B6 (although for the participants, the important issue was what *they* had learned). Furthermore, there is some similarity between the participants' criterion and the sponsors' B5b criterion (concerning participants registering views), but also to some degree with B6 (stating that there should be 'interaction' as well as mutual learning) and B4 (dialogue with experts) – all of which imply that participation is a good thing in its own right. Indeed, we identified two criteria, which we termed *social reassurance* and *enlightenment*, which seem to indicate that participants welcomed the process of engagement in itself. In both respects, participants were generally fairly positive about the Tier 1 meetings – to a greater extent than they were regarding the other criteria.

Performance in terms of translation quality

In Chapter 7 we described how we concluded that what we term 'translation quality' is an important consideration in the evaluation of engagement processes. We regard this as an important finding of the evaluation exercise. We recognise that considerable work is needed to develop specific instruments and procedures in order to assess translation quality in ways more systematic than the simple narrative approach that we have adopted here.

Our analysis reveals that the performance of the debate was flawed in terms of this new criterion. In essence, the gains from good initial work in identifying public framings of GM issues were steadily eroded throughout the subsequent stages of the debate process. These framings were first transformed into stimulus materials that were rather bland, which failed to capture the contextual relevance of its sources, and which were, in any case, largely ignored by participants in the debate. Indeed, it was not at all clear to what extent these materials informed the deliberations that took place in the public meetings or Narrow-but-Deep groups, or their significance to those encountering the debate website. Furthermore, attempts to capture the richness of such deliberations were largely restricted to a small number of closed questions in the 'feedback' questionnaire, which focused on ratings of a number of pre-assigned attributes of GM. Arguably these somewhat limited data were then over-interpreted by a small number of time-pressured individuals during the process of producing the debate's final report.

After the final report was published, we note that additional translation mechanisms, in particular provided by the media (discussed in Chapter 8), politicians and pressure groups, rendered new possible understandings of what the debate had to say.

A summary of our findings

To conclude this section, we suggest that in the light of our findings the debate could reasonably be described in the following terms:

- The debate process was undermined by poorly drafted aims and objectives.
- It was methodologically innovative, though doubt might be cast on whether the budget was spent most effectively, and much of the debate process was not, strictly speaking, 'deliberative' in nature.
- A brave attempt was made to implement the objective of allowing the public to frame the terms of the debate, however, this was flawed by a far from perfect series of 'translations' of information between stages of the debate process.
- Stimulus materials produced specially for the debate were bland and unsatisfactory.
- There was a failure to engage with the broad mass of hitherto disengaged members of the lay public.
- The debate's component parts were meaningful and enjoyable for most participants, and meetings forming part of the debate were professionally facilitated. However, too little notice was given for public meetings, and stimulus materials were not available in advance. At these public meetings the stimulus materials made available were often largely ignored by participants.
- The preparation of the Steering Board's final report on the debate was over-hasty and under-resourced, and featured a methodologically inadequate analysis of the findings.
- A number of the key conclusions of the debate, particularly regarding the widespread levels of concern about the risks of this technology and the need for independent regulation, were broadly mirrored by our survey findings. However, our analysis also suggests that the extent of outright opposition to GM food and crops among the UK population is probably lower than indicated in the *GM Nation?* findings.
- In policy terms, it is not at all clear how the findings were used in the government's decision-making process, or what was the relative weight given to the debate in comparison with other factors.

Some methodological lessons from the evaluation exercise

So far, we have focused upon a number of aspects of the performance of the debate. Of course, this assessment relies upon the quality of the data we have gathered, and of the methods we used to acquire those data. With this assumption in mind, we now turn to a discussion of possible lessons of a methodological nature that we need to learn from the experience of evaluating the debate.

The first issue we consider is whether the normative framework was 'appropriate'. As discussed in the earlier chapters, there is no widely accepted evaluation framework and associated criteria. We chose to use one (of a limited number) of frameworks (see Rowe and Frewer, 2000), which has nine effectiveness criteria, although we only considered eight of these, and reformulated some of these slightly. It is clear that these were not completely appropriate for the evaluation of *all* of the processes within *GM Nation?*. They were originally formulated to address 'participation' exercises, yet some components of the debate, in particular the Foundation Discussion workshops, were public 'consultation' rather than 'participation' processes (cf. Rowe and Frewer, 2005), and hence ought to have been evaluated against different criteria. Nevertheless, we were not dogmatic in our implementation of these criteria, and were selective in our use and interpretation of these for the 'non-participatory' elements. Recognising potential limits to validation, we used two other sets of criteria in our evaluation – one from the sponsors, and one from participants. The overlap between these three sets suggests that the normative criteria were appropriate (at least for evaluating parts of the process), with the criteria of 'representativeness' and 'influence' being common across all three sets.

The next question we need to ask is: was the normative framework 'comprehensive'? We suggest that the normative criteria were to some degree valid, but clearly not comprehensive. Both the sponsors and the participants had additional criteria that they considered important in assessing the quality of the debate's processes. For the sponsors there were various functional requirements that needed to be attained; for the participants, learning and socialisation requirements were important. Our evaluation project has suggested that the normative criteria ought to be expanded, and further consideration should be given on when and whether each criterion is relevant. We suggest that our evaluation strategy as a whole allowed omissions to be identified and corrected. The one criterion that did not naturally emerge from our multi-criteria-set approach was that of 'translation quality' – a criterion that we were only able to identify after contact with the process, and from viewing the debate as a whole and from the outside. We suggest that our commitment to conduct a structured evaluation, and yet at the same time remain open to identifying alternative influences on effectiveness and wider issues, is an appropriate analytic stance with which to approach the difficult issue of evaluation of engagement processes.

One further issue concerns the quality of data itself. Much of this came from ethnographic monitoring, the use of participant questionnaires, and the MORI survey. We have described how we developed a protocol to ensure that different observers would attend to a common 'checklist' of issues, while not constraining their capacity to capture new ideas. Given the highly complex and uncontrolled nature of engagement approaches, there are no standardised, validated questionnaires to measure effectiveness. As such, we adopted and amended instruments used previously and 'validated' only in a rather informal sense. We have discussed the survey method in detail elsewhere (Pidgeon *et al.*, 2005). Importantly, by using a multi-method approach, we did not rely entirely upon any one method or set of data. We found that the results from these different datasets did generally give a consistent message about the different debate processes, so providing additional confidence about the overall validity of our findings.

In Chapter 3 we discussed a number of practical difficulties we encountered in implementing our evaluation exercise (see also Rowe *et al.*, 2005). We recognise that these arose from: our relatively late appointment as accredited evaluators; the structural nature of our relationship with the sponsors and their executive; the general experimental and untidy nature of the debate process; and the need for our data collection to be as unobtrusive as possible. One clear finding arising from this experience is that any future such engagement initiative should include an independent process of evaluation as part of its design and planning from its earliest stages. The other conclusion for would-be evaluators is to recognise that the practical implementation of a process of evaluation of this nature will almost inevitably entail the frustrations of working under multiple constraints. It will also necessitate a not inconsiderable amount of time and effort in order to maintain good working relations with the engagement sponsors, and those involved in implementing the process in question.

Some practical considerations for future engagement initiatives

On the basis of the experience of *GM Nation?*, it is possible to identify a number of areas where the organisation of a public debate of this nature might be improved. We have already discussed the key role of evaluation. Here, we outline some additional early conclusions and considerations arising from our evaluation of the GM debate, which we suggest are of more general relevance for future practice. In the final section of this chapter we will turn to wider questions about the role of deliberative engagement with stakeholders and the lay public in public policy development and decision-making.

Evidence of popular support for public debates

Our evaluation work provided evidence on how the GM debate was viewed by the lay public, and how the general idea of such a debate was received. On the question of its value, the debate attracted rather mixed views. On the one hand, people felt that the debate was a good way for the public to get more involved in making decisions about the complex issue of commercialisation of agricultural biotechnology. However, despite clear support for the debate itself, people were fairly sceptical about its impact. Many people felt that what would happen to GM agriculture was a foregone conclusion, because the government had already made up its mind on this matter, and also because 'in the end European and International Laws will determine what will happen'.

As reported in Chapter 8, our survey suggested that the lay public felt generally positive about public involvement exercises such as *GM Nation?*. It appeared that an overwhelming majority (77 per cent) of those surveyed took the view that public debates would be useful in the context of other new developments in science and technology. Clearly such apparent support is an important consideration for government. Of course, in generally approving of the notion of a public debate, respondents provided no firm commitment to participating in such initiatives. Neither did they consider the likely costs of such debates. Nevertheless, there appears to be a general sympathy for public examination of 'the facts' about such developments.

The management of public debates

In planning future public debates, there will be a need to carefully consider the organisational and practical aspects of their implementation. After all, a design might be elegant on paper, but how straightforward is it to put into practice? In this section and the following one, we consider questions regarding the workability of the process design, and the administrative arrangements put in place to implement that process. First we consider management issues.

The PDSB was based upon a subset of the AEBC, with the same Chair, and with a few additional members, appointed for their special experience. Without doubt, this body possessed a great deal of relevant expertise, although, given the extent to which members of the PDSB came to be involved in the detailed implementation of the debate, it might be argued that additional skills and experience might have been desirable. It should be recalled that the AEBC was purposefully constructed so as to embody inter-stakeholder tensions on issues concerned with GM agriculture. Although the possession of differences about GM does not imply that differences will exist on the organisation of public deliberation, it seems not unreasonable to suppose that some tensions may have emerged along stakeholder lines.

The PDSB's work was supported by the AEBC secretariat, and the detailed implementation of the debate carried out by a main contractor and a small number of sub-contractors. The central role of the main contractor and executive agency was provided by COI Communications. We suggest that examining the relationship between the PDSB and its executive provides useful insights of wider relevance to the management of public debates.

First, let us recall that in Chapter 1 we discussed what we know of the circumstances in which COI (an arm's length government agency) was appointed as the chief contractor for the debate. COI undoubtedly possesses considerable expertise in communication, event organisation and related matters. In addition it possesses an extensive roster of suppliers, thus making possible the speedy appointment of sub-contractors, without going through lengthy EU procurement procedures. In the context of the time pressure on the PDSB to organise the debate, this feature appears to have been seen as a particularly important consideration. Clearly COI is part of the government apparatus, however, we found no clear evidence to suggest that any political agendas were pursued in COI's appointment or in the way in which they implemented the debate.

At the start of this chapter, we recognised a number of important constraints that threatened to compromise the debate's effectiveness, in particular regarding its scale and novelty, lack of money and shortage of time. Within this already difficult context our evaluation work revealed some additional causes of concern regarding the management and execution of the debate. These appear to have arisen as a result of an unfortunate nexus of overlapping factors:

- There was a perception among some PDSB members of a notable degree of inexperience within COI over the management of the debate exercise. In particular this concerned the organisation of local meetings, the production of stimulus materials, and slippage between stated objectives and deliverables, for example in the production of the set of 'tool-kit' resources, and the relationship between Tier 1 and local events.
- Staff at COI (who were working under huge pressure) appear to have sensed that their professional competence was being questioned by the Steering Board.
- As the day-to-day (tactical and operational) management of the debate process became increasingly unacceptable to the PDSB, members of the Board became involved in detailed planning and decision-making, by means of the establishment of an ad hoc 'Technical Advisory Group'. For some members of the Board (most of whom also had full-time jobs) this level of commitment became punishing.

The initial intention was that the PDSB would collectively provide strategic management of the debate. However, as the situation evolved, members of the Board, a number of whom certainly possessed some relevant technical skills, but most of whom were also, in some sense, representing engaged stakeholder interests, became involved in the detailed implementation of strategic decisions. Therefore, a possibly unsatisfactory ambiguity arose over the roles being played by individual members in these tactical/operational roles.

We do not feel able to comment on the extent to which this shift in management practice influenced the final form of the debate process. However, we suggest that there are important structural lessons to be learnt here for the administrative design of future such public debates. There is a clear need for adequate funding, and for a realistic time-frame for the implementation of what will, inevitably, be a complex series of interlocking tasks. In addition, there is a need for:

- the detailed implementation of the debate to be managed by an independent executive;
- the availability of a requisite set of skills at the disposal of the executive to implement a diverse and demanding programme of work.

These suggestions are predicated upon the possibility of being able to appoint such a suitable executive body, and of the existence of individuals and organisations possessing such skills and knowledge. There may be an issue of capacity-building here, and there appears a need to foster the development of such capabilities within the sphere of corporate bodies and independent organisations.

Developing a tool-kit for appropriate deliberation

We now turn to consider certain detailed aspects of the design of the debate. We have noted that the organisers placed the notion of 'framing' at the heart of its construction. We have also noted that, especially in the preparation of stimulus materials, the organisers encountered severe difficulties in seeking to strike some kind of balance between 'factual' knowledge, and knowledge of a more ethical and political nature; in other words, value-based consider-ations. The debate was novel in terms of overall design, combining a number of group-based processes, a website, and so on. Yet, as we have noted, in the absence of a robust body of design knowledge about deliberative practice on which to draw, it was also a learning process for the organisers. Clearly, it will be unsatisfactory for organisers of future public debates to 'make it up as they go along' once again. Such an approach, although well-intentioned, is accompanied by the inevitable threat of ineffectiveness and inefficient use of resources. Rather, there is a need to develop systematic knowledge that can provide clear design options.

In the context of this discussion, it is interesting to revisit the overall aim of the debate, as agreed by the PDSB (2003: 11), namely: to 'promote an innovative, effective and deliberative programme of debate on GM issues'. It has never become entirely clear to us why the PDSB felt a need to be 'innovative'. It might be argued that the adoption of this aim was something of a high-risk strategy. After all, prima facie, the use of new, unproven methods is not necessarily the best way of delivering 'information to Government . . . to inform decision-making' (ibid.: 11).

Many of the issues in question during the GM debate were essentially about risk and uncertainty, and their management, and we suggest that future decision-making about such matters can fruitfully draw upon insights from both the research and policy literature that have begun to recognise that such problems necessitate decision processes that are neither wholly technical, nor social or political but, rather, something that combines these approaches: creating a design balance between a focus on processes and techniques (Eden, 1990; Horlick-Jones and Sime, 2004). Here we have in mind social processes of negotiation providing 'thinking support' that captures the technical and material nature of the issue in question. Such processes might draw upon, for example, multi-criteria, problem structuring, and computer modelling techniques, set within group-based processes (Andersen and Jaeger, 1999; Arvai *et al.*, 2001; DETR, 2000; Horlick-Jones *et al.*, 2001; Horlick-Jones and Rosenhead, 2006; Rosenhead and Mingers, 2001; Stirling and Meyer, 1999; Yearley, 1999). Further challenges are posed by how it might be possible to relate some of these interactive approaches to more traditional science and cost benefit-based approaches to decision-making (Chilton *et al.*, 2002; Pidgeon and Gregory, 2004).

While a set of such resources has the potential to provide a 'deliberation tool-kit', there is also a need to assemble a body of design knowledge that will allow *appropriate* forms of process/technique combinations to be utilised, given the character of the problem issue. This character will reflect a host of contextual features of the matters in question, together with the specific 'signature' of the associated risk issue (Horlick-Jones, 2007; Petts *et al.*, 2001). In this way possible topics for public debate will generate a variety of 'problem patterns'. They could, for instance, be deeply contentious, but relatively well understood, such as radioactive waste disposal. Others might be novel and relatively poorly understood, such as nanotechnology.

There is a need to build up a stock of practical understanding of these design and implementation issues. Such a need points to the essential role of rigorous evaluation across a range of experiments in deliberative participation so as to assemble such a body of knowledge.

Communications

In our discussion of knowledge-handling and 'translation' processes in Chapter 7, it became clear that communications are a pivotal consideration in the organisation and implementation of an effective deliberative participatory process. In this sense, public debates constitute not only organisational systems, but also *information* systems (see also Horlick-Jones *et al.*, in press, a).

In the case of *GM Nation?*, one might say that its information system extended beyond the limits established by its organisational design. This led to relevant discussions of the issues in question not only taking place in the face-to-face meetings organised as part of the debate, but also elsewhere: in a number of radio and television current affairs programmes, and on the message boards hosted by a range of websites. These websites included those hosted by major British daily newspapers, and broadcasting organisations (the BBC site being one of the most often used and highly trusted). This recognition has important implications for the gathering of knowledge generated by debates. It also offers opportunities for the promotion of such debates.

It seems clear that the most effective promotional strategy for a future public debate would involve the 'joining up' of these three various forms of engagement (see discussion in Chapter 8). We are aware that members of the PDSB made extensive efforts to interest television companies in the GM debate. Possible models for such involvement included the BBC television's *Great Britons* series. Here a series of profiles of historical celebrities, each presented by an 'advocate', led to a public vote on who was the 'greatest Briton'. Another recent BBC series, *Restoration*, which was concerned with architectural heritage, has shown how a hitherto low-profile issue can attract public interest if presented in a suitably engaging way. This series also led to a public vote; this time on which of a number of buildings should be 'saved' from demolition. The extent that future public debates can involve hitherto disengaged sections of the lay public may ultimately turn on whether the organisers can implement such a 'joined-up' media strategy.

A deliberative future?

In Chapter 1 we considered some wider questions concerning the increasing interest in policy circles around the world for processes of *citizen engagement*. We recognised that these developments may be understood in terms of attempts by governments to establish legitimacy for potentially controversial decisions, whilst seeking to promote economic competitiveness, and to repair a perceived loss of trust among the lay public. Other possible motivations may include an attempt to avoid potentially expensive future difficulties, as knowledge-gathering exercises, or possibly some kind of persuasive public-relations initiative.

We also noted that the academic literature contains a range of possible ways of understanding the emergence of what has been termed a 'deliberative democracy' (Dryzek, 2000). While, in practice, experiments such as *GM Nation?* fall well short of the wholesale 'transformation of the public sphere' (Habermas, 1989), it is relevant to reflect upon the potential scope for deliberation to play a more prominent role in the functioning of the democratic process.

In the UK, a wide range of initiatives is developing the practice of engagement, ranging from the Royal Society and Royal Academy of Engineering's (2004) recent study of nanoscience and nanotechnology, the government examination of the future for new 'smart' drugs (OST, 2005), and a host of local activities (Involve, 2005). All have entailed work with citizen groups, using a variety of engagement tools. On the basis of its work, the Royal Society report argued that the government should stage 'an adequately funded' and 'properly evaluated' public dialogue on nanotechnologies. In Chapter 1 we mentioned the current enthusiasm in some quarters for 'upstream' engagement, which would take place very early in the scientific development of potential technologies.

Although in this book we have no wish to wander very far into the realms of grand theory, it is worth briefly singling out the work of Jürgen Habermas (1987/1991, 1989, 1990). His writings have proved particularly influential in the work of a great many social scientists who have attempted to develop the notion of deliberation in practical ways; perhaps most notably in the programme of work associated with Ortwin Renn and his colleagues (1995). At the heart of Habermas' theorisation lies a broadly emancipatory agenda, and the notion of an *ideal speech situation* (discussed in White, 1988): a space for public discourse in which participation rights allow an unhindered exchange of views by all. This conception has not been without criticism, in fundamental ways, as being driven by an idealised notion of rationality out of kilter with the specific detail of everyday life (cf. Bogen, 1989; Lynch, 1993); and as a framework impossibly remote from the conditions under which contentious issues might actually be discussed in the real world (Schön and Rein, 1994; see also Horlick-Jones, 2007; Horlick-Jones *et al.*, 2001).

Such criticisms point to an alternative, and rather more modest, possible agenda for the development of citizen engagement; namely, one of simply seeking to enhance the quality of decisions, and making problem issues rather more workable (cf. Strong and Dingwall, 1989). 'Engagement' in these terms may be seen as a collective term for a range of initiatives that seeks to contextualise technical knowledge in order to relate problem issues more effectively with the specific features of the real world. In this way, by incorporating a wider range of knowledge, including 'unofficial expertise', into decision processes, this may allow contested values and uncertainties, as well as possible impacts on related policy areas to be taken into account (cf. Friend and Hickling, 2005; Funtowicz and Ravetz, 1992; Horlick-Jones, 1998; Petts, 1997; Rosenhead and Mingers, 2001; Wynne, 1991). As we pointed out in Chapter 7, according to this perspective, processes such as *GM Nation?* may be seen as attempts to incorporate and reconcile competing perspectives, subject to the constraints and opportunities afforded by the material characteristics of the issue in question.

We conclude this chapter by stressing the need to be cautious about some of the possible ways of thinking about citizen engagement. In Chapter 1 we recognised that some of the most energetic advocates for extended participation in public decision-making see engagement as a vehicle for achieving wider goals than the more modest agenda that we have identified. We also recognise a number of romantic perspectives within the discourse around engagement that have little or no evidence to support them. We will briefly consider three such perspectives. First, is the notion that engagement will resolve contentious issues by 'getting all the facts on the table and having a full and open discussion about them'. This is a rhetoric typical of calls in the UK for 'public inquiries' (Blackman, 1991; O'Riordan *et al.*, 1988). Such a resolution of difficulties is indeed one possible outcome, although one need only reflect for a moment about a range of international and domestic conflict situations to recognise that attempting a process of public engagement might well lead to impasse, and possibly to enhanced conflict (e.g. Butler *et al.*, 1994). Ultimately, this is a matter for empirical investigation.

A second example of romanticism has been identified by Steve Rayner (2003), who notes that all groups advocating more public participation tend to have within their arguments a particular tacit idea of the citizen. As Rayner notes, social scientists have been critical of conceptions of the citizenry in terms of the 'deficit model', which defines them in terms of their lack of technical understanding. However, he adds (ibid.: 165), such 'reflexive critics are often rather unreflexive about the standardised model of the citizen that is embodied in their own proposed citizen-science relationship', namely one in which the citizen is seen as 'socially embedded in a community', 'locally knowledgeable and intuitively reflexive', and 'focused on the common good as a core value of public life' (ibid.: 165). It seems not unreasonable to suppose that in the real world these assumptions may not be entirely valid. Once again, there is a need for such assumptions to be investigated empirically.

The construction of an idealised notion of a 'participant' raises an important question about the role of people who do not display such characteristics. Do they have a valid role in participation processes? Here it is pertinent to draw attention to some evidence we mentioned in Chapter 8, which reported an example of unease expressed by a representative of one of the engaged stakeholder groups about the involvement of the lay public who had not been appropriately 'immersed in the debates'.

Our third example has been partly addressed by Rayner in the previous example. However in this case, our evaluation exercise provides specific evidence that relates to it. One of the sponsors' objectives for the debate was to involve 'people at the grass-roots level whose voice has not been heard to participate in the programme'. The experience of the *GM Nation?* has shown how difficult that objective was to achieve. We note, however, with some concern, an apparent tendency within the policy community to construct a notion of 'the public', as a disengaged and even-handed majority of the laity. This population, we suggest, are seen in some quarters as legitimate representatives of the wider lay public to act as participants in stakeholder engagement exercises, in the sense that 'they do not have an axe to grind' (cf. Irwin, 2006).

We found that the participants in the open public aspects of the debate were quite atypical of the lay public as a whole. Many were politically engaged in the issue; in the sense that beliefs about GM appeared to form part of a wider *weltanschauung*. Of course, engaged people with clear views on GM issues had a legitimate contribution to make in the debate. Moreover, the exploration of their views was important, in view of their prominence within the political dynamics of wider debates about GM. Our survey work, in particular, also identified a substantial minority of our representative sample that were very strongly of the view that there were no potential benefits associated with GM. However, the extent to which this sub-group might be described as 'politically engaged' in the GM issue is not clear. There were also large numbers of people whose views might be described as 'ambivalent', a term that glosses over a number of possible underlying perspectives.

We conclude that attempting to make a clear distinction between 'an activist minority' and a 'disengaged, grass-roots, majority' is problematic. Rather, there are multiple publics, which exhibit varying degrees of engagement and modes of reasoning (cf. Horlick-Jones, 2005c). These observations lead us to pose a serious challenge to the policy community; namely, how to design public engagement processes that engage with the plurality of the lay public in appropriate ways.

The emerging practices of citizen engagement appear to bring with them the possibility of improving the quality of decision-making about some contentious and problematic issues, and enriching the democratic process. What, then, of the prospects for a 'deliberative future'? In this book we have documented the uneven performance of the *GM Nation?* public debate, and described the very real practical difficulties associated with an enterprise of this nature. However, we certainly do not advocate 'throwing the baby out with the bath water'. Rather, the experience of the GM debate offers a wealth of potential lessons for undertaking such initiatives more effectively. We conclude by stressing the need for systematic evaluations of such experiments in order to assemble a robust body of design knowledge. In this way, we hope, it will be possible to enhance the practicability of citizen engagement and its relevance for real-world problem issues. On this matter, only time will tell.

Annex A: Observational protocol

This protocol provides a guide for observational evaluation of events that form part of the government-sponsored public debate on the possible commercialisation of GM crops in the UK. It addresses this task by concentrating on the need to provide detailed descriptions of the ways in which the public discusses the issues raised in the context of interactions between participants, the facilitator and the stimulus material. The dimensions of behaviour set out below correspond to important aspects of deliberative processes which have been identified in the process evaluation literature.

Observer descriptions should provide as much detail as possible, including verbatim quotations of specific group exchanges and their dynamics. We will have access to the audio/video recordings that are being made, so *timing the reported events* would greatly assist subsequent analysis of these recordings. Observers should speak informally with participants if suitable opportunities arise (e.g. a break in the main event), subject to the schedule of observer behaviour agreed with the organisers which is set out in the appendix to this document.

Topics for observation

1 Task definition:
   - Is the nature and scope of the activity clearly defined?
   - Are the overall objectives of the exercise clearly set out (both for the event itself, and its wider impacts)?
   - Is it clear how these objectives have been derived?

2 Independence:
   - How do the facilitators describe themselves and their role in the workshop?
   - How do they describe their sponsor and the relationship between the two?
   - How was the agenda set and by whom? Is this made clear?
   - What reasons are given, if at all, for selecting workshop participants?

3 Resource accessibility:
- Does the style of moderation allow participants to fully take part in the workshop?
- How do people seem to be responding to the stimulus material? Did they find it useful as an educative tool? Which aspects were used, e.g. the CD-ROM/video etc?
- Are participants overwhelmed by the information?
- Is there sufficient time for issues to be discussed in depth and conclusions to be drawn? Is the discussion constrained by time limits?

4 Nature of the discourse:
- Disagreements – what form do they take? How are they resolved?
- How does the moderator arrive at a consensus (if at all)?
- What arguments are used by participants to make sense of the issues?
- What references are made to mediated sources – books, TV, radio – factual or drama? Make a rough estimate of the fraction of contributions informed by such material.
- How much reference is made to expert scientific views?

5 Structured decision-making:
- Are all the participants able to contribute and shape the discussion?
- Do some participants dominate the discussion?
- Are minority views allowed to be heard?
- How well did the use of cards/voting work?
- Is there evidence of non-participation or disruptive behaviour?
- Estimate the proportion of the workshop dominated by facilitator intervention rather than talk amongst the participants. Does this pattern change during the course of the workshop?
- Did people congregate around any of the six debating zones in particular? If so, which?

6 Transparency:
- Is there scope for future involvement of the participants in the GM public debate?
- Is it made clear how the participants can follow the course of the debate?
- Will participants be provided with any feedback on the findings of the workshop? If so, what form will this take?
- Is it made clear how these findings will be used, and who will be involved in determining these findings?
- Is it made clear how the workshop findings relate to the overall objectives of the exercise?

7   Views and experiences of participants:
    Is it possible to find evidence of:
    - Satisfaction or disappointment felt by participants about any aspects of the workshop?
    - The extent to which participants understood the workshop process and issues raised for discussion?
    - Support for, or scepticism towards, the GM debate, or, more generally, about the idea of public dialogue about such issues?

Appendix: Note on observer behaviour

The observer(s) will:

- work hard to present an unobtrusive presence (but not studiedly detached) at the workshops and will be sensitive to the possibility of inadvertent non-verbal signalling to the participants;
- not make tape or video recordings;
- take discreet notes by hand, and not use a laptop computer for this purpose;
- not interact verbally with participants unless directly addressed, or possibly informally during break times. In the latter case the observer will be careful not to ask leading or framing questions;
- not take photographs except for pictures of the flip-chart sheets produced during the workshop. These photographs will be taken after the event is over;
- collect copies of stimulus material used during the workshop.

Annex B: Short questionnaire – QS(FD)

Questionnaire on attitudes to GM foods

This is the first questionnaire. All you need to do is place a tick in one box for each of the seven questions. These are concerned with your views on GM foods. All information collected from you will be treated as anonymous. This should take you no more than five minutes.

1. How would you assess the *benefits*, if any, of GM food for British society as a whole?

   Very low   Some   Very high
   ☐   ☐   ☐   ☐   ☐   ☐   ☐

2. How would you assess the *risks*, if any, to human health of GM food for British society as a whole?

   Very low   Some   Very high
   ☐   ☐   ☐   ☐   ☐   ☐   ☐

3. How would you assess the *risks*, if any, to the environment from genetically modified food?

   Very low   Some   Very high
   ☐   ☐   ☐   ☐   ☐   ☐   ☐

4. How concerned or not are you about GM food?

   Not at all   Not really   Somewhat   Fairly   Very
   concerned   concerned   concerned   concerned   concerned
   ☐   ☐   ☐   ☐   ☐

5. How important or not important is GM food to you?

   Not at all   Not really   Somewhat   Fairly   Very
   important   important   important   important   important
   ☐   ☐   ☐   ☐   ☐

6. How much do you agree with the following statement?
   I feel that current rules and regulations in the UK are sufficient to control GM food

Strongly disagree	Tend to disagree	Neither agree nor disagree	Tend to agree	Strongly agree
☐	☐	☐	☐	☐

7. On the whole, how acceptable or unacceptable is GM food to you?

Very unacceptable	Fairly unacceptable	Neither acceptable nor unacceptable	Fairly acceptable	Very acceptable
☐	☐	☐	☐	☐

Thank you. Now please hand this questionnaire to the observer.

Annex C: Long questionnaire

GM event questionnaire

Section 1: Your views on the event

This first section of the questionnaire is about your views on the event you attended. Please write your comments in the space provided for each question or tick the relevant box. Once you have completed the questionnaire please place it in the freepost/self-addressed envelope – you do not need a stamp.

1. Why did you choose to participate in the event?

   ....
   ....
   ....
   ....

2. What did you see as your role in the event?

   ....
   ....
   ....
   ....

3. What did you hope to get out of participating in the event – what were your expectations?

   ....
   ....
   ....
   ....

4. What do you think the people who commissioned *GM Nation?* the public debate hope to get out of it?

....
....
....
....
....

5. Were you given a clear indication of what this event would involve?

☐ No   ☐ Yes   ☐ Don't know

6. What, if anything, would you say that you have learnt from taking part in the event?

....
....
....
....
....

7. What, if any, do you personally feel were the positive aspects of the event?

....
....
....
....
....

8. And what, if any, do you personally feel were the negative aspects of the event?

....
....
....
....
....

9. Based on your experience, please indicate whether you Strongly Agree, Agree, Disagree, Neither agree nor disagree or Strongly Disagree with each of the following statements (by placing a tick in the relevant box).

   1. *Strongly disagree*
   2. *Disagree*
   3. *Neither agree or disagree*
   4. *Strongly agree*
   5. *Don't know*

Please tick one box on each line	1.	2.	3.	4.	5.
There was not enough time to fully discuss all the relevant issues.	☐	☐	☐	☐	☐
All relevant issues were covered.	☐	☐	☐	☐	☐
The event was run in an unbiased way.	☐	☐	☐	☐	☐
I enjoyed taking part in the event.	☐	☐	☐	☐	☐
I didn't get the chance to say all that I wanted to say.	☐	☐	☐	☐	☐
The people who commissioned this event will not take any action on the views and recommendations made by participants.	☐	☐	☐	☐	☐
The people who attended the event were fairly typical of the sort of people who would be affected by GM issues.	☐	☐	☐	☐	☐
The facilitator encouraged everyone to have their say, no matter how little or how much they knew about the subject.	☐	☐	☐	☐	☐
It is not clear to me how the results of this event will be used.	☐	☐	☐	☐	☐
There was too much control by the facilitator over the way the event was run.	☐	☐	☐	☐	☐
The information that was given to participants was fair and balanced.	☐	☐	☐	☐	☐
The facilitators were biased by the views of the people who commissioned this event.	☐	☐	☐	☐	☐
I was confused at times about what I had to do.	☐	☐	☐	☐	☐
I felt there was so much information that it was difficult to assess it all.	☐	☐	☐	☐	☐

Feedback from this event will be influential on the future of GM food and crops in the UK.   ☐ ☐ ☐ ☐ ☐

It was not clear how participants in the event were selected.   ☐ ☐ ☐ ☐ ☐

The event was well-organised and structured.   ☐ ☐ ☐ ☐ ☐

The event was well-facilitated.   ☐ ☐ ☐ ☐ ☐

Participants had access to any information they wanted.   ☐ ☐ ☐ ☐ ☐

The event has taken place too late in the policy-making process to be influential.   ☐ ☐ ☐ ☐ ☐

10. How satisfied were you with the event?

    (Rate on a scale of 1–5 , where 1 is 'very satisfied', and 5 is 'not at all satisfied'.)

    1 Very satisfied   ☐

    2 Fairly satisfied   ☐

    3 Neither satisfied nor dissatisfied   ☐

    4 Not very satisfied   ☐

    5 Not at all satisfied   ☐

    Don't know   ☐

11. Do you expect to get any feedback on the results of these events?

    ☐ No   ☐ Yes   ☐ Don't know

12. How do you think these types of events could be improved?

    ....

    ....

    ....

    ....

13. Do you think it would be useful to have other events like this in the future?

    ☐ No   ☐ Yes   ☐ Don't know

14. If yes, please describe:

   ....

   ....

   ....

   ....

15. How did participating in the event match up to what you expected?

   As I expected   ☐

   Better than I expected   ☐

   Worse than I expected   ☐

16. Why do you say that? Please give reasons for your answer at Q.15. (If the event was as you expected, go to Q.17.)

   ....

   ....

   ....

   ....

17. Would you be willing to participate in a similar activity again?

   ☐ No   ☐ Yes   ☐ Don't know

18. Do you have any additional comments?

Section 2: Your Attitudes to GM Foods

This second section of the questionnaire is about your views on GM foods. All you need to do is place a tick in one box for each of the seven questions.

1. How would you assess the benefits, if any, of GM food for British society as a whole?

Very low			Some			Very high
☐	☐	☐	☐	☐	☐	☐

2. How would you assess the risks, if any, to human health of GM food for British society as a whole?

Very low			Some			Very high
☐	☐	☐	☐	☐	☐	☐

3. How would you assess the risks, if any, to the environment from genetically modified food?

Very low			Some			Very high
☐	☐	☐	☐	☐	☐	☐

4. How concerned or not are you about GM food?

Not at all concerned	Not really concerned	Somewhat concerned	Fairly concerned	Very concerned
☐	☐	☐	☐	☐

5. How important or not important is GM food to you?

Not at all important	Not really important	Somewhat important	Fairly important	Very important
☐	☐	☐	☐	☐

6. How much do you agree with the following statement?
I feel that current rules and regulations in the UK are sufficient to control GM food

Strongly disagree	Tend to disagree	Neither agree nor disagree	Tend to agree	Strongly agree
☐	☐	☐	☐	☐

7. On the whole, how acceptable or unacceptable is GM food to you?

Very unacceptable	Fairly unacceptable	Neither acceptable nor unacceptable	Fairly acceptable	Very acceptable
☐	☐	☐	☐	☐

Section 3: Additional information

We would be grateful if you would also provide us with some additional information about yourself to aid in the analysis of the event. All information collected from you will be treated as anonymous and confidential, and we will not pass this on to any third party.

Gender   Female ☐   Male ☐

Occupation ....

Organisation ....
(if applicable)

Years in education ....
(from age 11)

Which of the following age brackets do you belong to?
- ☐ 15–18 years   ☐ 45–54 years
- ☐ 18–24 years   ☐ 55–59 years
- ☐ 25–34 years   ☐ 60–64 years
- ☐ 35–44 years   ☐ 65 years or above

What is the highest level of qualification you have obtained?
1 ☐   None/No formal qualifications
2 ☐   Bachelor degree or equivalent
3 ☐   GCSEs/O-level/CSE
4 ☐   Postgraduate qualification (Masters or PhD)
5 ☐   Vocational qualifications (e.g. NVQ1+2)
6 ☐   A-levels or equivalent
7 ☐   Other, please specify: ....

Finally, we would like to contact some of the participants again in the near future in order to conduct some follow-up interviews by telephone. If you would be willing to be contacted again please complete the following section. If you are unwilling to be contacted again, just leave this next section blank and return the questionnaire.

Name ....

Day time number ....

Evening number ....

Mobile number ....

Address ....

     ....

Thank you for giving up your time to complete this questionnaire. Now please return it to us in the envelope provided. You do not need a stamp.

Notes

1 The origins of the debate

1 'Organic' is a legally defined term, regulated by the EU. Products must be certified by a recognised organic agency. There are a handful of such agencies in the UK, all of which are registered and monitored by the government's organic watchdog, the United Kingdom Register of Organic Food Standards (UKROFS). The Soil Association, the best known of these agencies, certifies up to 70 per cent of all the organic food produced in the UK. Genetic modification is prohibited in organic farming and food production, and organic products must be produced and processed without the use of such organisms or their derivatives. Infringement of this condition can lead to the loss of organic certification from specific land, crops or products, and therefore 'GM contamination' may have severe economic consequences for those involved in organic production.

2 'EU fear huge payout for GM export "ban"', *The Guardian*, 9 February 2006.

3 'Shops "unlikely" to stock GM food', *The Guardian*, 16 September 2003.

4 Details on Lord Sainsbury's alleged commercial links with GM companies may be found at www.gmwatch.org; see also Cook, 2004; Toke, 2004.

5 'Call to sack biotech advisers', *The Guardian*, 8 July 1998.

6 This request for advice came in the form of a letter from Margaret Beckett, Secretary of State at DEFRA. The quote we have used is taken from paragraph 30 of that communication.

7 The *GM Nation?* debate website was at: http://www.gmnation.org.uk.

2 Our approach to evaluating the debate

1 This document appeared in mid-October 2002. It should be noted that a month after our appointment as accredited evaluators, the debate's overall objectives had still to be finalised by the PDSB.

3 The unfolding of the debate and the implementation of the evaluation exercise

1 The Public Debate Steering Board (PDSB) was chaired by Professor Malcolm Grant CBE. In addition to Professor Grant, the Board drew on a number of AEBC members, namely: Anna Bradley, Dr Dave Carmichael, Professor Phil Dale, Professor Robin Grove-White, Judith Hann and Professor Jeff Maxwell OBE. There were four additional members: the late Stephen Smith, then the Chair of the Agricultural Biotechnology Council (ABC, an industry association), Clare Devereux, Director of the Five Year FREEZE (an umbrella organisation of pressure groups), Gary Kass,

from the Parliamentary Office of Science and Technology, and Lucian Hudson, Director of Communications at DEFRA, who sat on the PDSB to ensure proper accountability for expenditure of public funds. Stephen Smith resigned from the Board because of illness, and was replaced by Dr Paul Rylott, Deputy Chair of the ABC.

2   We note that two citizens' juries on GM were run in 2003: by the Food Standards Agency, as part of an independent examination of consumer views on GM foods; and by PEALS at the University of Newcastle (sponsored by the Consumers' Association, Greenpeace, the Co-operative group and Unilever).

3   COI Communications is an 'advisory non-departmental public body'. Its Chief Executive reports to the Minister for the Cabinet Office. See http://www.coi.gov.uk.

4   Both pieces of work were contained in the report *Desk Research for GM Public Debate Steering Board* (COI Communications, 17 December 2002).

5   The issue of representativeness

1   UK 2001 Census details and other background statistics may be found at http://www.statistics.gov.uk.

2   The scales for the 'benefits', 'health risks', and 'environment risks' questions were slightly different in the UEA/MORI Risk Survey 2002 and the UEA/MORI GM Food Survey 2003. In these two studies people could respond using a 7-point scale, ranging from 'none' (0) to 'very high' (6), with 'some' (3) as the scale mid-point (see appendices to Poortinga and Pidgeon, 2003a; 2004a). To make comparisons possible, all entries in this table have been recoded on a 1–7 scale.

3   The 'regulation' question was different in the 2003 survey. In that survey people were asked to indicate on a 5-point scale to what extent they agreed or disagreed with the statement 'I feel confident that the British government adequately regulates GM food'. As a consequence, the results are not strictly comparable.

4   Although we do not report direct significance tests here, the approximate statistical effect sizes are substantial (of the order of 0.5 to 1, calculated as the ratio of group mean difference to the average standard deviation).

5   The figures may not sum to 100 per cent due to missing values or rounding. NBD-1: 'Narrow-but-Deep' reconvened focus groups, 1st session. NBD-2: 'Narrow-but-Deep' reconvened focus groups, 2nd session. OPEN GMN: Open *GM Nation?* submissions through website and paper questionnaire. MORI 2003: University of East Anglia/MORI GM Survey 2003. Response categories for NBD-1, NBD-2 and OPEN GMN were 'Agree strongly', 'Agree', 'Don't know/unsure', 'Disagree' and 'Disagree strongly'. Response categories for the MORI 2003 survey were 'Strongly agree', 'Tend to agree', 'Neither agree nor disagree', 'Tend to disagree', 'Strongly disagree' and 'No opinion'. To make the responses comparable, the MORI data combines the 'Neither agree nor disagree' and 'No opinion' categories as 'Neutral'. 'Net' gives the percentage difference 'agree' over 'disagree'. The MORI 2003 percentages are weighted to the GB national profile.

6   To make these data comparable, the responses were recoded as: 1: 'Disagree strongly', 2: 'Disagree', 3: 'Don't know/unsure', 4: 'Agree', and 5: 'Agree strongly'.

7   The management and translation of knowledge

1   We note that the term 'knowledge translation' has been also used by researchers in a number of additional areas. Specifically, we are aware of work that uses this term in health care research (see e.g. the activities of the Canadian Institutes of Health Research, and the Faculty of Medicine at the University of Toronto), and in risk management research (see the special issue of *Risk Management: An International Journal*, 6(2), 2004).

2   The initial advice provided to government by the AEBC took the form of a memorandum entitled 'A debate about the possible commercialisation of GM crops', dated 26 April 2002. This was subsequently posted on the AEBC website (http://www.aebc.gov.uk/aebc/public_attitudes_advice.html).

3   It should be mentioned, *en passant*, that other researchers in this area have argued that this more 'worldly' version of the nature of scientific activity is revealed in everyday scientific work and discourse, whilst being masked in formal accounts of such practices (Gilbert and Mulkay, 1984; Lynch, 1993). We also note that empirical investigations of patterns of practical reasoning about risk issues suggest that the categorical differences between 'expert' and 'lay' behaviour (implied in much of the literature critical of the deficit model) are not nearly so pronounced in real-world settings. Indeed, members of the lay public may be as narrowly defined in their thinking as any stereotype image of a technical 'expert'. Conversely, in the real world, experts often display regard to a range of considerations beyond the purely technical (Horlick-Jones, 2005c; Mulkay, 1997).

4   This quote is taken from the contractor's brief, prepared by COI in December 2002.

5   These questions were adopted by the GM Science Review as a basis for structuring its work (GM Science Review Panel, 2003). In this way, a commitment to allowing the Foundation Discussion workshops to 'frame' the terms of the science review took on this 'deficit' form. The six frames identified by Corr Willbourn (2003a: 13; which we reproduce at Box 7.2) were included in the Cabinet Office economic review report (2003: 42). Interestingly, a seventh frame, 'progress', is also included there. This additional frame was included in the presentation made by Corr Willbourn to the PDSB on 17 December 2002, but was absent from its subsequent report, and indeed from the PDSB's final report (2003: paragraph 16). Whatever, it is not clear how, in substantive terms, these framings shaped the Cabinet Office review work. More generally, there is little evidence to suggest that the formal commitment to 'interaction' between all three strands of the GM dialogue (set out in a memorandum circulated by the *GM Nation?* secretariat on 28 May 2003) delivered much in the way of 'cross-fertilisation'.

6   The 'workbook' formed part of the stimulus materials produced to support the debate. It was a glossy 48-page pamphlet. In addition to for/against perspectives on a range of GM-related issues, it provided some background information on the debate, a glossary, and details of a number of different organisations' websites.

7   We also note that the debate failed to utilise the potentially significant capacity of the NBD diaries to reveal rich details of the participants' engagement with 'factual' accounts of GM-related issues (cf. Alaszewski, 2006).

8   The letter put together by the NBD group that met at King's Lynn (see PDSB, 2003), and which contains sentiments expressing a strongly cautious and outspoken position on GM, may have arisen from such an instability in views. Our observational data contain some evidence of the disproportionate influence on second meeting of a NBD group of participants who returned from the 'diary' exercise particularly 'fired up' by what they had found. Here we note a well-established phenomenon in the behaviour of groups that is contained in the psychological literature; namely, that they have a tendency to make more extreme decisions than individuals. It seems that group interactions have the capacity to move people towards polar extremes of 'risky' or 'risk-averse' decisions (Myers and Lamm, 1976).

References

Abelson, J., Forest, P.-G., Eyles, J., Smith, P., Martin, E. and Gauvin, F.-P. (2003) 'Deliberations about deliberative methods: issues in the design and evaluation of public participation processes', *Social Science & Medicine*, 57, pp. 239–251.

AEBC (2001) *Crops on Trial*, Agriculture and Environment Biotechnology Commission report, Department of Trade and Industry, London.

Alaszewski, A. (2006) *Using Diaries in Social Research*, Sage, London.

Alvesson, M. (2004) *Knowledge Work and Knowledge-Intensive Firms*, Oxford University Press, Oxford.

Andersen, I. and Jaeger, B. (1999) 'Scenario workshops and consensus conferences: towards more democratic decision-making', *Science and Public Policy*, 26(5) pp. 331–340.

Anderson, L. (1999) *Genetic Engineering, Food, and Our Environment*, Green Books, Dartington.

Arnstein, S.R. (1969) 'A ladder of citizen participation', *Journal of the American Institute of Planners*, 35 pp. 215–224.

Arvai, J., Gregory, R. and McDaniels, T. (2001) 'Testing a structured decision-aiding approach: value-focused thinking for deliberative risk communication', *Risk Analysis*, 21, pp. 1065–1076.

Bauer, M. (2005) 'Public perceptions and mass media in the biotechnology controversy', *International Journal of Public Opinion Research*, 17(1) pp. 5–22.

Bauer, M. and Gaskell, G. (eds) (2002) *Biotechnology: The Making of a Global Controversy*, Cambridge University Press, Cambridge.

Beck, U. (1992) *Risk Society: Towards a New Modernity*, Sage, London.

Beck, U. (1995) *Ecological Politics in an Age of Risk*, Polity, Cambridge.

Becker, H. (1963) *Outsiders: Studies in the Sociology of Deviance*, Free Press, New York.

Beierle, T. and Konisky, D. (2000) 'Values, conflict and trust in participatory environmental planning', *Journal of Policy Analysis and Management*, 19(4) pp. 587–602.

Bennett, D., Glasner, P. and Travis, D. (1986) *The Politics of Uncertainty: Regulating Recombinant DNA Research in Britain*, Routledge & Kegan Paul, London.

Berger, P. (1987) *The Capitalist Revolution*, Wildwood House, Aldershot.

Blackman, T. (1991) 'Planning inquiries: a socio-legal study', *Sociology*, 25(2) pp. 311–327.

Blair, T. (1998) *The Third Way: New Politics for a New Century*, Pamphlet 588, The Fabian Society, London.

Blair, T. (2002) 'Science matters', speech to the Royal Society, London, 23 May.

Bloor, M. (1978) 'On the analysis of observational data: a discussion of the worth and uses of inductive techniques and respondent validation', *Sociology*, 12(3) pp. 545–557.

Bloor, M., Frankland, J., Thomas, M. and Robson, K. (2001) *Focus Groups in Social Research*, Sage, London.

Bogen, D. (1989) 'A reappraisal of Habermas' *Theory of Communicative Action* in light of detailed investigations of social praxis', *Journal for the Theory of Social Behaviour*, 19(1) pp. 47–77.

Burgess, A. (2004) *Cellular Phones, Public Fears and a Culture of Precaution*, Cambridge University Press, Cambridge.

Burke, K. (1969) *A Grammar of Motives*, University of California Press, Berkeley CA.

Butler, D., Adonis, A. and Travers, T. (1994) *Failure in British Government: The Politics of the Poll Tax*, Oxford University Press, Oxford.

Button, G. (1993) 'The curious case of the disappearing technology', in G. Button (ed.) *Technology in Working Order: Studies of Work, Interaction and Technology*, Routledge, London, pp. 10–28.

Cabinet Office (2002) *Risk: Improving Government's Ability to Handle Risk and Uncertainty*, Cabinet Office Strategy Unit, London.

Cabinet Office (2003) *Field Work: Weighing Up the Costs and Benefits of GM Crops*, Cabinet Office Strategy Unit, London.

Campbell, S. and Townsend, E. (2003) 'Flaws undermine results of UK biotech debate', *Nature*, 425, p. 559.

Carnes, S., Schweitzer, M., Peelle, E., Wolfe, A. and Munro, J. (1998) 'Measuring the success of public participation on environmental restoration and waste management activities in the US Department of Energy', *Technology in Society*, 20(4) pp. 385–406.

CEC (2001) *European Governance: a White Paper*, Commission of the European Communities, Brussels.

Checkland, P. and Scholes, J. (1990) *Soft Systems Methodology in Action*, Wiley, Chichester.

Checkoway, B. (1981) 'The politics of public hearings', *The Journal of Applied Behavioral Science*, 17(4) pp. 566–582.

Chess, C. and Purcell, K. (1999) 'Public participation and the environment: do we know what works?', *Environmental Science and Technology*, 33(16) pp. 2685–2692.

Chilton, S., Covey, J., Hopkins, L., Jones-Lee, M., Loomes, G., Pidgeon, N.F. and Spencer, A. (2002) 'Public perceptions of risk and preference-based values of safety', *Journal of Risk and Uncertainty*, 25, 211–232.

Clarke, A. with Dawson, R. (1999) *Evaluation Research: an Introduction to Principles, Methods and Practice*, Sage, London.

Cook, G. (2004) *Genetically Modified Language: the Discourse of Arguments for GM Crops and Food*, Routledge, London.

Cook, G., Robbins, P. and Pieri, E. (2006) '"Words of mass destruction": British newspaper coverage of the genetically modified food debate, expert and non-expert reactions', *Public Understanding of Science*, 14, pp. 5–29.

Coote, A. and Lenaghan, J. (1997) *Citizens' Juries: Theory into Practice*, Institute for Public Policy Research, London.

Corr Willbourn (2003a) *A Report on the Foundation Discussion Workshops Conducted to Inform the GM Public Debate*, Corr Willbourn Research and Development, London.

Corr Willbourn (2003b) *Qualitative Research on a Series of Reconvened Group Discussions for the 'Narrow but Deep' Strand of the GM Public Debate*, Corr Willbourn Research and Development, London.

DEFRA (2003) *Compendium of UK Organic Standards*, Department of Environment, Food and Rural Affairs, London.

Desvousges, W.H. and Smith, V.K. (1988) 'Focus groups and risk communication: the "science" of listening to data', *Risk Analysis*, 8(4) pp. 479–484.

DETR (1998) *Guidance on Enhancing Public Participation*, Department of the Environment, Transport and Rural Affairs, London.

DETR (2000) *Multi-Criteria Analysis: a Manual. DETR Appraisal Guidance*, Department of Transport, Environment and the Regions, London.

Dingwall, R. (1997) 'Accounts, interviews and observations', in G. Miller and R. Dingwall (eds) *Context and Method in Qualitative Research*, Sage, London, pp. 51–65.

Dingwall, R. (1999) 'Risk society: the cult of theory and the millennium', *Social Policy and Administration*, 33, pp. 474–491.

Dryzek, J. (2000) *Deliberative Democracy and Beyond*, Oxford University Press, Oxford.

Dunkerley, D. and Glasner, P. (1998) 'Empowering the public? Citizens' juries and the new genetic technologies', *Critical Public Health*, 8(3) pp. 181–192.

Durant, J. and Lindsey, N. (2000) *The Great GM Food Debate: a Survey of Media Coverage in the First Half of 1999*, House of Commons Parliamentary Office of Science and Technology (POST), London.

Eden, C. (1990) 'The unfolding nature of group decision support – two dimensions of skill', in C. Eden and J. Radford (eds) *Tackling Strategic Problems: the Role of Group Decision Support*, Sage, London, pp. 48–55.

Esogbue, A.O. and Ahipo, Z.M. (1982) 'A fuzzy sets model for measuring the effectiveness of public participation in water resources planning', *Water Resources Bulletin*, 18(3) pp. 451–456.

Feldman, M. (1989) *Order without Design: Information Processing and Policy Making*, Stanford University Press, Stanford CA.

Fielding, N.G. and Fielding, J.L. (1986) *Linking Data*, Sage Publications, Beverley Hills CA.

Fincham, J. and Ravetz, J. (1991) *Genetically Engineered Organisms: Benefits and Risks*, Open University Press, Buckingham.

Fiorino, D. (1990) 'Citizen participation and environmental risk: a survey of institutional mechanisms', *Science, Technology, & Human Values*, 15(2) pp. 226–243.

Friend, J.K. and Hickling, A. (2005) *Planning Under Pressure: the Strategic Choice Approach*, 3rd edition, Elsevier Butterworth-Heinemann, Oxford.

Funtowicz, S. and Ravetz, J. (1992) 'Risk management as a post-normal science', *Risk Analysis*, 12(1) pp. 95–97.

Gamson, W. and Modigliani, A. (1989) 'Media discourse and public opinion on nuclear power: a constructionist approach', *American Journal of Sociology*, 95(1) pp. 1–37.

Garfinkel, H. (1967) *Studies in Ethnomethodology*, Prentice-Hall, Englewood Cliffs NJ.

Gaskell, G. (2004) 'Science policy and society: the British debate over GM agriculture', *Current Opinion in Biotechnology*, 15, pp. 241–245.

Gaskell, G. and Bauer, M. (eds) (2001) *Biotechnology 1996–2000: The Years of Controversy*, The Science Museum, London.

Gaskell, G., Allum, N., Bauer, M., Jackson, J., Howard, S. and Lindsey, N. (2003) *Ambivalent GM Nation? Public attitudes to biotechnology in the UK, 1991–2002*, Life Sciences in European Society Report, London School of Economics and Political Science, London.

Gephart, R. (1988) *Ethnostatistics: Qualitative Foundations for Quantitative Research*, Sage, Newbury Park CA.

Giddens, A. (1990) *The Consequences of Modernity*, Polity, Cambridge.

Giddens, A. (1991) *Modernity and Self-Identity*, Polity, Cambridge.

Gilbert, G.N. and Mulkay, M. (1984) *Opening Pandora's Box: a Sociological Analysis of Scientists' Discourse*, Cambridge University Press, Cambridge.

Glaser, B. and Strauss, A. (1967) *The Discovery of Grounded Theory: Strategies for Qualitative Research*, Weidenfeld & Nicholson, London.

Glassner, B. (1999) *The Culture of Fear: Why Americans are Afraid of the Wrong Things*, Basic Books, New York.

GM Science Review Panel (2003) *GM Science Review: First Report*, Department of Trade and Industry, London.

Goffman, E. (1975) *Frame Analysis: an Essay on the Organization of Experience*, Penguin, Harmondsworth.

Grabner, P., Hampel, J., Lindsey, N. and Torgersen, H. (2001) 'Biotechnology diversity: the challenge of multilevel policy-making', in G. Gaskell and M. Bauer (eds) *Biotechnology 1996–2000: the Years of Controversy*, Science Museum, London, pp. 15–34.

Grove-White, R. (2003) 'GM debate methodology works in the real world', *Nature*, 426, p. 495.

Grove-White, R., Macnaghten, P., Mayer, S. and Wynne, B. (1997) *Uncertain World: Genetically Modified Organisms, Food and Public Attitudes in Britain*, Centre for the Study of Environmental Change, Lancaster.

Habermas, J. (1987/1991) *The Theory of Communicative Action* (Parts I and II), Polity, Cambridge.

Habermas, J. (1989) *The Structural Transformation of the Public Sphere*, Polity, Cambridge.

Habermas, J. (1990) *Moral Consciousness and Communicative Action*, MIT Press, Cambridge MA.

Hammersley, M. and Atkinson, P. (1995) *Ethnography: Principles in Practice*, 2nd edition, Routledge, London.

Harper, R. (1998) *Inside the IMF: an Ethnography of Documents, Technology and Organisational Action*, Academic Press, San Diego CA.

Hawes, C., Haughton, A., Osborne, J., Roy, S., Clark, S. *et al.* (2003) 'Responses of plants and invertebrate trophic groups to contrasting herbicide regimes in the farm scale evaluations of genetically modified herbicide-tolerant crops', *Philosophical Transactions of the Royal Society of London*, B358, pp. 1899–1913.

Heberlein, T. (1976) 'Some observations on alternative mechanisms for public involvement: the hearing, public opinion poll, the workshop and the quasi-experiment', *Natural Resources Journal*, 16(1) pp. 197–212.

Her Majesty's Government (1999) *Modernising Government*, Cm 4310, The Stationery Office, London.

Hood, C. (1991) 'A public administration for all seasons?', *Public Administration*, 69, pp. 3–19.

Horlick-Jones, T. (1998) 'Meaning and contextualisation in risk assessment', *Reliability Engineering & System Safety*, 59, pp. 79–89.

Horlick-Jones, T. (2004) 'Experts in risk? . . . do they exist?', *Health, Risk & Society*, 6(2) pp. 107–114.

Horlick-Jones, T. (2005a) 'On "risk work": professional discourse, accountability and everyday action', *Health, Risk & Society*, 7(3) pp. 293–307.

Horlick-Jones, T. (2005b) 'On the governance of risk and the risk of governance: corporate-style risk management and British state institutions', paper presented to an *Understanding Risk* programme workshop on *The Governance of Risk and New Technologies*, held at the Royal Society, London, 21 November.

Horlick-Jones, T. (2005c) 'Informal logics of risk: contingency and modes of practical reasoning', *Journal of Risk Research*, 8(3) pp. 253–272.

Horlick-Jones, T. (2007) 'On the signature of new technologies: materiality, sociality and practical reasoning' in R. Flynn and P. Bellaby (eds), *Risk and the Public Acceptability of New Technologies,* Palgrave, Basingstoke.

Horlick-Jones, T. and Rosenhead, J. (2006) 'The uses of observation: combining problem structuring methods and ethnography', *Journal of the Operational Research Society*, in press.

Horlick-Jones, T. and Sime, J. (2004) 'Living on the border: knowledge, risk and transdisciplinarity', *Futures*, 36, pp. 441–456.

Horlick-Jones, T. and Walls, J. (2005) 'Learning about, making sense of, and discussing issues about transgenic crops and food', paper presented to the *14th Annual Conference of the Society for Risk Analysis (Europe)*, Como, 12–14 September.

Horlick-Jones, T., Kitzinger, J. and Walls, J. (2006a) 'Bricolage in audience reception: mediated knowledge and the work of making sense about GM crops and food', paper presented to the *4th Communications, Medicine & Ethics (COMET) Conference*, Cardiff, June–July.

Horlick-Jones, T., Rowe, G. and Walls, J. (in press, a) 'Citizen engagement processes as information systems: the role of knowledge and the concept of translation quality', *Public Understanding of Science*.

Horlick-Jones, T., Walls, J. and Kitzinger, J. (in press, b) '*Bricolage* in action: learning about, making sense of, and discussing issues about GM crops and food'. *Health, Risk & Society*.

Horlick-Jones, T., Walls, J., Pidgeon, N. and Weyman, A. (2003a) 'Trust in UK health and safety regulators: the role of practical reasoning strategies in the formation of public attitudes', paper delivered to an ESRC workshop on trust, forming part of the 1st *Medicine, Communication & Ethics (COMET) Conference*, Cardiff, June.

Horlick-Jones, T., Rosenhead, J., Georgiou, I., Ravetz, J. and Löfstedt, R. (2001) 'Decision support for organisational risk management by problem structuring', *Health, Risk & Society*, 3(2) pp. 141–165.

Horlick-Jones, T., Rowe, G., Walls, J., O'Riordan, T. and Pidgeon, N. (2002) *Proposals for the Evaluation of the UK Public Debate on the Possible Commercialisation of Genetically Modified Crops*, memorandum considered by the *GM Nation?* Public Debate Steering Board, September.

Horlick-Jones, T., Walls, J., Rowe, G., Pidgeon, N., Poortinga, W. and O'Riordan, T. (2004) *A Deliberative Future? An Independent Evaluation of the GM Nation? Public Debate about the Possible Commercialisation of Transgenic Crops in Britain 2003*, Understanding Risk Working Paper 04–02, Norwich.

Horlick-Jones, T., Walls, J., Rowe, G., Pidgeon, N., Poortinga, W. and O'Riordan, T. (2006b) 'On evaluating the *GM Nation?* public debate about the commercialisation of transgenic crops in Britain', *New Genetics & Society*, in press.

Horlick-Jones, T., Walls, J., Rowe, G., Pidgeon, N., Poortinga, W. and O'Riordan, T., Murdock, G., Tait, J. and Bruce, A. (2003b) 'Memorandum submitted by the Understanding Risk Team and Collaborators' in House of Commons Environment, Food and Rural Affairs Committee, *Conduct of the GM Public Debate*, Eighteenth Report of the Session 2002–03, HC 1220, The Stationery Office, London, pp. Ev50–Ev56.

House of Lords (2000) *Science and Society*, Select Committee on Science and Technology Third Report, HL Paper 38, The Stationery Office, London.

Houtkoop-Steenstra, H. (2000) *Interaction and the Standardized Survey Interview*, Cambridge University Press, Cambridge.

Huber, P. (1991) *Galileo's Revenge: Junk Science in the Courtroom*, Basic Books, New York.

Hutchby, I. (2001) 'Technologies, texts and affordances', *Sociology*, 35(2) pp. 441–456.

Involve (2005) *People & Participation: How to Put Citizens at the Heart of Decision-Making*, Involve, London.

Irwin, A. (2006) 'The politics of talk: coming to terms with the "new" scientific governance', *Social Studies of Science*, 36(2) pp. 299–320.

Irwin, A. and Wynne, B. (eds) (1996) *Misunderstanding Science: the Public Reconstruction of Science and Technology*, Cambridge University Press, Cambridge.

Jasanoff, S. (1997) Civilization and madness: the great BSE scare of 1996, *Public Understanding of Science*, 6, pp. 221–232.

Jasanoff, S., Markle, G., Petersen, J. and Pinch, T. (eds) (1995) *Handbook of Science and Technology Studies*, Sage, Thousand Oaks CA.

Jensen, P.E. (2005) 'A contextual theory of learning and the learning organization', *Knowledge and Process Management*, 12(1) pp. 53–64.

Jessop, B. (2002) *The Future of the Capitalist State*, Polity, Cambridge.

Johnson, B. (1987) 'The environmentalist movement and grid/group analysis: a modest critique', in B. Johnson and V. Covello (eds) *The Social and Cultural Construction of Risk*, Reidel, Dordrecht, pp. 147–178.

Joss, S. (1995) 'Evaluating consensus conferences: necessity or luxury?', in S. Joss and J. Durant (eds) *Public Participation in Science: the Role of Consensus Conferences in Europe*, The Science Museum, London, pp. 89–108.

Joss, S. and Durant, J. (eds) (1995) *Public Participation in Science: the Role of Consensus Conferences in Europe*, The Science Museum, London.

Kitzinger, J. (2000) 'Media templates: patterns of association and the (re)construction of meaning over time', *Media, Culture & Society*, 22, pp. 61–84.

Kuhn, T. (1970) *The Structure of Scientific Revolutions*, 2nd edition, Chicago University Press, Chicago IL.

Laird, F. (1993) 'Participatory analysis, democracy, and technological decision making', *Science, Technology, & Human Values*, 18(3) pp. 341–361.

Lauber, T. and Knuth, B. (1999) 'Measuring fairness in citizen participation: a case study of moose management', *Society and Natural Resources*, 11(1) pp. 19–37.

Levidow, L. and Carr, S. (2000) 'Unsound science? Transatlantic regulatory disputes', *International Journal of Biotechnology*, 2(1/2/3) pp. 257–273.

Levidow, L. and Carr, S. (2001) 'UK: precautionary commercialization', *Journal of Risk Research*, 3(3) pp. 261–270.

Linell, P. (1998) 'Discourse across boundaries: on recontextualizations and the blending of voices in professional discourse', *Text*, 18(2) pp. 143–157.

Löfstedt, R. and Horlick-Jones, T. (1999) 'Environmental politics in the UK: politics, institutional change and public trust', in G. Cvetkovich and R. Löfstedt (eds) *Social Trust and Risk Management*, Earthscan, London, pp. 73–88.

Löfstedt, R. and Renn, O. (1997) 'The Brent Spar controversy: an example of risk communication gone wrong', *Risk Analysis*, 17(2) pp. 131–136.

Lynch, M. (1993) *Scientific Practice and Ordinary Action: Ethnomethodology and Social Studies of Science*, Cambridge University Press, Cambridge.

McHoul, A. and Watson, D.R. (1984) 'Two axes for the analysis of "commonsense" and "formal" geographical knowledge in classroom talk', *British Journal of Sociology of Education*, 5(3) pp. 281–302.

Manning, P. (1988) *Symbolic Communication: Signifying Calls and the Police Response*, MIT Press, Cambridge MA.

Marquand, D. (2004) *Decline of the Public: the Hollowing Out of Citizenship*, Polity Press, Cambridge.

Marris, C., Wynne, B., Simmons, P., Weldon, S., *et al.* (2001) *Public Perceptions of Agricultural Biotechnology in Europe (PABE)*, Final Report to the European Commission, FAIR CT98–3844, DG12-SSMI.

Maxwell, R. (1997) *An Unplayable Hand? BSE, CJD and British Government*, Kings' Fund, London.

Milbraith, L. (1981) 'Citizen surveys as citizen participation mechanisms', *Journal of Applied Behavioral Science*, 17(4) pp. 478–496.

Moore, S. (1996) 'Defining "successful" environmental dispute resolution: case studies from public land planning in the United States and Australia', *Environmental Impact Assessment Review*, 16, pp. 151–169.

Mulkay, M. (1997) 'Review of A. Irwin and B. Wynne (eds) *Misunderstanding Science? The Public Reconstruction of Science and Technology*', in *Science, Technology & Human Values*, 22(2) pp. 254–264.

Munton, R. (2003) 'Deliberative democracy', in F. Berkout, I. Scoones and M. Leach (eds) *Negotiating Environmental Change: New Perspectives from the Social Sciences*, Edward Elgar, Cheltenham, pp. 109–136.

Murdock, G. (2004) 'Popular representation and post-normal science: the struggle over genetically modified foods', in S. Braman (ed.) *Biotechnology and Communication: the Meta-Technologies of Information*, Lawrence Erlbaum Associates, Mahwah NJ, pp. 227–259.

Murdock, G., Petts, J. and Horlick-Jones, T. (2003) 'After amplification: rethinking the role of the media in risk communication', in N. Pidgeon, P. Slovic and R. Kasperson (eds) *The Social Amplification of Risk*, Cambridge University Press, Cambridge, pp. 156–178.

Myers, D. and Lamm, H. (1976) 'The group polarisation phenomenon', *Psychological Bulletin*, 83, pp. 602–627.

NAO (2000) *Supporting Innovation: Managing Risk in Government Departments*, National Audit Office report by the Comptroller and Auditor General, HC 864, Session 1999–2000, The Stationery Office, London.

NAO (2004) *Managing Risks to Improve Public Services*, National Audit Office report by the Comptroller and Auditor General, HC 1078-I, Session 2003–2004, The Stationery Office, London.

National Research Council (1996) *Understanding Risk: Informing Decisions in a Democratic Society*, P. Stern and H. Fineberg (eds), National Academy Press, Washington DC.

OECD (2001) 'Engaging Citizens in Policy-Making: Information, Consultation and Public Participation', PUMA Policy briefing No. 10, Organisation of Economic Co-operation and Development, Paris.

OFCOM (2006) *Consumers and the Communications Market: 2006*, Office of Communications, London.

Oreszczyn, S. (2005) 'GM crops in the United Kingdom: precaution as process', *Science and Public Policy*, 32(4) pp. 317–424.

O'Riordan, T. (1976) *Environmentalism*, Pion, London.

O'Riordan, T., Kemp, R. and Purdue, M. (1988) *Sizewell B: an Anatomy of the Inquiry*, Macmillan, Basingstoke.

Osborne, D. and Gaebler, T. (1992) *Reinventing Government: How the Entrepreneurial Spirit is Transforming the Public Sector*, Addison-Wesley, Reading MA.

Osmond, J. (1988) *The Divided Kingdom*, Constable, London.

OST (1999) *The Advisory and Regulatory Framework for Biotechnology: Report from the Government's Review*, Cabinet Office/Office Science and Technology, London.

OST (2005) *Drugs Futures 2025?*, Foresight report, Office of Science and Technology, London (www.foresight.gov.uk).

Patton, M. (1990) *Qualitative Evaluation and Research Methods*, 2nd edition, Sage, London.

PDSB (2003) *GM Nation? The Findings of the Public Debate*, Public Debate Steering Board, Department of Trade and Industry, London.

Petts, J. (1997) 'The public-expert interface in local waste management decisions: expertise, credibility and process', *Public Understanding of Science*, 6, pp. 359–381.

Petts, J., Horlick-Jones, T. and Murdock, G. (2001) *Social Amplification of Risk: the Media and the Public*, HSE Books, Sudbury.

Lord Phillips of Worth Matravers, Bridgeman, J. and Ferguson-Smith, M. (2000) *The BSE Inquiry ('The Phillips Inquiry')*, The Stationery Office, London.

Pichardo, N. (1997) 'New social movements: a critical review', *Annual Reviews of Sociology*, 23, pp. 411–430.

Pidgeon, N. and Gregory, R. (2004) 'Judgement, decision making and public policy', in D. Koehler and N. Harvey (eds) *The Blackwell Handbook of Judgement and Decision-Making*, Blackwell, Oxford, pp. 604–623.

Pidgeon, N. and Poortinga, W. (2006) 'British public attitudes to agricultural biotechnology and the 2003 *GM Nation?* public debate: distrust, ambivalence and risk', in P. Glasner and H. Greenslade, P. Atkinson. (eds) *New Genetics, New Social Formations*, Routledge, London.

Pidgeon, N., Slovic, P. and Kasperson, R. (eds) (2003) *The Social Amplification of Risk*, Cambridge University Press, Cambridge.

Pidgeon, N., Poortinga, W., Rowe, G., Horlick-Jones, T., Walls, J. and O'Riordan, T. (2005) 'Using surveys in public participation processes for risk decision-making: the case of the 2003 British GM Nation public debate', *Risk Analysis*, 25(2) pp. 467–479.

Poisner, J. (1996) 'A civic republican perspective on the National Environmental Policy Act's process for citizen participation', *Environmental Law*, 26, pp. 53–94.

Poortinga, W. and Pidgeon, N.F. (2003a) *Public Perceptions of Risk, Science and Governance: Main Findings of a British Survey on Five Risk Cases*, University of East Anglia Centre for Environmental Risk, Norwich.

Poortinga, W. and Pidgeon, N.F. (2003b) 'Exploring the dimensionality of trust in risk regulation', *Risk Analysis*, 23(5) pp. 961–972.

Poortinga, W. and Pidgeon, N.F. (2004a) *Public Perceptions of Genetically Modified Food and Crops, and the GM Nation? public debate on the commercialisation of agricultural biotechnology in the UK*, Understanding Risk Working Paper 04–01, Norwich.

Poortinga, W. and Pidgeon, N.F. (2004b) 'Trust, the asymmetry principle, and the role of prior beliefs', *Risk Analysis*, 24(6) pp. 1475–1486.

POST (2001) *Open Channels: Public Dialogue in Science and Technology*, Parliamentary Office of Science and Technology, London.

Prior, L. (2003) 'Belief, knowledge and expertise: the emergence of the lay expert in medical sociology', *Sociology of Health & illness*, 25, pp. 41–57.

Purdue, D. (1999) 'Experiments in the governance of biotechnology: a case study of the UK consensus conference', *New Genetics and Society*, 18(1) pp. 79–99.

Rayner, S. (2003) 'Democracy in an age of assessment: reflections on the roles of expertise and democracy in public-sector decision making', *Science and Public Policy*, 30(3) pp. 163–170.

Renn, O., Webler, T. and Wiedemann, P. (eds) (1995) *Fairness and Competence in Citizens' Participation: Evaluating Models For Environmental Discourse*, Kluwer, Dordrecht.

Rhodes, R. (1997) *Understanding Governance: Policy Networks, Governance, Reflexivity and Accountability*, Open University Press, Buckingham.

Rissler, J. and Mellon, M. (1996) *The Ecological Risks of Engineered Crops*, MIT Press, Cambridge MA.

Rose, N. (1999) *Powers of Freedom: Reframing Political Thought*, Cambridge University Press, Cambridge.

Rosener, J. (1975) 'A cafeteria of techniques and critiques', *Public Management*, December, pp. 16–19.

Rosenhead, J. and Mingers, J. (eds) (2001) *Rational Analysis for a Problematic World Revisited: Problem Structuring Methods for Complexity, Uncertainty and Conflict*, Wiley, Chichester.

Rossi, P.H., Freeman, H.E. and Lipsey, M.W. (1999) *Evaluation: a Systematic Approach*, 6th edition, Sage Publications, London.

Rothstein, H., Huber, M. and Gaskell, G. (2006) 'A theory of risk colonization: the spiralling regulatory logics of societal and institutional risk', *Economy and Society*, 35(1) pp. 91–112.

Rowe, G. and Frewer, L. (2000) 'Public participation methods: a framework for evaluation', *Science, Technology, & Human Values*, 25(1) pp. 3–29.

Rowe, G. and Frewer, L. (2004) 'Evaluating public participation exercises: a research agenda', *Science, Technology, & Human Values*, 29(2) pp. 512–556.

Rowe, G. and Frewer, L. (2005) 'A typology of public engagement mechanisms', *Science, Technology, & Human Values*, 30(2) pp. 251–290.

Rowe, G., Horlick-Jones, T., Walls, J. and Pidgeon, N.F. (2005) 'Difficulties in evaluating public engagement initiatives: reflections on an evaluation of the UK *GM Nation?* public debate', *Public Understanding of Science*, 14(4) pp. 331–352.

Rowe, G., Horlick-Jones, T., Walls, J., Poortinga, W. and Pidgeon, N. (in press) 'Analysis of a normative framework for evaluating public engagement exercises: reliability, validity and limitations'. *Public Understanding of Science*.

Rowe, G., Marsh, R. and Frewer, L. (2001) *Public Participation Methods: Evolving and Operationalising an Evaluation Framework. Final Report*, Report to the Department of Health and Health & Safety Executive, Institute of Food Research, Norwich.

Rowe, G., Marsh, R. and Frewer, L. (2004) 'Evaluation of a deliberative conference', *Science, Technology, & Human Values*, 29(1) pp. 88–121.

Rowe, G., Poortinga, W. and Pidgeon, N. (2006) 'A comparison of responses to internet and postal surveys in a public engagement context', *Science Communication*, 27(3) pp. 352–375.

Rowell, A. (2003) *Don't Worry: It's Safe to Eat*, Earthscan, London.

Royal Society and Royal Academy of Engineering (2004) *Nanoscience and Nanotechnologies: Opportunties and Uncertainties*, Royal Society and Royal Academy of Engineering, London (www.royalsoc.ac.uk).

Schön, D. and Rein, M. (1994) *Frame Reflection: Toward the Resolution of Intractable Policy Controversies*, New York: Basic.

Seale, C. (1999) *The Quality of Qualitative Research*, Sage, London.

Sewell, W. and Phillips, S. (1979) 'Models for the evaluation of public participation programmes', *Natural Resources Journal*, 19, pp. 337–358.

Shaw, I. (1999) *Qualitative Evaluation*, Sage Publications, London.

Shindler, B. and Neburka, J. (1997) 'Public participation in forest planning: 8 attributes of success', *Journal of Forestry*, pp. 17–19.

Silverman, D. (1993) *Interpreting Qualitative Data: Methods for Analysing Talk, Text and Interaction*, Sage Publications, London.

Stirling, A. and Meyer, S. (1999) *Rethinking Risk*, Science and Technology Policy Research Unit, Brighton.

Strong, P. and Dingwall, R. (1989) 'Romantics and Stoics', in J. Gubrium and D. Silverman (eds) *The Politics of Field Research: Sociology Beyond Enlightenment*, Sage, London, pp. 49–69.

Sturgis, P. and Allum, N. (2004) 'Science in society: re-evaluating the deficit model of public attitudes', *Public Understanding of Science*, 13, pp. 55–74.

Thompson, J. (1995) *The Media and Modernity: a Social Theory of the Media*, Polity, Cambridge.

Timotijevic, L. and Barnett, J. (2006) 'Managing the possible health risks of mobile telecommunications: public understandings of precautionary action and advice', *Health, Risk & Society*, 8(2) pp. 143–164.

Toke, D. (2004) *The Politics of GM Food: A Comparative Study of the UK, USA and EU*, Routledge, London.

Toke, D. and Marsh, D. (2003) 'Policy networks and the GM crops issue: assessing the utility of a dialectical model of policy networks', *Public Administration*, 81(2) pp. 229–251.

Tuler, S. and Webler, T. (1999) 'Voices from the forest: what participants expect of a public participation process', *Society and Natural Resources*, 12(5) pp. 437–453.

Walls, J., Horlick-Jones, T., Niewöhner, J. and O'Riordan, T. (2005a) 'The meta-governance of risk: GM crops and mobile telephones', *Journal of Risk Research*, 8(7–8) pp. 635–661.

Walls, J., Pidgeon, N., Weyman, A. and Horlick-Jones, T. (2004) 'Critical trust: understanding lay perceptions of health and safety risk regulation', *Health, Risk & Society*, 6, pp. 133–150.

Walls, J., Rogers-Hayden, T., Mohr, A. and O'Riordan, T. (2005b) 'Seeking citizen's views on GM crops: experiences from the United Kingdom, Australia and New Zealand', *Environment*, 47(7) pp. 22–36.

Webler, T. (1995) '"Right" discourse in citizen participation: an evaluative yardstick', in O. Renn, T. Webler and P. Wiedemann (eds) *Fairness and Competence in Citizen Participation: Evaluating Models for Environmental Discourse*, Kluwer, Dordrecht, pp. 35–86.

White, S. (1988) *The Recent Work of Jürgen Habermas: Reason, Justice and Modernity*, Cambridge University Press, Cambridge.

Wiedemann, P. and Femers, S. (1993) 'Public-participation in waste management decision-making – analysis and management of conflicts', *Journal of Hazardous Materials*, 33(3) pp. 355–368.

Wiener, J. and Rogers, M. (2002) 'Comparing precaution in the US and Europe', *Journal of Risk Research*, 5(4) pp. 317–349.

Williams, G. and Popay, J. (1994) 'Lay knowledge and the privilege of experience', in J. Gabe, D. Kelleher and G. Williams (eds) *Challenging Medicine*, Routledge, London, pp. 118–139.

Wilsdon, J. and Willis, R. (2004) *See-Through Science: Why Public Engagement Needs to Move Upstream*, Demos, London.

Woolgar, S. (1988) *Science: the Very Idea*, Ellis Horwood and Tavistock, Chichester and London.

Wynne, B. (1987) *Risk Management and Hazardous Waste: Implementation and the Dialectics of Credibility*, Springer-Verlag, Berlin.

Wynne, B. (1991) 'Knowledges in context', *Science, Technology & Human Values*, 16(1) pp. 111–121.

Wynne, B. (1992) 'Misunderstood misunderstandings: social identities and public uptake of science', *Public Understanding of Science*, 1, pp. 281–304.

Wynne, B. (1995) 'Public understanding of science', in S. Jasanoff, G. Markle, J. Petersen and T. Pinch (eds) *Handbook of Science and Technology Studies*, Sage, Thousand Oaks CA, pp. 361–388.

Yearley, S. (1999) 'Computer models and the public's understanding of science', *Social Studies of Science*, 29(6) pp. 845–866.

Index

Pages containing relevant illustrations are indicated in *italic* type.